I0759803

“There is no better conduit of ancient Sephardic tradition than my friend, Hélène Jawhara Piñer. She has dedicated her life to this work to bring us the history and recipes of medieval Spanish Jewry with this fascinating cookbook. A must read—*Matzah and Flour* is historically eye-opening and of course, delicious.”

— Mike Solomonov, Co-Owner and Chef at Zahav and other restaurants,
James Beard Foundation Award winner

“What a brilliant concept for a Jewish cookbook! Leave it to Helène to find a way to offer her groundbreaking scholarly work through such a delicious, accessible lens. Through her concise writing and beautifully photographed recipes, she shows us just how essential flour in all its forms has been to Sephardic cooking, and how it reflects the community’s rich history from ancient to modern timeline.”

— Adeena Sussman, author of *Shabbat: Recipes and Rituals From My Kitchen To Yours*
and *Sababa: Fresh, Sunny Flavors from My Israeli Kitchen*

“Hélène’s ability to teach me about the history of Jewish food-ways always has me at the edge of my seat, the fact that I want to make every recipe in this book is just a bonus!”

— Jake Cohen, New York Times bestselling author of *Jew-ish* and *I Could Nosh*

“In this deeply researched book, Hélène has done an amazing job weaving together history, culture, religion, and food to tell the story of how flour is at the root of so much spirituality and is the heart of Sephardic Jewish cooking.”

— Chef José Andrés, Owner and Chef at Jaleo and other restaurants,
James Beard Foundation Award winner

“Piñer’s *Matzah and Flour* is a brilliant culinary journey. Piñer takes the reader on her quest for Sephardic bread recipes. Leaving no stone unturned, she time travels throughout history using ancient primary sources as a guide. The result is a fascinating foray, rich with stunning photographs and irresistible recipes that beautifully showcase the breadth of the Sephardic diaspora.”

— Sari Kamin, Public Programming at the James Beard Foundation

“Only an erudite food historian could give us this unique treasure of recipes from ancient Judea, medieval Europe, and the worldwide Sephardic diaspora. *Matzah and Flour* makes Sephardic history edible. This is a cookbook like no other. A revelation!”

— Barbara Kirshenblatt-Gimblett, Ronald S. Lauder Chief Curator, Core Exhibition,
POLIN Museum of the History of Polish Jews

"*Matzah and Flour* is an exceptional work that intertwines tradition and modernity with unique mastery. Helene Jawara Piñer takes us on a culinary journey that not only explores the cultural roots of cuisine but also reinterprets ancestral ingredients with surprising creativity and sensitivity. As a chef, I am deeply inspired to see how this book reimagines classic recipes for a new generation, while preserving the soul of each dish."

— Chef Daniel Ovadía, Owner and Chef at Merkava and other restaurants

"Hélène Jawhara Piñer masterfully demonstrates how a quotidian ingredient like flour can reveal multifaceted aspects of Jewish life and culinary practices throughout the ages. Add to that historic recipes that are as intriguing as they are mouthwatering."

— Gabriella Gershenson, co-author of *Love Japan: Recipes from Our Japanese American Kitchen*

"*Matzah and Flour* is more than just a cookbook; it's a culinary journey that blends the vibrant flavors of Sephardic heritage with Mexican cuisine. It is a celebration of diversity and tradition, with each carefully curated recipe telling a story of cultural fusion and Jewish culinary heritage. As someone who loves both Mexican cuisine and the rich tapestry of Jewish food, I was thrilled to explore this delightful cookbook."

— Pati Jinich, James Beard Award Winning Chef & TV Host; author of *Treasures of the Mexican Table*

"*Matzah and Flour* is a marvelous book—at once scholarly, practical, and fun. Hélène Jawhara Piñer traces the Sephardic diaspora through the Old World and into the New, from Spain and Morocco to Mexico, Brazil, and beyond. Drawing on sources that range from the Bible and Maimonides to the records of Inquisition tribunals, she tells stories through matza and muffins, noodles and couscous, tortillas and empanadas. Her easy-to-follow recipes feature flours made from wheat, barley, chickpeas, chestnuts, rice, and more. She takes readers on a journey to see the existential, emotive, and practical importance of food for Jewish peoples and their neighbors across the ages."

— Heather J. Sharkey, Professor of Modern Middle Eastern and North African History, University of Pennsylvania.

MATZAH AND FLOUR

Library of Congress Cataloging-in-Publication Data

Names: Piñer, Hélène Jawhara, author.
Title: Matzah and flour : recipes from the history of the Sephardic Jews / Hélène Jawhara Piñer.
Description: Boston : Cherry Orchard Books, an imprint of Academic Studies Press, 2024. | Includes bibliographical references and index.
Identifiers: LCCN 2024007962 (print) | LCCN 2024007963 (ebook) | ISBN 9798887195445 (hardback) | ISBN 9798887195452 (adobe pdf) | ISBN 9798887195469 (epub)
Subjects: LCSH: Sephardic cooking. | Matzos. | Flatbreads. | Jews--Food--Spain. | Jews--Food--History. | Fasts and feasts--Judaism. | LCGFT: Cookbooks.
Classification: LCC TX724.2.S47 P559 2024 (print) | LCC TX724.2.S47 (ebook) | DDC 641.5/676--dc23/eng/20240304
LC record available at https://lccn.loc.gov/2024007962
LC ebook record available at https://lccn.loc.gov/2024007963

Book design by PHi Business Solutions
Photographs by Hélène Jawhara Piñer, Mathilde Boclet, Stéphan Langrée, Martin de Arriba, and Laly Jawhara Piñer

Published by Cherry Orchard Books, and imprint of Academic Studies Press
1007 Chestnut St.
Newton, MA 02464, USA

press@academicstudiespress.com
www.academicstudiespress.com

Hélène Jawhara Piñer

MATZAH AND FLOUR

Recipes from the History of the Sephardic Jews

Cherry Orchard Books
Boston
2024

TABLE OF CONTENTS

Spain

Mexico

Morocco

SHAVUOT

Italy

SHABBAT

MARZIPAN
THE ICONIC SEPHARDIC ALMOND SWEET

Spain

EVERY OCCASION

Italy

Thessaloniki

Spain

MAIMONIDES

Morocco

THE PORTRAIT OF LOZANA: THE LUSTY ANDALUSIAN WOMAN

From Cordova to Rome

CREATIONS

WORLD SEPHARDIC FOOD MAP

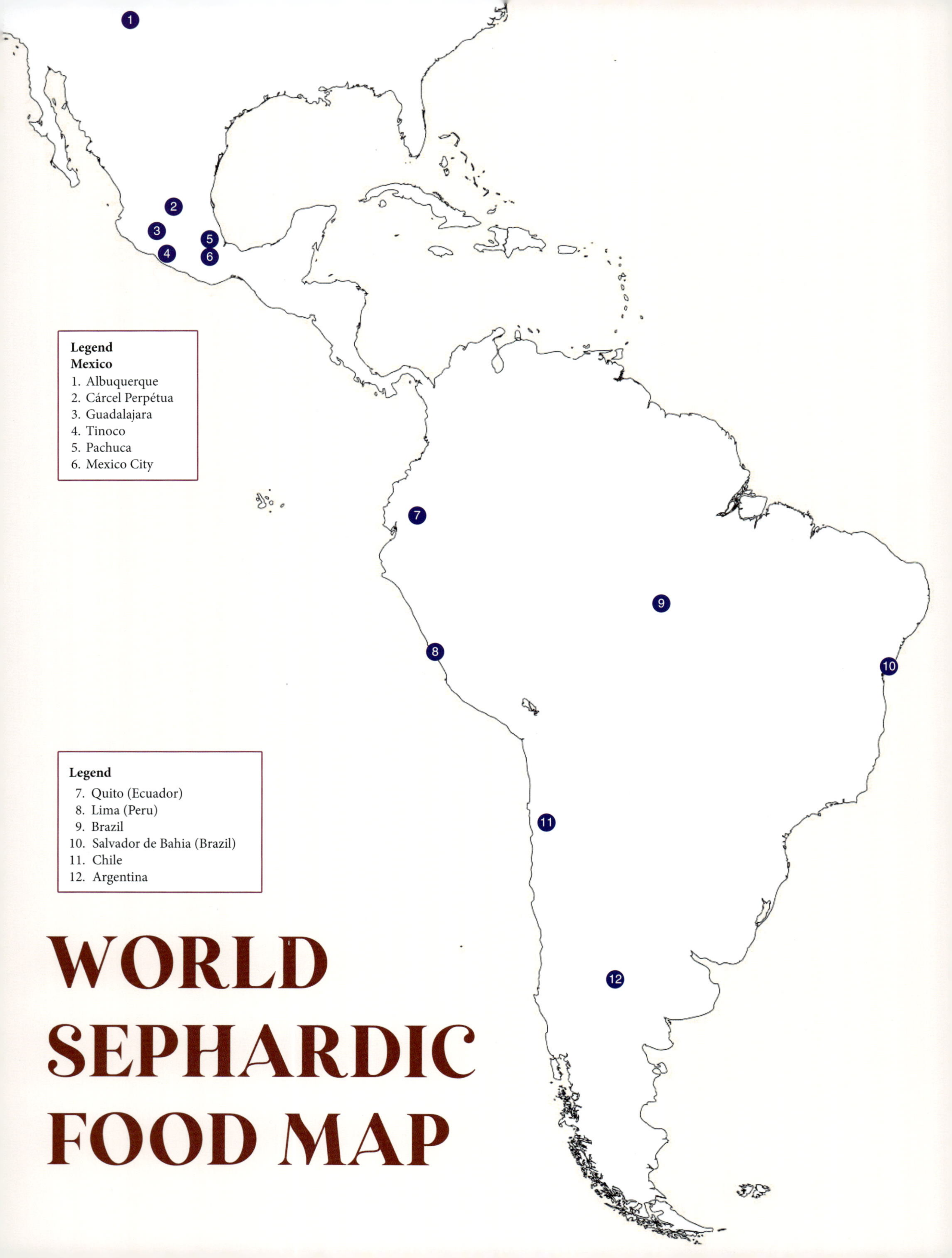

Legend
Mexico
1. Albuquerque
2. Cárcel Perpétua
3. Guadalajara
4. Tinoco
5. Pachuca
6. Mexico City

Legend
7. Quito (Ecuador)
8. Lima (Peru)
9. Brazil
10. Salvador de Bahia (Brazil)
11. Chile
12. Argentina

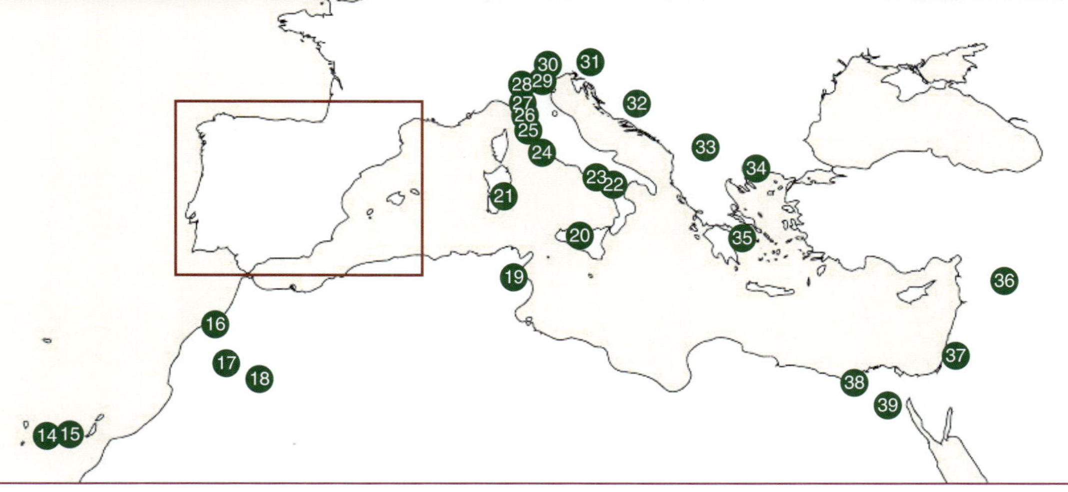

Legend

13. Azores Islands (Portugal)
14. Canary Islands (Spain)
15. Las Palmas (Canaria Island, Spain)
16. Rabat (Morocco)
17. Morocco
18. Fes (Morocco)
19. Qayrawan (Tunisia)
20. Palermo (Sicily, Italy)
21. Cagliari (Sardinia, Italy)
22. Campania (Italy)
23. Naples (Italy)
24. Terracina (Italy)
25. Rome (Italy)
26. Livorno (Italy)
27. Siena (Italy)
28. Mantua (Italy)
29. Ferrara (Italy)
30. Venice (Italy)
31. Trieste (Italy)
32. Croatia
33. Balkans
34. Salonika/Thessaloniki (Greece)
35. Aegina Island (Greece)
36. Syria
37. Ancient Judah
38. Alexandria (Egypt)
39. Cairo (Egypt)
40. Yemen

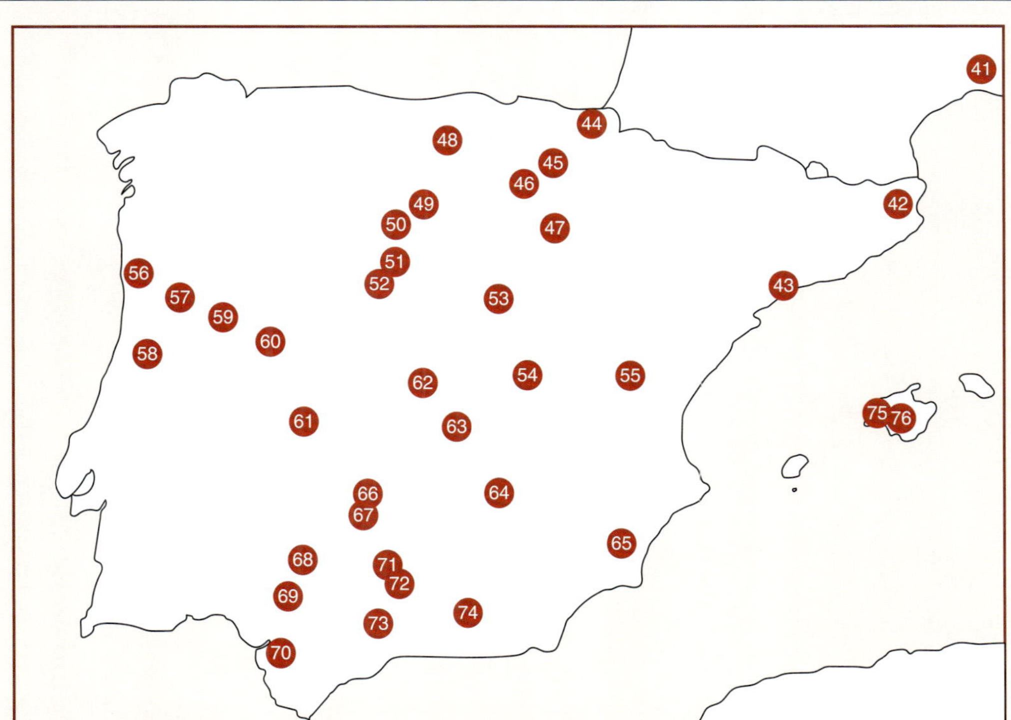

Legend

41. Lunel (France)
42. Gerona (Spain)
43. Tarragona (Spain)
44. Tolosa (Spain)
45. Logroño (Spain)
46. Matute (Spain)
47. Almazan (Spain)
48. Cervera del Río Pisuerga (Spain)
49. Palenzuela (Spain)
50. Palencia (Spain)
51. Rosadillo (Spain)
52. Medina de Campo (Spain)
53. Sigüenza (Spain)
54. Cuenca (Spain)
55. Teruel (Spain)
56. Porto (Portugal)
57. Lamego (Portugal)
58. Coimbra (Portugal)
59. Trancoso (Portugal)
60. Ciudad Rodrigo (Spain)
61. Casar de Cáceres (Spain)
62. Toledo (Spain)
63. Ciudad Real (Spain)
64. Villahermosa (Spain)
65. Murcia (Spain)
66. Andalusia (Spain)
67. Cordova (Spain)
68. Carmona (Spain)
69. Seville (Spain)
70. Jerez de la Frontera (Spain)
71. Lucena (Spain)
72. Archidona (Spain)
73. Antequera (Spain)
74. Granada (Spain)
75. Palma (Spain)
76. Mallorca (Spain)

INTRODUCTION

At the core of Sephardic cuisine lies the transformative potential of flour. From this unassuming ingredient emerges a diverse array of delicacies, each steeped in tradition and history. The recipes that follow will delve deep into the captivating journey of how flour and matzah have been a steady yet evolving influence on Sephardic cuisine, ultimately emerging as timeless symbols, embodying a history of resilience, faith, and community. The story of matzah is one of Exodus and freedom, transcending its physical form to represent the unbroken chain of Sephardic identity. This book is a tribute to this journey, where each recipe serves as a culinary link between generations, preserving the flavors that have accompanied Sephardic families through time.

I remain astonished and fascinated by the number of recipes I discovered throughout my research in which flour constituted a major element in Sephardic Jewish cuisine. But perhaps the most captivating realization was understanding how different types of flour (chickpea flour, corn flour, chestnut flour, wheat flour, barley flour, freekeh flour, almond flour, starch, semolina, etc.) could be used, finding their way into both sweet and savory dishes, shaping Sephardic food through a play of textures, colors, and flavors. However, where the use of flour has played (and continues to play) a predominant role is through its symbolic value.

MATZAH IN JEWISH HISTORY: ORIGINS, TRADITION, AND SYMBOLISM

Matzah refers to unleavened bread—bread made without yeast, from a simple mixture of flour and water—which is usually flat and similar in appearance to a cracker. It is meticulously prepared to ensure that it does not rise or ferment, a process that distinguishes it from regular bread. In Jewish history, matzah (מצה in Hebrew, or מצות "matzot" in the plural) is most closely associated with the observance of Passover (Pesach), one of the most important holidays in the Jewish calendar.

The significance of matzah in Jewish history can be traced back to the Hebrew Bible, the formative text of Judaism. Matzah is explicitly mentioned in several parts of the Bible, where it is called לחם מצות (*lechem matzot,* "matzot bread") or simply מצות *mazot*—and particularly in relation to the Passover story and its associated regulations.

In Exodus 12, the story of the Exodus from Egypt is described, including the institution of the Passover meal. According to the story, the Israelites left Egypt in haste, and they did not have time for their bread to rise. As a result, they baked unleavened bread, and the Israelites are commanded to eat unleavened bread thereafter as part of the Passover observance. In Exodus 12:15, we read: "Seven days you shall eat *matzot*, but on the first day you shall remove leaven from your houses. For whoever eats leaven from the first day until the seventh day, that person shall be cut off from Israel." It is also specifically stated that this observance is permanent and binding: "You shall observe the Feast of Unleavened Bread, for on this very day I brought your hosts out of the land of Egypt; thus, you shall observe this day throughout your generations as a permanent ordinance" (Exodus 12:17). This story of the Exodus is central to the Passover holiday, commemorated annually by the Jewish community.

During the week-long Passover festival, which typically falls in the spring, Jewish households refrain from consuming leavened bread or any products containing yeast or other leavening agents (chametz). Instead, they eat matzah as a tangible reminder of the Israelites' journey to freedom and their dependence on God during that period. Because of this, matzah is rich in symbolism. Its flat and simple appearance reflects humility and the absence of excess, which are important spiritual themes during Passover. It also represents purity, as it contains only basic ingredients and lacks any fermentation. In Jewish tradition, matzah is often referred to as the "bread of affliction" (lechem oni) and the "bread of freedom."

The use of unleavened bread in the context of Passover and the Feast of Unleavened Bread continued in Jewish tradition during the Second Temple period (circa 516 BCE to 70 CE) and afterward in Rabbinic literature. The Mishnah, a central text of Rabbinic Judaism which was written by Rabbi Yehudah HaNasi—also known as Judah the Prince—was redacted around the 2nd century CE. It discusses the preparation and consumption of matzah during the Passover Seder, thus solidifying matzah's central role in Rabbinic Jewish practice.

The study of flour and its historical context can provide valuable insights into various aspects of human history, including agriculture, economics, culture, and technology. Flour is derived from grains, which have been a fundamental part of human agriculture for thousands of years. The cultivation and processing of grains into flour played a crucial role in the development of early agricultural societies. Examining how different societies used flour in their cuisines provides insights into cultural preferences, dietary habits, and the development

of culinary traditions. Flour is a primary ingredient in many food products, and understanding its preparation, sources, and uses is crucial for determining whether a particular food item is kosher. The study of flour in Jewish scholarship is closely tied to the practical applications of Jewish law, rituals, and traditions, making it a relevant and significant subject for those interested in understanding the intricacies of Jewish life.

ANCIENT SOURCES

The recipes in this book—for both matzah and other Sephardic dishes made with different kinds of flours—are based upon an extensive array of historical sources. These sources, which encompass medical writings, legal documents, literary pieces, and liturgical texts, come together to create a mosaic that reflects the existence of a long, rich Sephardic culinary culture.

Maimonides, for instance (also known as Rabbi Moses ben Maimon or Rambam), wrote about matzah in his comprehensive legal work known as the Mishneh Torah in the 12th century CE. The Mishneh Torah is one of Maimonides' most renowned writings and is a comprehensive code of Jewish law that covers a wide range of topics, including the laws and customs related to Passover (Pesach) and the consumption of matzah. In this work, Maimonides dedicated a section called "Hilchot Chametz u'Matzah" (Laws of Leavened and Unleavened Bread) to the laws and regulations surrounding the preparation, consumption, and observance of Passover, which includes the requirement to eat matzah during the holiday. Maimonides outlines the specific rules for ensuring that the matzah used during Passover is unleavened, discusses the timing of eating matzah during the Seder, and provides details on the various types of matzot used. Maimonides' inclusion of Passover and matzah-related laws in the "Mishneh Torah" is significant because it demonstrates his commitment to providing a comprehensive and authoritative source for Jewish legal and religious practices during the Middle Ages. His writings on matzah and Passover continue to be studied and referenced by Jewish scholars and practitioners to this day. Maimonides attributes a key role to flour in his writings. In his book The Regimen of Health, he says that bread is the best food if it is made with sifted wheat flour, salted, well kneaded, and baked in a *tannūr* oven. Dishes made with boiled flour dishes, on the other hand, he does not consider good food, since he believes that dough should be baked.

The Shulchan Arukh ("Set Table"), another widely-respected and authoritative work on Jewish law, also mentions matzah in its section on the laws for Passover. It was authored by Rabbi Yosef Karo in the 16th century and has served as a comprehensive guide to Jewish religious and legal practices. In the Shulchan Arukh, one can find detailed discussions of the laws and customs related to Passover, including the consumption of matzah. The section on Passover is found in the "Orach Chayim" (Way of Life) portion of the book. Rabbi Karo discusses various aspects about the observance of Passover, such as the prohibition of *chametz* (leavened products) during the holiday, the specific requirements for the matzah used during the Seder, and the timing of the Seder meal. The "Yoreh De'ah" section of the Shulchan Arukh primarily deals with Jewish religious laws related to dietary regulations, kosher food, and other related topics. Specific details about wheat and flour can be found in various chapters and sections throughout "Yoreh De'ah" such as Siman 112, Siman 331, and Siman 112:4. This last subsection specifically discusses the requirement to separate challah when making a dough with wheat flour.

Non-liturgical sources concerning the daily life and dietary habits of Sephardic Jews, such as the medical writings of Maimonides, other literary works, and even records of inquisition trials, are equally revealing of the significance of consuming unleavened bread and various types of flours among the *conversos* or "crypto-Jews"—those who had officially converted to Christianism, but who in fact kept celebrating Judaism in secret. The unleavened bread of Sephardic Jews from the 13th to the 18th century, spanning the Mediterranean basin to Mexico, bears little resemblance to the present-day matzah, both in composition and in the time of year it was prepared and consumed. Firstly, the term "matzah" was not used during the Middle Ages or the pre-modern era. There is no mention of it in inquisition records. Instead, terms like "pan cenceño," "pan cotazo," "pan de judíos," "pão asmo," "pão dos judeus," "pan sin levadura," "pan cuez," "pan de Pascua," "pa alis," and more were employed to refer to this unleavened bread that only Jews ate, making its consumption an indicator of the Jewish identity of the person consuming it.

The *Responsa* (*Responsum* in singular) are the answers given by medieval rabbis or Talmudic scholars to questions that had been posed to them about Jewish law. We are fortunate that many such responsa have survived, since they offer a treasure trove of information about Jewish customs and law. Those written by Shlomo ben Avraham ibn Aderet (13th-14th century, Catalonia) reveal the complexity of living together with non-Jews, especially concerning

food practices. For example, one of the *responsa* which dates back to between 1235 and 1310 contains the answer given by the Rashba regarding whether it was permissible or not for Jews to accept sourdough bread (which was made with yeast) which was offered to them as a gift by gentiles (non-Jews, mainly Christians) for the last day of Passover. In short, the answer was negative. Another *responsum* from the same period questions the possibility of asking a non-Jewish servant to bring them hot bread from the market on Shabbat. The Rashba's answer is that "this is prohibited, and one who wishes to save his soul will refrain from doing so. Firstly, because it was said, 'It is forbidden to instruct a gentile to perform prohibited labor due to shebuth' (Babylonian Talmud, Shabbat 150a), and a person who refrains from working on Shabbat is not permitted to instruct a non-Jew to perform forbidden labor."

ON THE STRUCTURE OF THIS COOKBOOK

This cookbook isn't arranged with a conventional structure, because this isn't an ordinary cookbook. Instead, I've arranged it in an attempt to highlight the Jewish holidays, the diasporic homelands of Sephardic Jews, and the different historical periods in which they lived. This resulted in an eight-chapter structure, starting with the "Old and Holy Breads," and ending with some of my own "Creations."

The book begins with a map showcasing the locations of the historical sources I've used in creating this cookbook; its goal is to convey to the reader the vast and diverse diasporic Sephardic culinary heritage. This book commemorates the shared heritage of Sephardic foods—a symbol of unity amidst the dispersal of the Sephardic diaspora.

In some ways, the core of the cookbook lies within its second chapter, entitled "Matzah and Flour: Food and Holidays." This chapter not only presents recipes organized by Jewish holidays but also by the locations where these celebrations took place. This emphasizes the importance of Sephardic recipes in the diaspora, including places like Brazil, Portugal, Spain, Italy, Mexico, Morocco, Arabia, Greece, and Egypt, where Sephardim have historically lived. Inquisition trials served as the primary sources for this chapter. Regardless of the language in which they were written (Portuguese, Spanish, Catalan, Italian, etc.) or the location of the courts (Spain, Portugal, Mexico, etc.), they provide invaluable insights into Jewish food practices that deal with flour.

There is also a dedicated section that focuses on Shabbat, for the simple reason that it stands apart from other Jewish holidays in terms of its frequency: it is observed every week, beginning on Friday night and continuing until the following day, throughout the entire year. This frequent occurrence, incidentally, made it easier for those who wished to identify and denounce Jewish families for their religious practices. Various aspects of Shabbat food practices contributed to this ease of identification. For example: the practice of preparing dishes like *adafina* or other meals which needed to be cooked in a sealed pot on Friday evenings; consuming food that was either served cold or lukewarm for lunch on Saturday; families gathering in one Jewish home to partake in a communal meal; refraining from cooking on Friday nights and Saturdays; and the distinctive aromas of ingredients like garlic, olive oil, and eggplants. All of these played roles in recognizing *converso* families as Jewish and subsequently reporting them. Consequently, it is understandable why the majority of legal proceedings against Jewish food practices were associated with Shabbat observance.

The chapters "Marzipan" and "Every Occasion" are shorter but necessary because they are still part of contemporary Jewish culinary practices and because it's essential to convey that unleavened bread is not exclusively reserved for Passover. The two remaining chapters, "Maimonides" and "The Portrait of Lozana: The Lusty Andalusian Woman," are quite distinct in terms of sources and deserve special attention. Maimonides, in my view, is a pioneer of Jewish dietary principles. From his commentary on the Mishnah to his "Book of Simple Drugs," Maimonides' writings illuminate the profound connections between food, health, and Jewish traditions in which flour played a key role to sustaining good health. On the other hand, "The Portrait of Lozana," a literary work, illustrates how Jewish practices persisted in the diaspora when Sephardic Jews had no choice but to leave Spain and settle in other countries. This novel presents examples of the enduring Sephardic culinary practices in Italy, as evidenced by descriptions of 21 dishes brought there by the Andalusian woman.

The world of Jewish cuisine is a testament to its rich history of adaptation, evolution, and the passing down of traditions. This cookbook is a reflection of that journey, where I not only celebrate time-honored recipes but also introduce some dishes of my own invention in the final chapter, called "Creations." These original dishes are crafted in accordance with the principles of Kashrut and the enduring traditions of Jewish holidays, and they bear the mark of my Sephardic sensibilities.

THE SEPHARDIC DIASPORA AND MY CULINARY HERITAGE

Cooking runs deep in my family, particularly on my mother's side, where bakers, pastry chefs, cooks, butchers, and caterers have shaped my culinary heritage. It was from them that I inherited my passion for crafting exquisite French pastries. On my father's side, my grandmother has remained a profound source of culinary inspiration. Her mastery lies in the art of creating simple yet delectable dishes, skillfully combining flavors to perfection. Many of my fellow chefs and my travels have, of course, also informed and inspired my Sephardic recipes.

Historical sources have also played a significant role in shaping my culinary repertoire. They are particularly influential in crafting dishes for cherished holidays like Shabbat, Yom Kippur, Rosh Hashanah, Hanukkah, Purim, Sukkot, and Shavuot. These celebrations often feature my favorite vegetables and fruits, including eggplant, spinach, citron, dates, chickpeas and beans, herbs, olive oil, cheese, coriander, cinnamon, garlic, and honey. Yet, no matter how exquisite the dish, it cannot be fully appreciated without the presence of fresh bread, whether leavened or unleavened. In essence, bread is the cornerstone of these culinary traditions, symbolizing sustenance, tradition, and the heart of every meal.

This book aims to offer a journey into Sephardic culinary history. Through 125 recipes, I extend an invitation to join me on a gastronomic and historical voyage that intricately intertwines flavors, narratives, and traditions, immersing you in the story of matzah, flour, and the Sephardic Jewish experience. I hope that it provides an enjoyable, practical, and delicious portrayal of Jewish cuisines throughout history, where matzah and flour played a pivotal role in accentuating Jewish identity and history.

Our culinary heritage lives in us.

Take flour, make matzah, and bite into Jewish history.

freekeh
wheat
barley
chickpea
chestnut
rice
potato starch
tapioca starch
kernel blue corn
kernel yellow corn
kernel white corn
kernel pink corn
kernel purple corn
corn starch

mace
ginger
turmeric
cumin seeds
cinnamon
star anise
allspice berries
cardamom pods
pepper black long
coriander seeds
white peppercorns
orris
nutmeg
fennel seeds

The Ancient Judah Bread
Rambam Passover first day "poor man's bread" (Lechem Oni)
Rambam Passover Sweet Matzah for the other holy days of the week
Rambam Passover savory Matzah for the other holy days of the week
The Shulchan Arukh Orach Chayim Matzah 455:6
The Shulchan Arukh Orach Chayim 453:2 Matzah
The Shulchan Arukh Orach Chayim 444:1 The rich man's bread or Egg Matzah Matza ashirah
Pascoa do pão asmo
Bolos asmos prepared for Jejum das filhós (the Fast of the flat cakes)
Isabel Gomes five flat breads of the salvation
Felipa Cardos chestnut Matzah for Passover
Unleave flat snow cakes of María Gonzále
Blanca Enríquez's Mexican Small Unleavened breads
Passover Wine flat cakes from Juana de la Fuente and Beatriz Días Laínez
Cecilia Cardosa matza and Sweet Lamb for her Passover dish
Salamancan Isabel Núñez "dirty" bread
Sprinkled salted matza breads
Shmira Matza: The Freekeh Bread
The Suares fried tortillas of unleavened bread for Rosh Hashanah, from the spanish city of Matute
Cristóbal and Angelina de León' round tortillas
Matza from potato starch
Purple Corn Tortilla
Cheese Matzah from tapioca

SA'ADIA IBN DANAAN

*(Mid-Fifteenth Century–*1505*)*
"Back to the south and Muslim Spain. Sa'adia Ibn Danaan was born and raised in the last remaining Muslim territory on the Iberian peninsula, the kingdom of Granada, which at that time would have had a Jewish population of perhaps one thousand souls. After the city fell to the Christian Reconquest and the sentence of Expulsion was pronounced over all of Spain's Jews in 1492, Ibn Danaan fled to North Africa and settled in Morocco, where he became a leading transmitter of the Andalusian legacy and a religious authority known for his *responsa* literature and his wide learning. Apart from religious law and poetry, he wrote on history, linguistics, philosophy, biblical commentary, and poetics. He died in 1505. [. . .] Ibn Danaan is best known for his 1468 composition about the Spanish-Hebrew meters, which has been called the most detailed work of its kind written in the Middle Ages."

Pete Cole, *The Dream of the Poem. Hebrew Poetry from Muslim and Christian Spain 950–1492*, p. 333

SHE TRAPPED ME

She trapped me with temptation's **bread**;

with stolen waters she hunted me down.

Her angel's eyes looking at me

were archers slowly taking aim.

Now her cheeks are the breaking dawn.

Now her hair brings evening on.

THE OLD AND HOLY BREADS

ANCIENT JUDEAN BREAD

In *Food in Ancient Judah*, Dr. Cynthia Shafer-Elliott offers a fascinating work on domestic cooking in the time of the Hebrew Bible. The recipe below is based on her research.

SERVES: 4 flatbreads

TIME: 2 hours

3¼ cups (440 g) wheat flour

¼ cup (50 ml) whole milk

1 cup (210 ml) brine (2 tsp/10 g salt dissolved in 1 cup/200 ml lukewarm water)

½ cup (100 g) sourdough (if you are making leavened flat bread)

1 cup (200 ml) water

2 shallots, peeled

1 leek, small, washed and cut into short pieces

1 clove garlic, peeled

1. Put the wheat flour in a big bowl. Pour the milk over it, mix lightly with a spoon, and add the brine. Mix it all together with a spoon for about one minute, adding the sourdough (if desired). Knead the dough for about 15 minutes (or 10 minutes in a stand mixer). Cover it in a bowl and let it rise for about 30 minutes.

2. Add the water to a sauce pan. Once it is boiling, add the whole shallots, the leek, and the whole garlic clove. Cook over medium heat for about 15 minutes, and then remove from the water. Mash the vegetables with a fork, and press them one more time to drain.

3. Add the mashed vegetables to the dough and knead for about 10 minutes. Add ¼ cup flour if the dough is too wet. It should be sticky. Put the dough back in the bowl, cover it, and cool it in the fridge for about 20 minutes. Preheat the oven to 392°F (200°C).

4. Flour a cloth napkin, and form the dough into 4 balls the size of a tennis ball (7⅝ oz or 215 g). Put a dough ball on the floured napkin and add flour on the top. Flatten the ball with the palm of your hand until it is about 0.4 inch/1 cm thick. Repeat with all the balls.

5. Flour the flattened patties and cover them with a large napkin. If you are making the bread with sourdough, let the bread rise for about 30 minutes. For unleavened bread, do not let them rise.

6. Take a skillet and heat it over medium-high heat (or use a wood oven if you have one).

7. Put a dough patty in the skillet to cook for 3 minutes. Flip it and cook for 3 more minutes. Repeat for all of the patties.

8. Lay parchment paper in a baking tray and arrange the flatbreads on top. Bake in the oven for about 6 minutes on each side.

RAMBAM'S "POOR MAN'S BREAD" *(LECHEM ONI)*

FOR THE FIRST DAY OF PASSOVER

> "Hence even though we may put sesame seeds and nuts into honey, one may not mix them in his hand."
>
> "Mishneh Torah," Sabbath 21:17

From the third book of Rambam's *Mishneh Torah* (12th century CE), "Zemanim" (Times), *Hametz u-Matzah*, the laws of Passover:

5:20: "On the first day, it is forbidden to knead or baste [the matzot] with any other substance besides water; not because of the prohibition against chametz [yeast], but rather so [the matzah] will be 'poor man's bread.' It is only on the first day that the 'poor man's bread' must be commemorated."

6:5: "Matzah that was kneaded with fruit juice, one may fulfill one's obligation with it on Pesach. However, [the dough] should not be kneaded with wine, oil, honey, or milk, because of the requirement for poor man's bread, as explained above. A person who kneaded [dough with one of these liquids] does not fulfill his obligation. One cannot fulfill his obligation with matzah made from thin bran or coarse bran. However, one may knead flour together with its bran and make it into a loaf and fulfill one's obligation with it. Similarly, a loaf made with very fine flour is permitted, and a person may fulfill his obligation with it. We do not say: this is not poor man's bread."

Serves: 4 matzot

Time: 15 minutes

1 cup + 4 tbsp (180 g) wheat flour (not from thin bran or coarse bran)

½ cup (125 ml) fresh orange juice (or pomegranate juice, grape juice, any fresh fruit juice or water)

1. Preheat the oven to 536°F (280°C) and line a baking tray with aluminum foil. Keep a rolling pin and a fork close to you; according to the rabbinic law above, for the matzah to be kosher for Passover the preparation should not be longer than 18 minutes from beginning to end.

2. Mix together the flour and the liquid, and knead the dough for 2 minutes. Cut the dough into 4 pieces and roll them into balls. Each ball should fit in the palm of your hand. Put them in the freezer for 2 minutes.

3. Lightly flour a work surface and a rolling pin, and spread each ball into a very thin layer of dough (about 6 inches in diameter). You can use a large cookie cutter if you would like a round shape.

4. Place the matzah on the foil-lined baking sheet, and prick it with a fork across its surface. Bake for 2 and a half minutes on one side and 30 seconds on the other side.

5. Remove from the oven and put on a cooling rack.

RAMBAM'S SWEET PASSOVER MATZAH

FOR THE OTHER HOLY DAYS OF PASSOVER

5:20: "It is permissible to place spices, sesame seeds, poppy seeds, and the like into dough. Similarly, it is permissible to knead the dough with water and oil, honey or milk, or to baste with them."

6:5: "Matzah that was kneaded with fruit juice, one may fulfill one's obligation with it on Pesach."

SERVES: 6 medium matzot

TIME: 15 minutes

1 cup + 4 tbsp (180 g) wheat flour

½ cup (160 g) honey, liquid

1 tbsp sesame seeds

1 tsp anise seeds

1 tsp ground cinnamon

1 tsp ground cardamom

1. Preheat the oven to 536°F (280°C), and line a baking tray with aluminum foil. Keep a rolling pin and a fork close to you; according to the rabbinic law above, for the matzah to be kosher for Passover the preparation should not be longer than 18 minutes from beginning to end.

2. Mix together the flour and the honey, and knead the dough for 3 minutes. Add the seeds and the spices, and knead for another 1 minute. The dough will be sticky because of the honey.

3. Cut the dough into 6 pieces and roll them into balls. Each ball should fit in the palm of your hand. Put them in the freezer for 2 minutes.

4. Lightly flour a work surface and a rolling pin, and spread each ball into a very thin layer of dough (0.07 inch/2 mm, or around 4 inches/10 cm in diameter). You can use a small cookie cutter if you would like a round shape.

5. Sprinkle with ground cinnamon and ground cardamom. Place the matzah on the aluminum foil-lined baking sheet, and prick it with a fork across its surface. Bake for 2 minutes on one side, and flip them using a wood spatula. Be careful, they stick to the tray. Bake for 1 minute 30 seconds on the other side. Remove from the oven and place on a cooling rack.

RAMBAM'S SAVORY PASSOVER MATZAH
FOR THE OTHER HOLY DAYS OF PASSOVER

SERVES: 4 matzot

TIME: 15 minutes

1 cup + 4 tbsp (180 g) wheat flour

¼ cup (50 ml) dry white wine

¼ cup (50 ml) water

1 tbsp poppy seeds

1 tbsp flax seeds

1 tbsp sesame oil

2 tsp sumac

1. Prepare the oven and baking tray as above.

2. Mix together the flour and the white wine and water, and knead the dough for 3 minutes. Add the seeds, and knead for another 2 minutes.

3. Cut the dough into 4 pieces (2¼ oz/65 g each) and roll them into balls. Each ball should fit in the palm of your hand. Spread each ball with a rolling pin (or your hand) into a very thin layer of dough (6 inches/15 cm diameter).

4. Place the matzah on the aluminum foil-lined baking sheet, and prick it with a fork across its surface. Bake for 2 minutes on one side and 30 seconds on the other side.

5. Remove from the oven, brush lightly with 1 tbsp sesame oil and sprinkle with sumac. Put on a shelf to cool.

שולחן ערוך, אורח חיים

א׳

ין השכמת הבוקר ובו ט סעיפים:

תגבר כארי לעמוד בבוקר לעבודת בוראו ש

עורר השחר: הגה ועכ״פ לא יאחר זמן התפלה שהצ

טור) הגה שויתי ה׳ לנגדי תמיד הוא כלל גדול בתו

הצדיקים אשר הולכים לפני האלהים כי אין ישיבת הא

עסקיו והוא לבדו בביתו כישיבתו ותנועותיו ועסקיו וה

דול ולא דבורו והרחבת פיו כרצונו והוא עם אנשי

דבורו במושב המלך כ״ש כשישים האדם אל לבו ש

הקב״ה אשר מלא כל הארץ כבודו עומד עליו ורואה

THE "SHULCHAN ARUKH"

THE "SHULCHAN ARUKH" ORACH CHAYIM 455:6 MATZAH

Shulchan Arukh Orach Chayim 455:6: "[Regarding] kneading with caraway, sesame and other types of seasonings, it's kosher [for the Mitzvah] since there is the taste of Matzah. Nevertheless, one shouldn't place in seasonings, as they are focused [spicy] and will heat the dough."

SERVES: 4 matzot

TIME: 15 minutes

1 cup (150 g) wheat flour

2 tbsp (20 g) rice flour

¼ cup (50 ml) white wine

¼ cup (50 ml) water

1 tbsp olive oil (to brush)

1 tbsp caraway seeds (to sprinkle)

1 tbsp sesame seeds (to sprinkle)

1. Preheat the oven to 536°F (280°C), and line a baking tray with aluminum foil. Keep a rolling pin and a fork close to you.

2. Mix together the two flours, white wine and water, and knead the dough for 3 minutes.

3. Cut the dough into 4 pieces (2¼ oz/65 g each) and roll them into balls. Each ball should fit in the palm of your hand.

4. Take the rolling pin (or your hands) and spread each ball into a very thin layer of dough (6 inches in diameter). Place the matzah on the aluminum foil-lined baking sheet, and prick it with a fork across its surface.

5. Bake for 1 minutes 30 seconds on one side and 30 seconds on the other side. They should remain white and soft.

6. Remove from the oven and brush it with olive oil. Sprinkle with the caraway and sesame seeds and place on a cooling rack.

THE "SHULCHAN ARUKH" ORACH CHAYIM 453:2 MATZAH

> "If one makes dough from both wheat and rice, if it has the taste of [wheat] grain, one can fulfill the obligation with it on Pesach."

Serves: 4 large matzot

Time: 15 minutes

1 cup (150 g) wheat flour

⅛ cup (20 g) rice flour

½ cup (100 ml) water

1. Preheat the oven to 536°F (280°C), and line a baking tray with aluminum foil. Keep a rolling pin and a fork close to you.

2. Mix together the flours and water, and knead the dough for 1 minute. Place in the freezer for 2 minutes.

3. Cut the dough into 4 pieces (2¼ oz/65 g each) and roll them into balls. Each ball should fit in the palm of your hand. Roll each ball in rice flour.

4. Take a rolling pin (or your hands) and spread each ball into a very thin layer of dough (8 inches/20 cm diameter). According to the liturgy, for the matzah to be kosher for Passover, the preparation should not be longer than 18 minutes from beginning to end.

5. Place the matzah on the foil-lined baking sheet, and prick it with a fork over its surface.

6. Bake for 1 and a half minutes on one side and 30 seconds on the other side.

7. Remove from the oven and place on a cooling rack.

MATZAH ASHIRAH: RICH MAN'S EGG MATZAH

FROM "SHULCHAN ARUKH" ORACH CHAYIM 444:1

> "When the 14th of Nissan (the eve of the Passover holiday) occurs on Shabbat we search for *hametz* on the 13th and burn everything before Shabbat and we leave over enough food for the first two Shabbat meals, for the timing of the third meal is after Mincha time and at that time we are not able to have the meal with either matzah or hametz rather with *matzah ashirah* (egg matzah) and the meal should be eaten before the tenth hour."

SERVES: 8 matzot

TIME: 25 minutes

2 cups (300 g) wheat flour

1 egg beaten

½ cup (100 ml) water

1 tbsp date syrup (aka silan) (see recipe page 337)

1. Preheat your oven to 536°F (280°C), and place aluminum foil in a baking tray. Take a rolling pin and a fork, and keep them close to you.

2. Mix all the ingredients together, and knead the dough for 5 minutes. Cut the dough into 4 pieces (3⅞ oz/113 g each) and roll them into balls. Each ball should fit in the palm of your hand.

3. Take the rolling pin (or your hands) and spread each ball into a very thin layer of dough (6 inches in diameter).

4. Place the matzah on the aluminum foil on the baking sheet, and prick it with a fork over its surface. Bake for 2 minutes on one side and 30 seconds on the other side.

FOOD & HOLIDAYS

ROSH HASHANAH

Rosh Hashanah ("the head of the year") marks the beginning of the Jewish year. Rosh Hashanah occurs on the first day of the Hebrew month of Tishri and opens the Jewish holiday month, which includes Yom Kippur and Succot. Nowadays, Rosh Hashanah is one of the main Jewish Holidays, synonymous with joy and happiness.

During the Inquisition in the Middle Ages, however, Rosh Hashanah did not have the same importance for the crypto-Jews of Spain and Portugal. During this period, Rosh Hashanah was referred to alternately as "the feast of the horn," "Roxiaxana," "capdany," "Roçana," "the festival of the eighth month and fifteenth days," or "Rofagana." It was paid little attention by the *conversos*—Jews who were forced to convert to Catholicism and hide their Jewish identity. Given the circumstances, they focused their attention on Yom Kippur and other fasts, believing that the salvation of their souls was more important than the celebration of any feast. Because of this, culinary references to Rosh Hashanah celebrations during this period are particularly rare. Nevertheless, I identified some scattered references to food made during Inquisition trials. Eggs, oil and honey seem to be the foods used to be the foods used to celebrate Rosh Hashanah.

SUARES' FRIED UNLEAVENED TORTILLAS
FOR ROSH HASHANAH (MATUTE, SPAIN)

María García Redondo reported to the court in Almazan on June 6, 1505, that the wife of Francisco Suares, who lived in Matute (La Rioja, Spain), was preparing unleavened bread dough, kneading it with an egg, and adding oil to the dough. She remembers that it was for the period of San Miguel [a feast that falls on September 29, during Rosh Hashanah] and that she made three tortillas and a small cake, and that the cake with meat in it was eaten by a child she saw.

"[Maria] saw the wife of the aforementioned Francisco [Suares], whose name is unknown, kneading unleavened bread [*pan cenceño*], that is to say, bread without yeast. She kneaded it with one egg and added oil to the [. . .] dough. And she remembers it was for San Miguel, and that she made three *tortillas*."

SERVES: 12 tortillas

TIME: 1 hour 30 minutes

2½ cups (375 g) flour

½ teaspoon of salt

2 tablespoons (20 ml) olive oil

⅔ cup + 1 tbsp (150 ml) warm water

1 egg

⅛ cup (30 g) pomegranate syrup, to drizzle

⅛ cup fresh cheese, like labneh (see recipe p. 352)

3 figs, dried or fresh

Oil for frying (such as vegetable or canola oil)

1. In a large mixing bowl, whisk together the flour and salt. Add the olive oil, warm water, and egg to the bowl and mix until a dough forms. Knead the dough on a lightly floured surface for 5–7 minutes, until it is smooth and elastic.

2. Divide the dough into small pieces. Each one should be 1⅛ oz (30 g), the size of a ping-pong ball. Put them in a plastic bag and cool in the fridge for 1 hour. Roll the dough balls out into thin circles (about 6 inches/15 cm in diameter).

3. Heat a large skillet over medium-high heat and add a small amount of oil. Fry the matzah tortillas one at a time, flipping once, until they are lightly browned on both sides (about 1 minute on each side).

4. Remove the matzot from the skillet, drizzle with pomegranate syrup, and dip into fresh cheese and eat with figs. If desired, you can break the matzot into small pieces and fry them in oil until they are crispy.

YOM KIPPUR

Yom Kippur, a Jewish holiday observed on the 10th day of the Jewish month of Tishri, is commonly referred to as "the Day of Atonement." This day holds great significance as it symbolizes a fresh start and the purification of the soul for the Jewish community. Yom Kippur marks the culmination of the "10 days of repentance," which commence with Rosh Hashanah. In the Bible, Yom Kippur is often described as the "Sabbath of Sabbaths." One of the distinctive features of Yom Kippur is the practice of abstaining from food, drink, and sexual relations.

Yom Kippur holds a particularly special place in the hearts of Jews from the Iberian Peninsula. When the Inquisition began in 1478 and the Decree of Expulsion was issued 14 years after, Yom Kippur took on even greater significance and became a deeply meaningful holiday to celebrate. In the New World, where Judaism was initially not widely observed due to a lack of knowledgeable Jewish leaders and resources, crypto-Jews had to rely on alternative methods to determine the timing of Yom Kippur. They used various reference points such as the moon, the Christian feast of Saint Matthew, and the grape harvest to pinpoint the precise date for observing Yom Kippur. Consequently, Yom Kippur was often the most prominent holiday in their makeshift calendars. This historical fact is supported by evidence from trials held in places like Chile (1602), Quito (Ecuador), and Lima (Peru) (1635).

Before 1492, Yom Kippur was cherished for its symbolism of atonement. However, after this pivotal year, Jewish conversos regarded Yom Kippur as the most solemn and essential festival in their religious calendar, with a particular focus on the importance of fasting as a means to safeguard their souls. Yom Kippur goes by various names, but the ones most frequently mentioned in Inquisition trials are "el día grande" (The Great Day) or "Quipur." Other names include "equipuz," "antepur," "el ayuno del día grande/mayor"

(The Fast of the Greatest Day), and "The 10th day of the September moon."

MARÍA GARCÍA'S MATZAH AND CHICKEN SOUP TO PREPARE FOR THE YOM KIPPUR FAST

María García from Almazán was denounced because "a witness saw her eating eggs the day before fasting and unleavened cakes [*tortas*] made with meat broth on said days prior to fasting."

In his book "The Regimen of Health" (1198), Maimonides advocates for a diet that sustains one's strength through the consumption of light foods, such as chicken soup, meat broth, soft egg yolk, and wine for those who can tolerate it. He even mentions the inclusion of slightly stronger elements like chicken meat. Maimonides' reference to chicken soup evokes memories of the dish my Andalusian grandmother, Ana Guillen Palma Torres, used to prepare, which interestingly has historical roots dating back to the Spanish Inquisition trial records of the sixteenth century. This dish has since evolved and is now known as "puchero."

Serves: 4 people

Time: 30 minutes

For the puchero soup:

½ pound (220 g) of chicken breast

2 or 3 tbsp olive oil

1 clove garlic, chopped

3 carrots

2 stalks of celery, with leaves

½ cup (100 g) cooked chickpeas

1 onion

1 tsp salt

½ tsp black pepper

5 cups (1.5 liters) water

½ cup (100 g) rice

4 eggs

1 fresh lemon's juice + 1 tsp salt

For the broth matzah:

½ cup (125 ml) chicken broth taken from the puchero

1 cup + 4 tbsp (180 g) wheat flour (not from thin bran or coarse bran)

1. Preheat your oven to 536°F (280°C), and place aluminum foil in a baking tray. Take a rolling pin and a fork, and keep them handy.

2. Soften the chicken breasts by beating them, and cut them into thin, small strips. Peel and wash the carrots. Cut them in half lengthwise, then cut them into pieces that are ¾ of an inch (2 cm) long. Wash the celery stalks, cut them into pieces that are ¾ of an inch (2 cm) long as well, and keep their leaves. Cut the onion into thin slices.

3. In a pot, heat the olive oil over medium heat. Add the chopped garlic clove and the pieces of chicken breast, and brown for 5 minutes.

4. Add the carrots, celery (including the leaves), cooked chickpeas, onion, salt, pepper, and water to the pot. Cook covered for 15 minutes. Then add the rice and cook uncovered for 10 minutes. Add a little water if the mixture thickens.

5. While the puchero is simmering, mix together the flour and ½ cup of the puchero broth, and knead the dough for 2 minutes. Cut the dough into 4 pieces and roll them into balls. Each ball should fit in the palm of your hand. Put them in the freezer for 2 minutes.

6. Lightly flour a working surface, and using the rolling pin or your hands, spread each ball into a very thin layer of dough (6 inches in diameter).

7. Place the matzah on the foil-lined baking sheet, and prick it with a fork across its surface.

8. Bake for 1 minute and 30 seconds on one side and 30 seconds on the other side.

9. Remove from the oven and place on a cooling rack.

10. In a separate small saucepan, take 2 cups of the broth and bring to a boil. Crack an egg in the saucepan and move the egg around the pan so that the broth cooks it for 2 minutes, until soft boiled. Remove the egg and place it aside in a serving bowl, and do the same for the other 3 eggs in three additional bowls. Ladle the *puchero* into each bowl around the egg.

11. Pour fresh lemon juice in a small bowl, and add 1 tsp salt.

12. Break the matzah into pieces, and dip your matzah chunk into the lemon juice and then dip it into the egg of the puchero. Eat everything while it's hot.

SPAIN

ISABEL RODRÍGUEZ'S *HOJUELAS*

TO BREAK THE FAST (TOLEDO, 1677)

To break the fast, Isabel de Luna's family had, for several generations, eaten "fruits [. . .] and fried thin rolled [*hojuelas*] honeyed [*con miel*] pastries and chocolate with biscuits [*bizcochos*]." Converso Jews from the Mexican city of Guadalajara used to break the fast drinking chocolate.

Hojuelas take us on a long journey from Spain to Argentina. All Sephardim are familiar with these rolled thin strips of pastry that are quickly fried and deliciously covered in sugar: they are impossibly tender and melt in your mouth. Though they are known under many names (*fijuelas*, *fazuelos*, *hojuelas*), their characteristic shape reminds one of the megillah of Esther and the scroll read during the Jewish holiday of Purim. *Hojuelas* are traditionally prepared to celebrate this Jewish holiday.

In memory of Esther's story and prowess, roll up your sleeves, warm up your wrists, and get ready to prepare these wonderful hojuelas. These will be tastier and smoother if you prepare the dough the day before frying it.

SERVES: 10 pieces

TIME: 40 minutes

For the dough:

2 cups (300 g) flour

1 tsp baking powder

3 eggs, beaten

½ cup (50 g) sugar

2 tsp water

½ tsp salt

7 tsp neutral oil for frying

For the syrup:

½ cup (100 ml) water

¼ cup (50 ml) orange blossom water

½ cup (100 g) sugar

To decorate:

½ cup (50 g) icing sugar

¼ cup (30 g) sesame seeds

1. Place the flour, the baking powder, the beaten eggs, the sugar, the water, the salt, and the oil in a bowl and mix with a spoon. Finish mixing with your hands. The dough should be smooth, without lumps.

2. Wrap the dough in plastic wrap and cool for 15 minutes in the refrigerator. Sprinkle flour on your working surface and roll out the dough into a thin layer. The dough should not be sticky.

3. Cut strips 1 generous inch (3 cm) wide and about 15 inches (40 cm) long, and heat the oil over medium heat.

4. Take a strip in your hand. Gently stick the teeth of a fork into one end of the strip, and put the fork in the oil to cook this portion of the strip while keeping the rest out of the pan. Small bubbles will form on the dough. Every two seconds, gently twist the fork to roll up a little more of the strip, and fry that bit. Continue like this until the entire strip of dough has been wrapped around the fork and fried. Set aside and continue in the same way for all *hojuelas*.

5. Prepare the syrup: pour the water, orange blossom and sugar into a pan. Stir over low heat for 5 minutes. The mixture should remain very liquid and transparent.

6. Put the sesame seeds and the icing sugar on two separate plates. Soak the fried *hojuelas* in the sugar syrup, being careful not to break them, and then dip one side of the *hojuela* into the sesame seeds. Take another hojuela and instead of diping it into the sesame seeds, dip it lightly into icing sugar.

TOLEDAN BISCUITS AND HOT CHOCOLATE

FROM ISABEL RODRÍGUEZ TO BREAK THE FAST (1677)

The use of chocolate among Sephardic Jews of Spain was rather rare. Cocoa beans had been cultivated by the Maya in Mesoamerica for at least a few thousand years, but were not brought back to the Old World before the arrival of Christopher Columbus in 1492. In *Living in Silverado*, David Gitlitz explains that Columbus became aware of cocoa in 1502 when he saw the natives on the coast of Honduras drinking it, and he brought back cocoa beans to Spain. Its trade to Spain began in the early 1530 s and cocoa then spread throughout Europe. Originally, the drink was made from ground cocoa beans mixed with cornmeal and water. It was not sweetened.

The cocoa drink mentioned 150 years after the arrival of cocoa beans in Spain likely has nothing to do with the original bitter version. This sweetened version accompanied by treats such as biscuits and hojuelas goes perfectly with the period of sweet celebrations that begins with Rosh Hashanah and Yom Kippur.

SERVES: 10 people

TIME: 30 minutes + 1 h cooling

- 1¼ (180 g) flour
- 10 tbsp (125 g) butter, softened
- 3 tbsp (20 g) corn starch
- 2 egg yolks
- ½ + ⅓ cups (137 g) icing sugar
- 4 tbsp (50 g) ground almonds
- 1 tsp ground cinnamon
- 1 tbsp honey (to brush)

1. In a bowl, mix together the softened butter, flour, and starch until the mixture is homogeneous. Add the icing sugar, the cinnamon and the ground almonds. Stir until mixed but don't over stir.

2. Add the egg yolks, mix everything with a rubber spatula, and put the dough in a plastic bag. Put it in the fridge for about 1 hour.

3. Roll out the dough and shape it as a log (1.6 inch/4 cm) diameter. Heat the oven at 392°F (200°C), and line a baking tray with parchment paper.

4. With a knife, cut slices 0.4 inch (1 cm) thick, and put them on the parchment paper. Leave about ¾ of an inch (2 cm) of space between them. Brush them with honey, and bake for 15 minutes or until golden.

5. Let them cool out of the oven without moving them for about 10 minutes.

6. Enjoy these biscuits at room temperature. You can store them in an airtight container.

CREAMY HOT CHOCOLATE

SPAIN

SERVES: 4 glasses

TIME: 20 minutes

2 cups (475 ml) whole milk

½ cup (120 ml) heavy cream

4 oz (115 g) bittersweet chocolate, chopped

¼ cup (50 g) granulated sugar

½ tsp vanilla extract

Pinch of salt

Whipped cream, for topping (optional)

1. In a medium saucepan, heat the milk and cream over medium heat until it starts to steam. Add the chopped chocolate and sugar to the saucepan, and stir until the chocolate is melted and the sugar is dissolved.

2. Stir in the vanilla extract and salt. Continue to cook the hot chocolate, stirring occasionally, until it thickens slightly and coats the back of a spoon, about 5–7 minutes. Remove the hot chocolate from heat and let it cool slightly before serving.

3. If you want a foamy chocolate, wait until it is lukewarm (not hot!) and pour the liquid into a glass bottle. Shake for 30 seconds. Pour into a glass and serve topped with whipped cream, if desired.

GASPAR VÁEZ'S FISH EMPANADAS
FOR AFTER YOM KIPPUR

Gaspar Váez, a well-known converso who was living in Mexico used to break the fast of Yom Kippur by dining on eggs, salad, empanadas, fish, olives and hot chocolate, avoiding any meat. Chocolate could be substituted for the wine used for the Kiddush of Shabbat because it was seen as a drink used to celebrate holidays. Because of this, drinking chocolate was another telltale sign of converso customs, along with fasting and secretive behavior.

Fish pies were also significant in the culinary customs of the converso Jews in Mexico and Brazil and were typically consumed after the Yom Kippur holiday to conclude the fast. I didn't find a recipe for fish pie among the historical records, but the dish was recognized as one of the various means by which conversos were exposed and reported.

SERVES: 10 small pies

TIME: 1 hour

For the dough:

2½ cups (375 g) flour
1 egg
½ tsp salt
⅓ cup (75 g) soft butter or margarine or olive oil
½ cup (110 g) water
1 egg, beaten (to brush)

For the filling:

¼ cup (50 g) olive oil
1 garlic clove, chopped
1 onion
1 lb (400 g) fresh white fish (cod or hake)
1 cup (100 g to 150 g) grated cheese (like Emmental)
3 eggs, beaten
½ tsp salt
1 tsp black pepper

1. To make the dough, beat the eggs, and add flour and salt. Add the soft butter (or oil). Mix all the ingredients together. Knead the dough for 5 minutes until even and smooth. Cover and put in the fridge for 30 minutes.

2. Meanwhile, prepare the filling: add the olive oil, garlic, and chopped onion to a pan, and fry for 3 minutes until golden. Add the fish and sauté for 5 minutes at medium heat. Transfer to a big bowl to cool.

3. In another bowl, mix the grated cheese and egg. Add salt and black pepper. Then, add the fish mixture.

4. Roll out the dough between two pieces of parchment paper until it is a tenth of an inch thick (a couple of millimeters). To prepare the first individual pie, cut out a circle with a round cookie cutter (2 inches/5 cm in diameter, or in any case larger than your pie dish). Grease each small pie dish, lay the first disk of dough in it and raise it around the edges to the top. Add in the filling, leaving some room at the top. Cut out another dough circle and cover the top of the pie. Flatten the edges. Do the same for the rest of your small pies. Once finished, refrigerate for at least 30 minutes.

5. Turn on the oven to 400°F (200°C). Take your cold fish pies out of the fridge and put them on a tray. Brush them with egg wash, and prick the top with a knife. Once the oven is hot, cook them for 25 minutes. Wait until the pies have cooled to remove them from their molds.

MEXICO

MANUEL DE LUCENA AND ÁLVARO DE CARRIÓN

YOM KIPPUR TORTILLAS

Álvaro de Carrión was a converso of Spanish origin who later emigrated to northern Portugal and whose parents later returned to the Spanish town of Cervera del Río Pisuerga, in the mountains north of the city of Palencia. This town was known for its sheep and goat farms, and most likely for its production of milk and cheese. Carrión then emigrated to Mexico in 1580. He lived on a ranch in the countryside of Mexico City, not far from the Mexican town of Pachuca. Luis de Carvajal was a friend of his and he used to visit Carrión at his farm where he produced, among other products, goat milk and goat cheese, which were sold in the store of the crypto-Jew Manuel de Lucena, in Pachuca. When Luis de Carvajal decided to celebrate Yom Kippur for an entire week—he fasted during the day and dined after dark—he asked his friend Carrión for a favor. We thus know that "Lucena had provisioned him with two candles, a box of fruit preserves, and a dish of fried eggs and cheese called 'frutas de sartén.'" This was in September 1594.

As David Gitlitz explains in his book *Living in Silverado*, Carvajal (who had run out of food) asked Álvaro de Carrión—who was living close by in his farm—"for more fried eggs, fresh cheese and tortillas, cautioning him that they must not include any bacon, lard or other pork product."

Serves: 10

Time: 1 hour

For the dough:

2 cups (300 g) nixtamalized red corn flour/masa harina (or any color you prefer)

1½ tsp salt

1⅓ cups (260 ml) hot water

½ green Serrano chili pepper, chopped

½ red jalapeño chili pepper, chopped

¼ tsp smoked paprika

1 tsp olive oil

1. Wash the green and red chiles. Cut them into a half and remove the pits, and dice them very finely.

2. To make the dough, mix together corn flour and salt in a large bowl. Add the olive oil, the smoked paprika, the chopped chiles and the hot water.

3. Mix the preparation with a spoon until all the water is absorbed. Make balls of dough the size of a golf ball (1⅛ oz (30 g). Let them to rest on a plate for 20 minutes, covered so they do not dry out.

4. To flatten and cook the tortillas, you can use a tortilla press if you have one (remember to put the dough ball between two pieces of parchment paper so it does not stick to the press): place the dough in the center of the bottom part of the press, push the top down until the dough is spread thin, and then open it and carefully remove the tortilla from the parchment paper. If you don't have a tortilla press, you can use the bottom of a heavy saucepan with parchment paper and press down hard.

5. Cook in a preheated (medium-high heat) nonstick skillet for 20 seconds. Then flip the tortilla over and cook the other side for 20 seconds more. Repeat the operation once more until the tortilla has golden-brown marks.

6. Keep the tortillas in a plastic bag but do not close it completely.

SUKKOT

Sukkot, also spelled as Succot or Succoth, is a Jewish holiday that is often referred to as the Feast of Tabernacles or the Feast of Booths. It is one of the three major Jewish pilgrimage festivals, along with Passover (Pesach) and Shavuot. Sukkot occurs in the fall and typically lasts for seven days, with an additional day celebrated outside of Israel.

The central theme of Sukkot is to commemorate and celebrate the harvest season, as well as to remember the Israelites' journey through the desert after their exodus from Egypt, during which they lived in temporary shelters or booths (sukkot in Hebrew). To observe Sukkot, Jewish families build temporary outdoor structures called sukkot, which are typically made of natural materials like branches and leaves. The sukkah serves as a reminder of the temporary dwellings used by the Israelites in the wilderness.

During Sukkot, Jewish people eat their meals and sometimes sleep in the sukkah (the singular form of sukkot). It is customary to invite guests to the sukkah and to recite blessings over the Four Species (Lulav and Etrog), which include a palm branch, myrtle branches, willow branches, and a citron fruit. The Four Species represent different aspects of the natural world.

Sukkot is a joyous holiday, characterized by festive meals, singing, dancing, and expressing gratitude for the harvest and the protection provided by God during the Israelites' wanderings. It is a time for community and family gatherings, and it is also a reminder of the impermanence of material possessions and the importance of faith and trust in God.

BAKER´S STRIKE IN THE 13TH CENTURY, ALEXANDRIA (EGYPT)

The following letter sent from Alexandria to Fustat tells about a baker's strike that happened in September—October during the 13th century immediately after the autumn holidays. Goiten translated it as follows:

"On the second day of Sukkot feast there were great disturbances in Alexandria because of the bread, which could not be found all over the city, until God brought relief by the end of the day; the governor and the superintendent of the markets rode out and threatened to burn down [the houses of] the bakers because of the bread, after they had inquired with the people at one oven in the east and one in the west. At the end there remained fifty hundred weights of bread in the ovens that night. So do not worry."

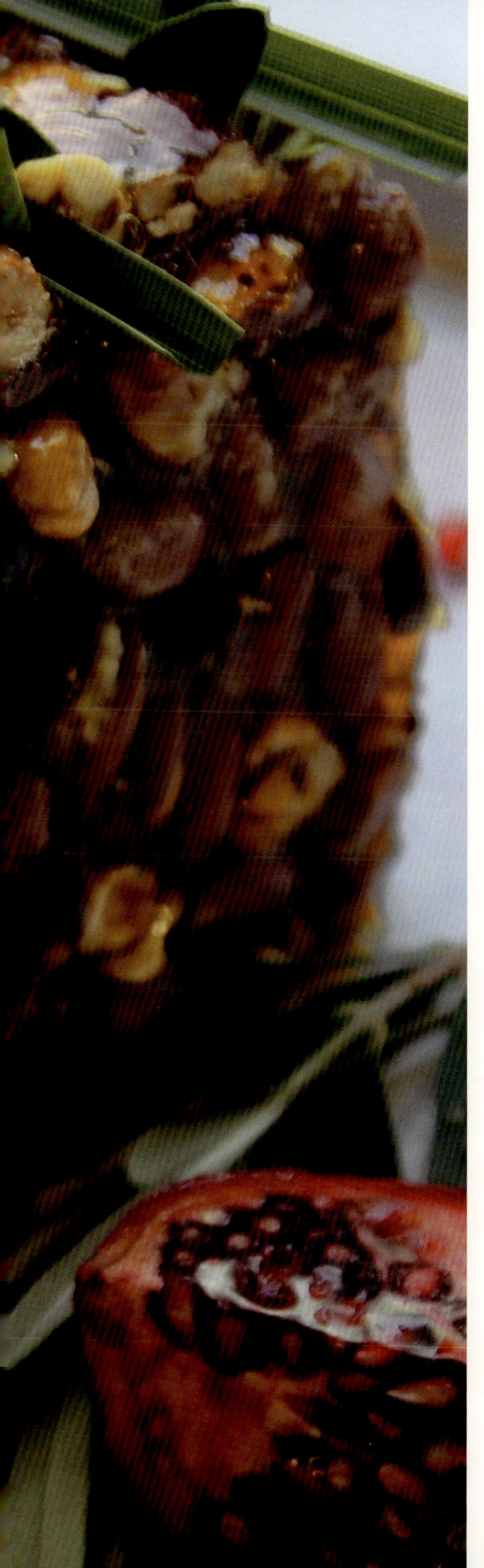

In Mexico City on September 21, 1603, Sebastián Rodríguez organized a grand event at Cárcel Perpétua, a mandatory boarding house where prisoners were required to sleep but had freedom during the day for their personal affairs. This establishment was likely situated near Plaza de Santo Domingo, the headquarters of the Court of the Inquisition in Mexico City. The purpose of this festive gathering was to celebrate Sukkot, during which a variety of dishes were prepared in Sebastián Rodríguez's personal kitchen, primarily by his wife and daughter.

The celebration was opulent and Rodríguez extended an invitation to the entire Portuguese prison community. In accordance with Sukkot traditions, which included constructing an outdoor hut and adorning it with fruits for meals, the prison was meticulously decorated. Rodríguez and the other attendees moved their tables outside into the prison courtyard, beneath the open sky. They embellished the corridor pillars with willow branches and leaves, which Rodríguez had purchased and arranged for four natives to deliver to the prison. However, three of Rodríguez's guests, namely Ruy Díaz Nieto, Héctor de Fonseca, and Antonio Díaz Márquez, declined the invitation. Gil de la Guarda speculated that their refusal stemmed from their insistence on consuming only kosher food, whereas "everyone else in the Cárcel Perpetua . . . eats salted pork without concern." While Ruy Díaz Nieto remained in his cell to pray, Héctor de Fonseca and Antonio Díaz Márquez adorned the corridor in front of their cell with branches and strewn twigs on the floor. The Mexican converso Sebastián Rodríguez and his companions commemorated Sukkot with a banquet, savoring sweet pastries, turcos, cakes, pies, and blanc-manger (*pasteles, turcos, tortas, empanadas y manjar blanco*).

This Jewish celebration of a major holiday appears to be the last one scheduled by the crypto-Jews living in Mexico.

QUINCE CAKE WITH HONEY

MEXICO

According to Professor Gerrit Bos, in his medical treatise *On Asthma*, Maimonides states that "to suck quinces after the meal is beneficial, but one should not take too much of them, because all the astringent things such as quinces, lotus fruits and medlars are harmful for this disease [asthma]."

SERVES: 10 people

TIME: 1 hour 30 minutes

5⅓ oz (150 g) softened unsalted butter (+ 1 tbsp for greasing the pan)

1⅔ cup (250 g) flour

¾ cup (150 g) sugar

1½ tsp baking powder

3 eggs

¾ cup (100 g) almond flour

3 quinces (or 4 hard peaches if preferred), peeled, cored, and halved

1 yellow or green lemon peel and juice from the lemon

¼ cup (75 g) honey

1 tsp vanilla extract

2½ cups (450 ml) water

1 orange's juice

½ cup almonds, slivered

For serving:

1 cup Labneh

1 cup icing sugar

1. To poach the quince, peel strips of lemon zest into a saucepan, and add a little squeeze of the juice. Stir in the honey, vanilla extract, and pour in water. Bring to a boil, stirring constantly and then cook over medium heat for about 10 minutes. (If you want to make caramelized quince sauce as a side, see the recipe below.)

2. Peel, halve and core the quince. Cut each half into 1 cm wedges, and place them into the pan. Poach for 25–35 minutes or until just tender—the time will depend on how ripe your quinces are. If using peaches, slice but do not peel them, and poach them for 3 minutes or until tender.

3. Remove the fruit from the sauce pan.

4. Remove the lemon peel from the syrup. Squeeze the juice of one orange into the syrup and cook over medium heat to thicken for about 5 to 10 minutes. Set aside to cool completely.

5. Preheat the oven to 330°F (170°C). Grease a 9-inches (23 cm) long cake pan. You can also make two cakes in smaller pans.

Place the flour in a large bowl with the almond flour, sugar, baking powder, butter, and ¼ cup of the cooled syrup. Mix until well blended.

6. In a separate bowl, beat the eggs for about 5 minutes until the mixture is fluffy. Add half of the cooked quinces, and fold through the mixture. Spoon the mixture into the baking pan and arrange the remaining fruits slices on top.

7. Bake the cake for about 33 minutes. If you are making muffins, bake them only for 23 minutes.

8. In a bowl, thoroughly mix the labneh and icing sugar; add the sugar slowly to avoid lumps. Cover and cool in the fridge.

9. Pour the remaining syrup over the finished cake. Sprinkle with the ½ cup of slivered almonds and bake for another 3 minutes. Leave to cool in the baking pan for about 20 minutes.

10. Serve lukewarm with a spoonful of sweet labneh.

CARAMELIZED QUINCE SAUCE

SERVES: 2–3 cups of sauce

TIME: approximately 1 hour 30 minutes

3–4 large quinces, peeled, cored, and diced

1 cup granulated sugar

½ cup water

1 cinnamon stick (optional)

1 lemon, juiced

Pinch of salt

1. Wash, peel, and core the quinces. Cut them into small, uniform pieces. In a large saucepan, combine the diced quinces, sugar, water, and a pinch of salt. If desired, add a cinnamon stick for extra flavor. Squeeze the lemon juice over the quinces to prevent browning and add a fresh citrus note. Stir the mixture to combine.

2. Place the saucepan over medium heat and bring the mixture to a simmer. Reduce the heat to low and let the quinces cook gently. Stir occasionally to prevent sticking.

3. As the quinces cook, they will release their natural pectin and slowly turn a beautiful caramel color. This process can take anywhere from 45 minutes to 1.5 hours, depending on the quinces' ripeness. Be patient and watch for the quinces to transform into a caramelized sauce with a thick, jam-like consistency.

4. To check if the quince sauce is ready, take a small spoonful and place it on a chilled plate. If it thickens and holds its shape without spreading too much, it's done. Remove the cinnamon stick if you added one.

5. Once the quince sauce has reached the desired caramelization, remove it from the heat and let it cool to room temperature.

6. This sauce is also delicious with a poultry dish and garlic and parsley challah croutons (see recipe on p. 225).

TURCOS

<u>Serves</u>: 20 pieces

<u>Time</u>: 45 minutes

For the dough:

3½ cups (490 g) all-purpose flour

7 tbsp (100 g) margarine

¾ cup (180 ml) water

2–3 inches of cinnamon stick (or ⅛ tsp ground cinnamon)

¼ tsp anise seeds

1 tsp (5 g) granulated sugar

1 tsp (5 g) baking powder

½ tsp salt

For the Lamb Filling:

500 g lamb, cut into small cubes

½ cup (100 g) olive oil (for the marinade)

1 tsp salt

1 short cinnamon stick

½ tsp anise seeds

¼ tsp ground nutmeg

¼ cup (40 g) raisins (in the marinade)

2 tbsp (40 g) honey

2 cloves garlic, chopped

Juice of ½ lemon

Water (enough to cover the meat + 1 cup)

1 apple (red or green), peeled and cut into small chunks

¼ cup (40 g) golden raisins (added at the end)

¼ cup (30 g) chopped almonds

1 egg (for egg wash)

1. In a saucepan, combine the water, cinnamon stick, anise seeds, and raisins for the filling. Bring to a boil and let it simmer for 5 minutes. Remove from heat and let it cool.

2. In a large bowl, combine the flour, sugar, baking powder, salt, and margarine. Remove the cinnamon stick and raisins from the saucepan and set them aside. Add the cooled water with the anise seeds to the dry ingredients and mix until a dough forms.

3. Knead the dough by hand for about 5 minutes until it becomes smooth and homogeneous.

4. Form the dough into a ball and place it in a plastic bag. Chill it in the refrigerator for at least 30 minutes, or overnight.

5. In a large bowl, make a marinade with the olive oil, salt, cinnamon stick, anise seeds, nutmeg, raisins, honey, chopped garlic, and lemon juice. Mix well and add the cubed lamb. Cover and refrigerate for at least 2 hours or overnight.

6. Heat a large pot over medium-high heat. Add a few tablespoons of oil and cook the lamb for about 10 minutes until golden-brown. Add the other ingredients of the marinade, add water until the ingredients are covered, and then add one more cup of water. Cover the pot and cook for about one hour.

7. Remove the cinnamon stick. Uncover the pot and cook for another 30 minutes, until there is very little water left and the meat is very tender. The color of the sauce should be dark.

8. Add the golden raisins, apple chunks, and chopped almonds. Mix and let the mixture cool.

Making the *turcos*:

1. Preheat the oven to 375°F (180°C), and line a baking tray with parchment paper. Cut the dough in half to make two balls. Place one ball on a parchment paper. Cover it with another parchment paper and roll it to ⅛ inch thickness.

2. Remove the top sheet of parchment paper and use a cookie cutter to make rounds 4 inches (10 cm) in diameter. Using a small bowl of water and your fingers, apply water to half of the outer edge of each round.

3. Place each round on the parchment-lined baking tray. Add one tablespoon of the lamb filling to the middle of the half round, fold the round over the filling, and press the edges of the round together to seal it. You can use a fork to press over the edges to seal it better or use your fingers for a more aesthetic look. Continue until all of the dough and filling are used.

4. Brush the egg wash over the *turcos*. Bake for about 20 minutes until golden.

FIG AND ALMOND *TORTAS*

Serves: 6 people

Time: 1 hour 30 minutes

For the Pastry Dough (for one 12-inch or two 8-inch pan tarts):

1 cup (150 g) icing sugar

1¾ cup (288 g) flour

1 tsp salt

9 tbsp (135 g) unsalted butter, softened

1 egg

2 tsp vanilla extract or ½ vanilla bean

For the Almond Custard:

⅔ cup (150 g) sugar

1 cup (150 g) ground almonds

8 tbsp (120 g) unsalted butter, softened

1 egg

1 egg yolk

1 tbsp flour

1 tsp almond extract

For the Fig Marmalade:

8 fresh figs

2 tbsp butter

½ vanilla bean (or ½ tbsp vanilla extract)

For the Egg Custard:

1 egg

2 tbsp (24 g) sugar

½ cup (132 g) heavy cream

To Decorate:

2 figs, sliced

2 tbsp almonds, chopped

For the Pastry Dough:

1. In a large bowl, sift together the icing sugar, flour, and salt to remove any lumps. In another bowl, mix the softened unsalted butter until smooth. Add the egg and vanilla extract (or split the ½ vanilla bean into two halves and add the seeds to the butter). Slowly mix the two bowls' ingredients until they form a homogeneous dough. Form the dough into one ball for one 12-inch pan tart or split the dough into two equal parts if making two tarts (8 inches each). Place the dough ball(s) in a plastic bag and cool in the fridge for about 30 minutes.

2. Take two parchment paper sheets. Lay the first one on a working surface and place the ball of dough on top. Cover the dough with the second parchment sheet and roll it out until it is about ⅛ of an inch (3 mm) thick. Remove the parchment paper from the top and put the dough (with the parchment paper still on the bottom) into a tart pan (ideally with a removable bottom). Make sure the dough reaches over the edges of the pan by about 1 to 1¼ inches (2.5 to 3 cm). Cool the pan with the dough for 15 minutes. If making two tarts (8 inches each), repeat the same process with the other ball of dough.

For the Almond Custard:

1. Preheat the oven to 365°F (185°C). In a bowl, mix together the sugar and ground almonds.

2. Add the softened unsalted butter and mix until well combined. Stir in the egg and egg yolk.

3. Add the flour and almond extract. Stir until the mixture is well combined, and cool in the fridge for 15 minutes.

4. Take the tart pan with the cooled dough and spread the almond custard across the dough on the bottom of the pan. If making two tarts, put the same amount of almond custard over the bottom of the dough of each pan. Bake for 13 minutes and remove from the oven. Set aside.

For the Fig Marmalade:

1. Open the fresh figs. Then, cut them into quarters and put them in a sauce pan. Add the butter and the vanilla, and cook over medium heat for about five minutes until it thickens. Take the baked tart and scrape the marmalade over the baked almond custard, setting the figs aside.

For the Egg Custard:

1. In a bowl, stir the egg, sugar and heavy cream until the mixture is homogeneous.

2. Pour it over the fig marmalade, and add the sliced figs and chopped almonds on top.

Baking:

1. Bake for 40 minutes at 350°F (180°C) until the top goldens. Remove from the oven and let it cool for at least 30 minutes without removing it from the pan.

---

*See the photo on the next page.

BEEF EMPANADAS

MEXICO

SERVES: 3 pies

TIME: 1 hour

For the dough:

2 eggs

1¾ cup + 1 tbsp (270 g) flour

½ tsp salt

⅓ cup (75 g) soft butter or margarine

egg wash

For the filling:

¼ cup (50 g) olive oil

2 cloves of garlic, chopped

2 onions, sliced

½ pound (220 g) ground beef

3 eggs, beaten

¼ cup (15 g) fresh coriander

2 tsp ground cumin

2 tbsp smoked paprika

2 tbsp cayenne pepper

1 tsp salt

1 tsp black pepper

1 egg (for egg wash)

1 tbsp oregano

1 tbsp sesame seeds

1. To make the dough, beat the eggs, and add the flour and salt. Add the soft margarine (or oil). Mix all the ingredients together. Knead the dough for 5 minutes until even and smooth. Wrap it in plastic wrap and cool the dough in the fridge for 30 minutes.

2. For the filling, pour the olive oil into a frying pan on medium-high heat, add the garlic and onions. Fry for 3 minutes until golden. Add the ground beef and cook for 5 minutes. Place the mixture in a big bowl to cool.

3. In another bowl, beat the 3 eggs. Add the salt, black pepper, smoked paprika, cayenne pepper, fresh coriander, and cumin, and mix. Then, add the cooked ground meat (drained of its liquid) to the mixture. Turn on the oven at 375°F (190°C).

4. Roll out the dough between two pieces of parchment paper, until it is a tenth of an inch thick (a couple of millimeters). Make individual pies using a cookie cutter to make 6-inch (15 cm) rounds. Lightly wet the edges of the dough rounds with water.

5. Add 1tbsp filling in the middle of the circle and close to make a small pie. Seal it using a fork, flattening the edges. Refrigerate for at least 30 minutes.

6. Brush the small pies with egg wash and sprinkle with oregano and sesame seeds. Prick the dough in the middle with the tip of a knife. Bake for 40 minutes, and let it cool for 15 minutes before serving.

MANJAR BLANCO (WHITE PUDDING)

Manjar blanco, or blancmange, is not a contemporary dessert. It dates back at least from the 13th century, and has the distinctive feature of having a jelly consistency. It looks like malabi, the famous fresh creamy-jelly dessert commonly known today throughout the Middle East.

Cassava starch, also known as tapioca flour, is often used to thicken or even jellify certain culinary preparations. This root has been consumed as early as 2500 BCE in Latin America (Peru), and utensils for grating cassava tubers have been found in Mexico (Tehuacán and Tamaulipas) dating back to the first millennium BCE. It is therefore entirely possible that the Manjar Blanco prepared by crypto-Jews in prison to celebrate the Sukkot festival may have been prepared using cassava starch to thicken the dessert. It's worth noting that this root did not arrive in Europe until the late 19th century.

The recipe prepared today in the Middle East by both Jewish and Muslim people has many different names and variations; it is also called sutlage, mḥalbiya, ksab, or muhallabiyye. What they all have in common is the use of rice or rice flour as a base. The dish is found in many cookbooks since the tenth century, often with the addition of sugar, saffron, and even chicken.

Blancmange and muhallabiyye are both white and delicious, but their consistency and thickness are a bit different, and I prefer the former. I also favor using agar to aid in the thickening of manjar blanco for several reasons. The first is that it is derived from seaweed, making agar a natural vegetable-based gelling agent (as opposed to animal-based gelatin). The second reason is that agar contains a significant amount of vitamins (A, B, C, and E) and minerals (iodine, etc.). Finally, agar can gel preparations that, when heated above 85°C, have a viscous texture but solidify as they cool. Therefore, it is not necessary to refrigerate to solidify. Below are recipes for both.

Muhallabiyye

SERVES: 6

TIME: 30 minutes

- 1 cup (150 g) rice flour
- 2 cups (500 ml) almond milk
- 2¾ cups (670 ml) whole milk (divided)
- ½ cup (120 g) sugar
- 2 tsp orange blossom water
- 2 tbsp pomegranate syrup
- 2 tbsp hibiscus syrup
- 1 tbsp coconut powder
- 1 tbsp pistachios, chopped

1. Prepare the small jars or cups in which the preparation will be served. In a bowl, using a fork, combine the rice flour and ¾ cup of whole milk.

2. In a saucepan, pour the almond milk and whole milk. Add the sugar and stir. Bring to a boil.

3. When it is boiling, lower the heat and add the rice flour and milk mixture. Stir constantly for 3 minutes, to obtain a smooth consistency. It will thicken. Add the orange blossom water.

4. Pour into the serving containers and let stand for 15 minutes. Then, drizzle pomegranate and hibiscus syrup over it. Sprinkle with coconut powder (preferably toasted) and the chopped pistachios. Serve cold or at room temperature.

Manjar Blanco

SERVES: 6

TIME: 30 minutes

1 short cinnamon stick

2 tbsp sugar

3¼ cups (650 ml) almond milk

1 tsp agar powder + ¼ cup (50 ml) almond milk

½ tsp rose water

½ tsp vanilla extract

For toppings:

Mexican Pinyon nuts, toasted (you can use pine nuts as a substitute)

2 Matzah toffee sheets, broke into chunks (see recipe p. 341)

Preserved orange, sliced

6 tbsp pomegranate syrup (1 tbsp per glass); you can add fresh seeds as well.

2 apricots, cut into quarters

1. Prepare 6 small crystal glasses in a tray.

2. In a pan, place the cinnamon stick, the sugar and pour over the almond milk. Stir, and bring to a boil over low-medium heat.

3. In a small bowl, combine the agar powder and the ¼ cup almond milk.

4. Once the almond milk is boiling, lower the heat and pour in the agar mixture. Stir constantly for about 3 minutes. Add the rose water and vanilla. You want the manjar blanco to thicken. It will look more runny while it is hot.

5. Remove the cinnamon stick, and pour the manjar blanco into the glasses; try to avoid touching the edges. Let them cool at room temperature without moving them.

6. Once they are cooled, you can place them in the fridge for a firmer consistency (or if you'd prefer it chilled, which is recommended).

7. Decorate the top of the manjar blanco with matzah toffee crumbles, the pomegranate syrup and seeds, and apricots. Finish by sprinkling with toasted pinyon nuts.

*See the photo on the next page.

MEXICO

ROASTED CHICKEN WITH PRESERVED LEMON AND DATES

SERVES: 8–10 people

TIME: 4.5–5 hours total (20–30 minutes prep, 3–4 hours roasting, 20–30 minutes resting)

1 whole large chicken or 2 medium chickens (12–15 pounds)

1 preserved lemon, quartered (found in specialty stores, or you can make your own)

2 onions, quartered

1 cup pitted dates

2 tablespoons olive oil

2 teaspoons salt

1 teaspoon black pepper

1 teaspoon ground cumin

1 teaspoon ground coriander

1 teaspoon ground paprika

1 teaspoon ground cinnamon

4–6 cloves garlic, peeled

Fresh herbs (rosemary, thyme, sage) for stuffing

¼ cup olive oil to coat the potatoes

10 potatoes with peel

1 tbsp salt

1 tbsp smoked paprika

1 tbsp pomegranate seeds (to decorate)

3 fresh figs (to decorate)

1. Thaw the chicken(s): If your chicken is frozen, make sure to thaw it in the refrigerator according to the package instructions. This can take several days, so plan ahead.

2. Preheat your oven to 325°F (163°C).

3. Remove the giblets and neck from the chicken's cavity. These are often packaged inside the chicken. Rinse the chicken inside and out with cold water and pat it dry with paper towels.

4. Place the chicken on a rack in a large roasting pan.

5. In a small bowl, combine the olive oil, salt, pepper, cumin, coriander, paprika, and cinnamon to create a spice rub. Rub the spice mixture evenly over the surface of the chicken, inside and out.

6. You can stuff the chicken with quartered onions, preserved lemon quarters, dates, garlic cloves, and fresh herbs for added flavor. Make sure not to overstuff, as this can affect cooking times. You can also prepare a separate stuffing, but it's important to cook it separately from the chicken(s) to ensure it reaches a safe temperature.

7. Once the chicken is in the roasting pan, cut the potatoes into quarters and place them around the chicken(s). Coat them with the oil and add 1 tbsp salt and 1 tbsp smoked paprika. Make sure they are all coated. Cover the chicken(s) with aluminum foil and roast it, allowing about 13–15 minutes of cooking time per pound (every 450 grams). Baste the chicken(s) with pan juices every 30 minutes.

8. Use a meat thermometer to check the internal temperature. The chicken is done when the thickest part of the thigh reaches 165°F (74°C), and the juices run clear. This usually takes around 3–4 hours for a 12–15-pound chicken(s). If you stuffed the chicken(s), make sure the stuffing also reaches a safe temperature of 165°F (74°C).

9. Once the chicken is done, remove it from the oven and let it rest for about 20–30 minutes before carving. This allows the juices to redistribute, resulting in a juicier chicken.

10. Carve the chicken and arrange the slices on a serving platter. Serve with the delicious stuffing and roasted potatoes.

11. Enjoy with leftover garlic and parsley challah croutons (see recipe of 13th Century Andalusian Challah p. 223) and caramelized quinces sauce (see recipe of Quince Cake with Honey p. 59)

Ruy Díaz Nieto remedy against hemorrhoids:

The active social and religious life of the Portuguese *conversos* in the Cárcel Perpetua in Mexico at the beginning of the 17th century allows us to know certain details concerning their food practices and preferences. In "Living in Silverado," David Gitlitz offers a few fascinating insights. Ruy Díaz Nieto and his converso friends Antonio Méndez, Duarte Rodríguez and Héctor de Fonseca were particularly proactive in keeping Jewish practices, and Manuel Gil de la Guarda—who knew about this fact—was asked by the Inquisitors to gather evidence against them. Thus, we know that Ruy Díaz Nieto who "suffered hemorrhoids was particularly fond of eating raisins, cheese and quince paste."

In the table hymn *Zemer Naeh* written by the Andalusian poet (1089–1164), Abraham Ibn Ezra lists special food prepared on Sabbath of Hanukkah, including "Fine flour, wine, doves, ducks, fatted geese" (compare *Encyclopedia of Jewish Food*, p. 476).

From the Middle Ages, we have little information in relation to Hanukkah practices, and even less concerning Hanukkah culinary practices. This is curious in comparison with the amount of interesting information available about Passover, Shabbat, and Yom Kippur food habits, in particular from records of Inquisition trials.

HANUKKAH

Hanukkah, also known as the "Festival of Lights," is a Jewish holiday that lasts for eight days and commemorates the rededication of the Second Temple in Jerusalem during the second century BCE. This occurred after the Jewish people successfully fought against their Greek-Syrian oppressors in the Maccabean Revolt. In Hebrew, Hanukkah means "dedication." The holiday begins on the fifth of Kislev on the Hebrew calendar and usually falls in November or December. In Talmud Shabbat, 23a (The William Davidson Talmud edition, Koren-Steinsaltz) one reads the following: "Rabbi Yehoshua ben Levi said: All the oils are suitable for the Hanukkah lamp, and olive oil is the most select of the oils. Abaye said: At first, my Master, Rabba, would seek sesame oil, as he said: The light of sesame oil lasts longer and does not burn as quickly as olive oil. Once he heard that statement of Rabbi Yehoshua ben Levi, he sought olive oil because he said: Its light is clearer."

We know that Hanukkah was called the "Festival of the 'little' lights" (Fiesta de las Candelillas). Of course, in medieval Spain there was no electricity and the only way to light your house was using candles. But the relationship between lighting candles and Judaism is interesting and nuanced. In most of the Spanish inquisition trials, conversos were denounced for lighting candles, but at the synagogue, not at their homes, and for Shabbat or Yom Kippur, not Hanukkah.

Jews were denounced by witnesses who saw the conversos bringing olive oil to the synagogue to light the candles. One explanation for the lack of information concerning Hanukkah practices could be, as David Gitlitz writes in *Secrecy and Deceit*, that after the expulsion, Jewish objects/artifacts disappeared or were hidden. Having and lighting a hanukkiah at home would have been the only evidence of practicing Judaism.

Nevertheless, some *conversos* were denounced because lighting the Hanukkiah candles requires a very particular technique, and they did it for an entire week, making it more easily identifiable as a crypto-Jewish practice. That is exactly what happened to the Spanish woman María Diaz, who was accused of having lighted nine candles to celebrate the "Pascua de las candeillas" (Passover of the Little Candles).

SPAIN

SUARES' FRIED *PASTELICOS*

The Suares family of Spain used to make this dough to make tortillas as well as for *pastelicos* for Rosh Hashanah. The dish described refers to a fried pastry stuffed with meat:

> "[Maria] saw the wife of the aforementioned Francisco [Suares], whose name is unknown, kneading unleavened bread [*pan cenceño*], that is to say, bread without yeast. She kneaded it with one egg and added oil to the [. . .] dough. And she remembers it was for San Miguel, and that she made three *tortillas* and a *pastelico*, and that she saw the child she had eating the meat from the paste."

In Ladino, *pasteliko* refers to a small pastry often made with meat. The word "pasteliko" is mentioned in a song that celebrates Hanukkah: "Ocho Kandelikas" by Flory Jagoda:

Hanukah linda sta aki,
ocho kandelas para mi,
Hanukah linda sta aki,
ocho kandelas para mi, O. . .

Muchas fiestas vo fazer, kon alegrias i plazer,
Muchas fiestas vo fazer, kon alegrias i plazer,
Los **pastelikos** vo kumer, kon almendrikas i la myel,
Los pastelikos vo kumer, kon almendrikas i la myel. O. . .

Serves: 12 pastelicos

Time: 1 hour 30 minutes

- 2½ cups (375 g) flour
- ½ teaspoon of salt
- 2 tablespoons (20 ml) olive oil
- ⅔ cup +1 tbsp (150 ml) warm water
- 1 egg
- Oil for frying (a neutral oil such as vegetable or canola)
- ⅛ cup (30 g) pomegranate syrup (to drizzle)

For the beef filling:

- ½ lb (250 g) ground beef
- ¼ tsp salt
- ¼ tsp ground black pepper
- 2 tsp ground cumin
- 2 tsp ground ginger
- 2 tbsp (15 g) chopped fresh coriander leaves
- ⅛ cup (30 g) honey (to drizzle)

---

1. To make the filling, mix the ground beef with salt, pepper, cumin, and ginger. Add the chopped coriander, and place the mixture in a plate and let it cool.

2. For the dough, whisk together the flour and salt in a large mixing bowl. Add the olive oil, warm water, and egg to the bowl and mix until a dough forms. Knead the dough on a lightly floured surface for 5–7 minutes, until it is smooth and elastic.

3. Divide the dough into 10 small pieces (each one should be 1⅛ oz/30 g). Roll them out into circles (about 6 inches/15 cm in diameter) that should be a little bit thick (1/10 of an inch/3 mm). Cool in the fridge for 30 minutes.

4. Take the dough out of the fridge and lay them out on parchment paper. Place two spoonfuls (each should be ¾ oz or 20 g) of the cold ground beef mixture in the middle of each dough circle, leaving about 2.5 inches (6 cm) of space from the edges to be able to close and seal the pastelico. Lightly wet the edge of the dough and fold the dough over to seal. Flatten a little with your hand, and let them cool in the fridge for about 10 minutes.

5. Heat oil in the frying pan over medium heat, and fry the pastelicos for about 5 minutes. Drizzle honey over the top, and serve hot.

BIMUELOS
FRIED SEPHARDIC ANISE DONUT BALLS

Bimuelo is a fried pastry coated with honey. It has the form of a golden ball, crispy on the outside and soft on the inside. This pastry is known throughout the Mediterranean Sephardic world, mainly on the western side of the Mediterranean.

This delicious pastry bears a variety of names, such as *bunuelo*, *binmuelo*, *bilmuelo*, *buñuelo*, and so on. One of the reasons this dish—still commonly prepared today—is known by so many different names is the enormous size and diversity of the Sephardic diaspora.

This dish, however, is not a contemporary dish at all. It may be described in the Bible in Numbers 11:8 as a "cake in oil," and mentioned in Exodus 16:31 to describe the taste of the manna that should have looked like *sapihit* in honey.

In a trial which dates to Monday, April 19, 1490 in the court of Segovia (close to Madrid), we learn that Diego Arias Davila, from a famous Jewish family, was denounced because a servant used to secretly bring foods like honeyed fritters ("frutas de nuegados e de sartén") to his home at Medina de Campo while he was on holidays ("estando en feria"). It is not stated that these were explicitly for Hanukkah, but we understand that it was for a Jewish holiday and that Diego Arias Davila observed this Jewish Holiday. We also know that it wasn't for Shabbat because in this trial it is also specified that the servant would bring a dish called "adafina"—already cooked—to Diego Arias Davila's house for Shabbat. The hypothesis that the "honeyed fritters" were for Hanukkah is therefore plausible.

Ladino, or the Judeo-Spanish language, originated from Spain. It is a mix of Spanish and Hebrew words, which is still spoken as the vernacular and as a literary language by the Sephardim from Spain and the diaspora (Turkey, the Balkans, Israel, North Africa etc.). Ladino has similarities with Old Spanish language of the fifteenth century, and contains words taken from Hebrew and Spaniolized. The text can be written in Latin letters or in square Hebrew characters.

One can read the following words in the first Ladino translation of the Torah printed in Hebrew characters and published in Istanbul in 1547 (and subsequently in Ferrara during 1553): "I yamaron kaza de Yisrael a su nomre magna; i el komo simiente de kolantro, blanko, i su savor komo bunuelo kon miel." This text refers to the manna which God provided to the children of Israel, and mentions that it tasted like *bunuelo* in honey. This could be the starting point to understand how the word "sapihit" came to refer to "bunuelo." The famous kabbalist Moshe Cordovero's son, Gedalia Cordovero, edited a glossary of non-Hebrew words mentioned in the Torah which he translated into Ladino. Thus, a glossary of non-Hebrew words in the Torah that were translated into Ladino—such as in the "Sefer Heshek Shelomo," first published in Venice in 1588—uses the term *binuelos* for the translation of *sapihit;* the English translation refers to "wafers with honey."

A Ladino Bible translation published later, in the 17th and 18th century, mainly in Turkey, shows that the word *binmuelo* was the translation of the Hebrew word *sapihit*.

The word "bimuelo," written in Ladino, also appears in a 16th-century source written in Italy. Verses written by Ḥayim Yom-Tob Magula in his book "Las malas costumbes" (Bad Habits) should be emphasized. This book from the 18th century strongly criticizes the author's fellow Jews for deviating from the path set by Mosaic law. One of the verses mentions *bimuelos* as a dish traditionally eaten during Hanukkah: "Comer en Purim hijuelas, y en Ḥanuká bimuelos" which means "eating *hijuelas* on Purim, and *bimuelos* on Ḥanuká."

SERVES: 12 bimuelos

TIME: 1 hour 30 minutes

- 1 tbsp olive oil
- 1 tbsp anise seeds
- 2 cups (300 g) flour
- 1 tbsp (20 g) fresh yeast (or 10 g) dry active yeast
- ¾ cup (177 ml) lukewarm water
- ½ orange (for juice, pulp and zest)
- ½ tsp salt
- 3 tbsp sugar
- 1 cup (340 g) honey
- 1 tbsp orange blossom water
- Neutral oil for frying

1. In a frying pan, place the anise seeds along with the olive oil and fry for about 3 minutes over medium heat (be careful, it burns very quickly). Add the ½ fresh orange juice with the zest. Mix with a spoon for about 1 minute and set aside.

2. Take lukewarm water and add the yeast. Mix to dissolve for 10 seconds. In a stand mixer (or by hand), mix the flour, salt and sugar. Then add the yeast-water mixture, the olive oil with the anise seeds. Mix slowly for about 4 minutes, and then cover it and let it rise for at least 1 hour.

3. Heat oil over medium heat (347°F/175°C) (not too hot). Oil your hand lightly and take small pieces of dough the size of a walnut. Fry them for about 3 minutes until they are golden brown.

4. In another pan heat the honey with the orange blossom water, over low heat. Stir the fried bimuelos in the honey for about 3 minutes, and enjoy!

*See the photo on the next page.

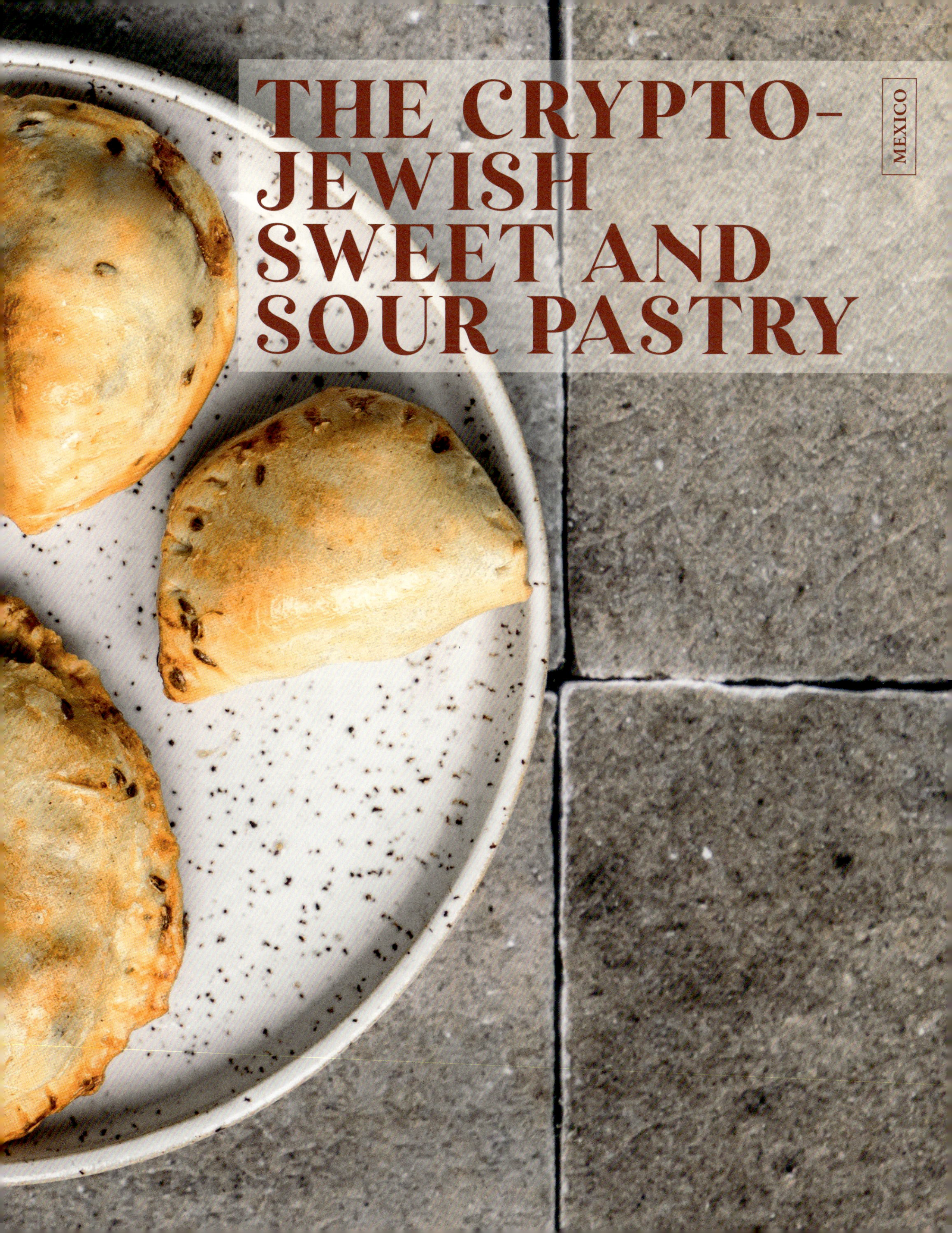

THE CRYPTO-JEWISH SWEET AND SOUR PASTRY

MEXICO

A Mexican trial which dates back to September 10, 1603 tells us about the consumption of meat pies/empanadas. While Rosh Hashanah is not explicitly mentioned, we can suppose that the *turcos* meat pies were made for this occasion. Nevertheless, this same trial also tells us about a Sukkot party which took place in prison. So, the *turcos* may have also been prepared for this celebration scheduled on September 21.

In Texas, people still make *turcos*, but for celebrating the Christian New Year. They prepare a dough that contains anise seeds, while the filling is made of crispy pork, cinnamon, raisins, apple, garlic, onions, sugar, nuts, and cloves. The vegetable ingredients are the same as those used in Mexico in the 17th century. Furthermore, the sweet and savory taste is frequent in Sephardi cuisine and Rosh Hashanah dishes.

Below I present two versions: one with lamb, and the other with beef.

Serves: 10 pieces

Time: 45 minutes

For the dough:

¾ cup (180 ml) water

2 or 3-inch cinnamon stick (or ⅛ tsp ground cinnamon)

¼ tsp anise seeds

3½ cups (490 g) all-purpose flour

1 tsp (5 g) granulated sugar

1 tsp (5 g) baking powder

½ tsp salt

7 tbsp (100 g) margarine

---

1. In a saucepan, combine the water, cinnamon stick, anise seeds, and raisins for the filling. Bring to a boil and let it simmer for 5 minutes. Remove from heat and let it cool.

2. In a large bowl, combine the flour, sugar, baking powder, salt, and margarine. Remove the cinnamon stick and drained raisins from the saucepan and set them aside. Add the cooled water with the anise seeds to the dry ingredients and mix until a dough forms.

3. Knead the dough by hand for about 5 minutes until it becomes smooth and homogeneous.

4. Form the dough into a ball, place it in a plastic bag, and chill it in the refrigerator for at least 30 minutes, or overnight.

For the beef filling:

⅓ cup almonds (+ ½ cup neutral oil for frying them)

¼ cup olive oil

1 medium onion diced fine

2 tbsp honey

¼ cup olive oil (to cook the meat)

1 pound (500 g) ground meat

½ tsp salt

1 tsp ground cinnamon

¼ tsp anise seeds or ground anise

¼ tsp ground cloves (or ground nutmeg)

¼ cup raisins

1 apple (green) diced into small pieces

1 egg (for egg wash)

To make the beef filling:

1. Take a small frying pan. Pour in the neutral oil and the almonds, and fry for about 3 minutes, until golden. Remove them from the oil, and put them on a paper towel to let them drain and cool. Once they are cooled and crunchy, chop them and set them aside.

2. In a frying pan, add the olive oil and onion, and cook on low-medium heat for about 5 minutes. Add the honey. Cook until the mixture is dry and thick. Set aside.

3. In the same frying pan, pour ¼ cup olive oil and add the ground meat and salt. Cook it on medium heat for about 5 minutes.

4. To the meat, add the ground cinnamon, ground anise, ground cloves/nutmeg, the raisins, the diced apple, the cooked onion-honey mixture, and the chopped almonds. Mix thoroughly with a spoon.

Lamb filling:

500 g lamb, cut into small cubes

½ cup (100 g) olive oil (for the marinade)

1 tsp salt

1 short cinnamon stick

½ tsp anise seeds

¼ tsp ground nutmeg

¼ cup (40 g) raisins (in the marinade)

2 tbsp (40 g) honey

2 cloves of garlic, chopped

Juice of ½ lemon

Water (enough to cover the meat + 1 cup)

1 apple (red or green), peeled and cut into small chunks

¼ cup (40 g) golden raisins (added at the end)

¼ cup (30 g) chopped almonds

1 egg (for egg wash)

---

1. In a large bowl, make a marinade with the olive oil, salt, cinnamon stick, anise seeds, nutmeg, raisins, honey, chopped garlic, and lemon juice. Mix well and add the cubed lamb. Cover and refrigerate for at least 2 hours or overnight.

2. Heat a large pot over medium-high heat. Add the lamb and cook for about 10 minutes until golden-brown. Add the other ingredients of the marinade, cover with water and add one more cup of water. Cover the pot and cook for about one hour.

3. Remove the cinnamon stick from the pot, uncover, and cook for another 30 minutes, until there is very little water left and the meat is very tender. The color of the sauce should be dark. Add the golden raisins, apple chunks, and chopped almonds. Mix and let the mixture cool.

Making the *turcos*:

1. Preheat oven to 375°F (180°C), and line a baking tray with parchment paper. Take the dough and cut it into two parts to make two balls of dough. Place one ball on a parchment paper. Cover it with another parchment paper and roll it to ⅛ of an inch thick.

2. Remove the top sheet of parchment paper and use a cookie cutter to make 4-inch diameter rounds. Spread a small amount of water along half of the edge of each round using a small bowl of water. Place each round on the parchment paper-lined baking tray. Add one tablespoon of the lamb filling to the middle of the half round. Fold the other half of the round on top and press the edges to seal. You can use a fork to press over the edges to seal it better or use your fingers for a more aesthetic look.

3. Brush the egg wash over the turcos.

4. Bake for about 20 minutes until golden.

MOROCCO

ISFENĞ
THE ANDALUSIAN DONUT

SERVES: 8 donuts

TIME: 20 min +
4 hours (or overnight) +
20 min

1 tbsp fresh yeast (or 1½ teaspoons fast-acting dried yeast) and ⅓ cup (70 ml) lukewarm water

3 cups (450 g) flour

2 tsp sugar

½ tbsp salt

1⅔ cup (330 ml) or less (300 ml) lukewarm water

Neutral oil for frying (such as sunflower, safflower, avocado or canola)

1. Also known as "sfenǧ," this fried pastry is a culinary tradition shared by both Jews and Muslims, particularly in Morocco and Israel. It is also referred to as *esponja* ("sponge" in Spanish), a term derived from the Arabic word "sjenǧ," which carries the same meaning. The origins of this recipe can be traced back to the thirteenth century when similar dishes were popular in al-Andalus. In modern-day Morocco, street vendors commonly prepare it, although Jewish communities often serve it during Hanukkah as well. This Jewish holiday, also known as the "Festival of Lights," spans eight nights and days, commemorating the miracle of the menorah candle in the Second Temple (164 BCE). The miracle lies in the fact that the candle had only enough oil to burn for a single day, yet it illuminated the temple for eight nights, providing ample time for the completion of the temple's construction. In remembrance of this sacred oil, it has become a tradition to enjoy fried foods during Hanukkah.

2. In a small bowl, dilute the fresh yeast with ⅓ cup of lukewarm water.

3. In a large bowl, or in the bowl of a stand mixer, place the dissolved yeast, flour, sugar, and salt. Mix with a wooden spoon or with the steel flat beater hook over medium speed, and gradually add the rest of the water. The dough should be sticky.

4. Mix or knead for about 10 to 15 minutes and cover the bowl with a kitchen towel. Let it rise for 1 hour on the counter. Degas the dough and place it again in the bowl. Cover it with the kitchen towel and rest the dough overnight (or for at least 4 hours) in the refrigerator.

5. Heat ½ inch of oil in a frying pan, over medium-high heat. Drop a small piece of the dough into the oil; if it rises quickly to the surface it means that the oil is hot enough to cook.

6. Lightly dip your hands into some water and take a golf ball-sized portion of the dough.

7. Make a hole in the middle of the dough and stretch it well. If you can, tilt your skillet to an angle and place something under the handle (such as an upturned pot) to hold it in place. Place the sfenj on the top portion of the skillet so it fries in only a small amount of oil. Fry it for 20 seconds and then slide the sfenj down into the deep-frying bath at the bottom of the skillet. Fry for another 30 seconds to one minute more, turning it over one more time. Using a large spoon, you can baste frying oil over the top of the sfenj while it is frying to help it cook evenly.

8. These are usually eaten on their own, but you can coat them with frosting sugar or lightly dip them in honey if you want them to be sweeter.

on SACRIFIED MEAT

«e que si algunas volateria manjava volia que fos degollada al modo judaich e que sempre fossen sublimades ab aygua e ab sal e oli e no ab sagi ni carn salada»

"and that if any poultry was consumed, it had to be slaughtered in the Jewish manner and always be prepared with water, salt, and oil, and not with fat or lard from pork."

Pedro Miguel Carbonell, *Opusculos inéditos del cronista catalan Pedro Miguel Carbonell*, Vol. 2, Barcelona, 1865.

PASSOVER

Passover is a sacred Jewish holiday that commemorates the liberation of enslaved Jews from Egypt, as recounted in the Bible's Exodus narrative (Exodus 12–14). This observance traditionally spans eight days, commencing on the fourteenth day of the Jewish month of Nissan, typically occurring in April. Central to the Passover celebration is the reading of the Haggadah, a timeless Jewish text dating back to the 3rd-4th century, which forms the foundation for the Passover seder—an elaborate ritual dinner and discussion held on the first or first two nights of Passover.

Passover, known as "Pesach" in Hebrew, holds a profound connection to the consumption of unleavened bread, now known as "matzah." This custom serves as a reminder of the flatbread that Hebrews brought with them during their hasty departure from Egypt, which did not have time to leaven (Exodus 12:39). Additionally, Passover involves partaking in haroset, a paste made from figs and dates—as a commemoration of the mortar employed by the Jews during their forced labor in Egypt—as well as consuming bitter herbs, referred to as "maror," during the Seder, which itself signifies "Order" in Hebrew. Passover and its associated dietary traditions are closely intertwined, and it often coincides with the Christian Holy Week.

Shabbat, due to its weekly recurrence, featured prominently in inquisition trials, making it easier for informants to identify crypto-Jews. However, Passover played a pivotal role in Sephardic Jewish practices, earning recognition as the most significant Jewish celebration. The fervor with which Jews observed Passover made it the most frequently cited Jewish holiday in denunciations of Jewish practices.

Within the Jewish community, Passover was known by various names. In Inquisition trials conducted in the Iberian Peninsula and among the Sephardic diaspora, Passover was referred to as "Pascua de los judíos" (The Jewish Passover), "Pascua del Cordero" (The Lamb Passover), "Pascua del pan cenceño" (Passover of the unleavened bread), "Pascua florida" (The flowered Passover), and "Fiesta del pan cenceño" (The Feast of the Unleavened bread). In Portuguese, where the focus was often on unleavened bread consumption, the term used was "Pascua do pão asmo" (The Feast of the Unleavened bread), while in Catalan, it was "Pasqua del pa alís" (Passover of the Unleavened bread). Notably, the term "matzah" does not appear in the records; instead, various terms like "pan cenceño," "pan cotazo," "pan de judíos," (The bread of the Jews), "pão asmo," "pão dos judeus," "pan sin levadura," "pan cuez," "pan de Pascua," "pa alís," and "pan de la aflicción" (The bread of affliction) were used to describe unleavened bread.

PASCUA DO PÃO ASMO

BRAZIL

PASSOVER OF THE UNLEAVENED BREAD (BAHIA, 1591-1592)

In Brazil, just like in other cities where Jews had settled, unleavened bread was consumed for other Jewish holidays besides Passover. This is evidenced by the Inquisition trial of Salvador de Bahia from the 16th century, in which the words of Abreu Capistrano read as follows:

"They celebrated, or celebrate, the Jewish Passovers, as well as the Passover of unleavened bread, and of the Tabernacles, and the Passover of the horn, eating unleavened bread on said Passover of unleavened bread, in new bowls and dishes, as a ceremony of said Passover."

«Item, se solenizaram, ou solenizam as Páscoas dos Judeus, assim como a Páscoa do pão asmo, e das Cabanas, e a Páscoa do corno, comendo o pão asmo na dita Páscoa do pão asmo, em bacios, e escudelas novas, por cerimônia da dita Páscoa.»

Serves: 4 matzot

Time: 18 minutes

1⅛ cup (170 g) flour

½ cup (100 ml) water

1. Preheat your oven to 536°F (280°C), and use aluminum foil to line a baking tray. Take a rolling pin and a fork, and keep them close to you.

2. Mix together the water and the flour, and knead the dough for 5 minutes. Cut the dough into 4 pieces (2⅛ oz/62 g each) and roll them into balls. Each ball should fit in the palm of your hand. Take a rolling pin (or your hands) and spread each ball into a very thin layer of dough (6 inches in diameter). According to Rabbinic rule, for the matzah to be kosher for Passover, the preparation should not be longer than 18 minutes from beginning to end.

3. Place the matzah on the foil-lined baking sheet, and prick it with a fork across its surface.

4. Bake for 30 seconds on one side and 30 seconds on the other side.

PORTUGAL

BOLOS ASMOS FOR *JEJUM DAS FILHÓS*

THE FAST OF THE FLAT CAKES

From the end of the 15th century, the consumption of unleavened bread was very often—and wrongly—only associated with the bread consumed during the Jewish Passover. In Coimbra and its surrounding area in the 16th century, Passover could last for 4 days, 5 or 6 days, 6 or 7 days, 7 or 8 days, or 10 days. Fasting was considered the most common practice for purification. Therefore, fasting by not consuming unleavened bread was a common practice. This is how in a Portuguese city near Coimbra in 1570, "bolos asmos" were prepared for the *Jejum das filhós*, the fast of the flat cakes. "Filhós" is a traditional dried dessert in Portugal, Northeastern Brazil and the Azores**.** They are usually made by forming balls from a mixture of flour and eggs. When the dough has risen, the balls are deep fried and sprinkled with a mixture of sugar and cinnamon. Interestingly, "filho" without an accent on the letter "o" means "son."

The fast of the firstborn (in Hebrew, *taanit bekhorim*) is observed just before the Passover holiday—that is, during the 14th of Nissan, which falls in March or April of the Gregorian calendar. The fast first appears historically between the end of Antiquity and the beginning of the Middle Ages, and it commemorates the 10th plague of Egypt, the death of the firstborn. According to the Torah, while the Hebrews were in captivity in Egypt, God inflicted on the Egyptians a series of successive calamities to compel Pharaoh to free his slaves. The 10th of these plagues is the death of the firstborn which struck all the Egyptians, including Pharaoh's own son, as well as their servants and their cattle. On the other hand, the plague spared the Hebrews, who followed the divine instructions to place a sign of recognition on the lintel of their house and were celebrating Passover at the same time. So, if we consider the possibility of an orthographic error made by the writer of the Inquisition records, this celebration could also refer to the Fast of the firstborn male born before Passover starts.

In *Sefaria* (a living library of Torah texts online), the term "bolos asmos" appears in: "e um cesto de bolos asmos, [bolos de flor de farinha com azeite]," which is the translation of Numbers 6:14–15: "As an offering to the LORD, that person shall present: [. . .] a basket of unleavened cakes of choice flour with oil mixed in." Relatedly, in Judges 6:19–20, we read: "So Gideon went in and prepared a kid, and [baked] unleavened bread from an *ephah* of flour. He put the meat in a basket and poured the broth into a pot, and he brought them out to Him under the terebinth. As he presented them, the angel of God said to him, 'Take the meat and the unleavened bread, put them on yonder rock, and spill out the broth.' And he did so."

Serves: 8 pieces

Time: 1 hour

2⅓ cup (350 g) wheat flour

⅔ cup (100 g) whole wheat flour

2 tbsp (25 ml) virgin olive oil

1¼ cup (250 ml) warm water

1 tbsp olive oil for brushing

½ tbsp salt flakes (optional)

1. Preheat your oven to 536°F (280°C), line a baking tray with aluminum foil, and lightly flour it. Take a rolling pin and a fork, and keep them handy.

2. In a large bowl, mix all the ingredients. Knead vigorously for five minutes. The dough should be soft. Cover and chill for thirty minutes, then divide the dough into eight equal balls (3 oz/86 g each).

3. Flour a working surface and place a ball of dough on it. Using a floured rolling pin, flatten each piece of dough into a 6-inch (15 cm) diameter disk. The dough should be thin.

4. Place the dough on the baking sheet, and lightly brush the bread with oil. Brush one more time and sprinkle with salt.

5. You can bake the bread right away or wait to put several on the sheet.

6. Bake for 1 minute 15 seconds on one side, and then flip the bread and cook for 15 seconds on the other side. The bread should be golden with brown spots.

*See the photo on the next page.

ISABEL GOMES' FIVE FLATBREADS OF SALVATION

PORTUGAL

Isabel Gomes was from the Portuguese town of Trancoso. She was accused in 1574 by the Inquisition Court of Coimbra of making and eating five unleavened breads for Passover. She did it for the salvation of her soul more than for respecting the seder.

Sefaria defines matzah as "the unleavened bread made from any of the five grains mentioned in the Torah: wheat, barley, spelt, rye, and oats. In the Torah, Jews were commanded by God to eat matzah before leaving Egypt and today are obligated to eat matzah during the Passover Seder."

Sefaria 6:4 states: "A person does not fulfill the obligation of eating matzah unless he partakes [of matzah made] from one of the five species [of grain], as [Deuteronomy 16:3] states: 'Do not eat chametz upon it . . . eat matzot for seven days.'"

Below is a receipt for 5 types of matzah made from all five grains.

SERVES: 5 matzot

TIME: 45 minutes

2¼ cup (340 g) flour

1½ cup (300 ml) hot water

1 tbsp olive oil

1 tsp salt

1 tbsp ground freekeh

1 tbsp ground barley

1 tbsp ground spelt

1 tbsp ground rye

1 tbsp oat flakes

1. Preheat your oven to 536°F (280°C), line a baking tray with aluminum foil, and lightly flour it. Take a rolling pin and a fork, and keep them close to you.

2. In a bowl, combine the flour, hot water, olive oil and salt. Mix with a spoon and then by hand for about 3 minutes. Separate the dough into five balls (4⅛ oz/110 g each). Add one tablespoon each of the different types of grain to each ball of dough in order to make five different kinds of unleavened bread. Knead each ball for about 3 minutes.

3. Lay out a piece of parchment paper and lightly flour it. Place a dough ball in the middle, lightly flour the top of the ball, and cover it with a second piece of parchment paper. Flatten the ball as thin as possible, flip it and do it a second time.

4. Remove the parchment paper and place the flattened dough on a baking tray. Repeat with the four other balls of dough. Once all the matzot are on the baking tray, bake them for about 2 minutes, and then flip them and cook for 30 more seconds.

FELIPA CARDOSA'S CHESTNUT MATZAH

FOR PASSOVER

Chestnut consumption for Passover in Portugal was common in the late 16th century. In the Portuguese city of Lamego, in 1550, Felipa Cardosa substituted cooked chestnuts that have been cooked in a new pot for matzah, as reported in the Inquisition trial: "Comendo nele castanhas cozidas em lugar do *pão asmo*" (eating boiled chestnuts in it instead of unleavened bread). Chestnuts are sweet, which lends a slightly sweet taste to the matzah.

SERVES: 8 matzot

TIME: 15 minutes

1 cup (20 pieces) (160 g) chestnuts, cooked, drained, and mashed

1 cup (100 g) chestnut flour

2 tsp salt

4 tbsp (60 g) water

1. Even if using canned chestnuts is easier, you can make your own cooked chestnuts. To do so, make a small X-shaped incision on the flat side of each chestnut using a sharp knife. This helps prevent them from bursting during boiling and makes them easier to peel later. Rinse the chestnuts under cold water to remove any dirt or debris. Place the prepared chestnuts in a large pot and cover them with enough water to submerge them completely. Bring the water to a boil over high heat.

2. Once the water is boiling, reduce the heat to medium-low and let the chestnuts simmer for about 20–30 minutes; he exact time will depend on the size of the chestnuts. They are ready when the shells begin to peel back, and the nuts inside are tender. Once boiled, drain the chestnuts and let them cool for a few minutes until they are safe to handle. Peel the chestnuts while they are still warm. The shells should come off easily, especially if you made the X-shaped incision.

3. If you are using canned chestnuts, drain and mash them thoroughly with a fork. Put the mixture in a large bowl, and add the salt and chestnut flour. Mix until there are no lumps.

4. Gradually add the water until the dough is homogeneous. It should remain a little bit thick.

5. Divide the dough into eight balls, each the size of a golf ball (1⅛ oz or 30 g).

6. Take two sheets of parchment paper. Lightly flour the surface of one with chestnut flour, and place a ball of dough in the middle. Flour the surface of the ball and cover with the other sheet of parchment paper. Flatten the ball until it is about 0.1 inch (2 mm) thick. You can use a cookie cutter if you want them to be perfectly round.

7. Heat a nonstick (iron) skillet over medium-high heat. Remove the top parchment sheet, and flip the bottom sheet over to lay the uncooked matzah into the skillet. Cook it for 30 seconds, flip it, and cook for another 30 seconds. Let them cool on cooling rack to ensure they remain crispy.

CECILIA CARDOSA´S MATZAH AND SWEET LAMB FOR PASSOVER

In 1569 in Porto, Cecilia Cardosa was accused of celebrating Passover by eating "a dish made of matzah [*pão asmo*], grains [*grãos*], and cooked chestnut [*castanhas cozidas*] cooked in a new pot [*louça nova*] for Passover." She was sentenced by wearing the *sambenito* (penitential robe) and forbidden to appear in public.

Serves: 4 people

Time: 45 minutes

¼ cup (50 g) olive oil

4 matzot, broken into medium pieces (Matzah recipe you prefer)

8 lamb chops

2 onions, sliced very thinly

2 tsp salt

1 tsp pepper

¼ cup (85 g) honey

2 tsp turmeric

2 tsp ginger

1 tsp cinnamon

8 tbsp water

3 cups chestnuts, cooked and drained

10 apricots, fresh (if they are dried, soaked them for 1 hour in hot water before using)

1 tbsp sesame seeds

1 tsp nigella seeds

---

1. In a large frying pan, pour the olive oil. Heat over medium heat and add the pieces of unleavened bread. Slightly brown them while stirring for 3–4 minutes. Then set them aside on a plate. Do not cover them, otherwise they will become soft.

2. In the same pan, lower the heat, add the sliced onions and cook until they are translucent. Add the lamb chops and brown them for two minutes on each side. Cover and cook for about 2 minutes over medium heat.

3. Remove the chops and put them on a separate plate. Cover them with aluminum foil to keep them warm. In the same pan, over low heat, add the salt, pepper, honey, powdered turmeric, powdered ginger, and powdered cinnamon. Stir the mixture, and add the 8 tbsp water. Cook for five minutes over medium heat.

4. In a separate pot, put the cooked chestnuts in boiling water for 30 seconds. This is not to cook them (as they are already cooked) but to warm them up. Add the halved apricots to the same water. Drain and add them to the honey-spice syrup in the pan. Cover and cook over low heat for 5 minutes.

5. Check the chestnuts to make sure they are tender, and return the meat to the sauce with the chestnuts and apricots so it can absorb the flavors.

6. Take four plates. Place two chops in each plate and arrange the chestnuts and apricots around them. Pour the sauce over them and sprinkle the meat with sesame and nigella seeds. Put the pieces of unleavened bread that were browned in oil on one side of the plate.

SPAIN

ROLLICOS DE ANGELINA

The celebration of the Jewish Passover was important for the Jews of the Iberian Peninsula. The continued respect for Jewish rituals and practices earned the conversos (Jews who converted to Christianity) to be denounced. The consumption of unleavened bread in particular attracted much attention and it constituted a clear identifying element of the Jewishness of those who consumed it. But the preparation of this bread, its acquisition, and its presence on the tables of Jews were just as symbolic as the consumption of this unleavened bread.

According to trial records dating back to 1488, Diego García Costello, a Spanish man, was reported to have gone door to door in search of pan cenceño (unleavened bread) for Passover. Additionally, he was accused of observing Shabbat.

On March 12, 1492, Yuda Rabinuça told the Inquisition court of Burgos that 34 or 35 years ago, when he was 11 years old, he saw Papudo, likely originally from the Spanish town of Rosadillo, spend the entire Passover of the unleavened bread (*pan cenceño*) at his father's house. He also ate celery and other bitter things eaten the day before the aforementioned Passover, and unleavened bread and meats, and that everyone was at the Jew's house, and he [Papudo] said Jewish prayers, as he knew how to pray.

The Jewish Passover (*Pesach*) and the Christian Holy Week (*Semana Santa* in Spanish) often take place at the same time or within a few days of each other. *Converso* Jews took advantage of this temporal overlap to mask their culinary practices related to the making of bread.

Angelina was denounced by the Inquisition for preparing rolled unleavened breads during this period. The record of her trial that occurred on June 17, 1505 in Almazan reads as follows:

"And she also saw her making during Holy Week . . . some cakes and rolls [*rollicos*], and she made them like she made *tortillas*, and she put those aforementioned things [pepper and honey and oil] on them, and baked them in the oven."

Serves: 4 people

Time: 1 hour

For 8 matzot:

2 cup (300 g) wheat flour

1 egg beaten

1 tsp black pepper

¼ cup (50 ml) water

1 tbsp honey

If using store-bought matzah, use 4 large matzot

For the filling:

1 tbsp olive oil

1 clove garlic, crushed

1¼ pound (600 g) fresh spinach

2 eggs

1½ cup (150 g) cheese (peynir or feta)

½ cup (110 g) heavy cream

2 tsp salt

2 tsp black pepper

1 tbsp butter, soft to butter the baking pan

1 egg beaten (for egg wash)

1 tbsp sesame seeds to sprinkle

For the pomegranate sauce:

¼ cup pomegranate syrup

1 small fresh ginger chunk

1 tsp lime juice

½ black pepper

1 tsp honey

1 tbsp pomegranate seeds

To make the matzot:

1. Preheat your oven to 536°F (280°C). Line a baking tray with aluminum foil and lightly flour it. Take a rolling pin and a fork, and keep them close to you.

2. Mix all the ingredients together, and knead the dough for 5 minutes. Cut the dough into 4 pieces and roll them into balls. Each ball should fit in the palm of your hand.

3. Take the rolling pin (or your hands) and spread each ball into a thin layer of dough, making a square that is 6 inches (15 cm) across.

4. Put the matzah on the aluminum foil on the baking sheet, and prick it with the fork across its surface. Bake for 30 seconds on one side and 30 seconds on the other side.

To make the filling:

1. Wash the fresh spinach leaves and drain. In a skillet, heat 1 tbsp of olive oil and add the crushed garlic clove. Cook for about 2 minutes over medium-high heat until golden.

2. Add the spinach leaves to the skillet and stir with a spoon. Lower the heat to medium and cook for about 3 minutes.

3. In a large bowl, mix together the eggs, cheese, heavy cream, salt, and pepper. Drain the cooked spinach and garlic and add it to the bowl mixture, stir the ingredients together until it forms a thick mixture, and set it aside.

To make the *rollicos*:

1. Preheat the oven to 375°F (190°C). If you are using store-bought matzah, start by soaking each square of matzah in lukewarm water for about 15 seconds on each side, and then place them on a paper towel to drain. Repeat the process for all of the matzot. (If you are making your own matzah, you do not need to soak them.)

2. Next, generously butter a baking pan. Take a square of matzah and add two spoonfuls of the spinach filling (without any liquid), spreading it in a line along the first third of the matzah. Then, tightly roll the matzah around the filling and place the *rollico* in the prepared baking pan. Repeat this step for the remaining matzot until all the filling is used.

3. Brush the *rollicos* with a beaten egg and sprinkle sesame seeds over the top. Bake for about 25 minutes, or until they are golden brown. Once done, remove the *rollicos* from the oven and let them cool before serving.

To make the sauce:

1. Mix together the pomegranate syrup, lime juice, ground black pepper, and honey. Grate the fresh ginger very thinly and add it to the other ingredients. Put everything in a small bowl and sprinkle the top with pomegranate seeds. Serve the *rollicos* with the hot pomegranate sauce on the side for dipping.

SPAIN

MADAM BERNAL'S EGG TORTAS

FOR THE EASTER OF THE FLOWERS

"During Semana Santa [the Holy Christian Week in Spanish, which often coincides with Passover], Sir Bernal and his wife made rolls and cakes with eggs for the Easter of the Flowers, and they were not seen eating them except during the aforementioned Easter." This is what one reads concerning the denunciations against the Bernal family. The record dates back to July 4th, 1505.

Passover was also called "Easter of the Flowers," as it corresponds to the Spring season, "Resurrection Sunday," or "Easter of the Resurrection." In 1501, the Inquisition court of the Spanish city of Sigüenza also mentions the preparation (by María Alvarez) of "rollillos" made from the same dough as she does the thin "*tortas*": "she made rollillos [*hormigos*], and from the same dough, she made thin cakes."

SERVES: 4 sandwiches

TIME: 45 minutes

For 8 matzot:

2 cups (300 g) wheat flour
1 tsp salt
2 eggs, beaten
1 tsp black pepper
⅛ cup (25 ml) water
2 tsp olive oil
1 tbsp fresh rosemary, chopped

For the filling:

3 eggs, beaten
½ tsp salt
½ cup (50 g) pine nuts, roasted
½ cup cilantro (leaves and stem) chopped
4 large Manchego cheese slices
2 tbsp lime juice
2 tsp honey
3 tsps olive oil, to fry the omelet
2 eggs beaten to coat the matzah tortas
1 cup breadcrumbs, coarse
1 tsp nigella seeds
1 tsp cumin seeds
3 tbsp neutral oil (for frying)
Fresh edible flowers to decorate

To make the matzah tortas:

1. In a large bowl, combine flour, salt, eggs, black pepper, water, and olive oil.

2. Stir with a spoon and once the dough starts to come together, add the chopped rosemary herb and knead by hand for about 3 minutes. Cover and set aside in the fridge for about 20 minutes.

3. Take the dough and, using a rolling pin, roll it out thin to about 1/10 of an inch (3 mm), but not too thin.

4. Cut it into squares of 4 inches (10 cm). Bake according to the instructions on page 21.

5. (If using store-bought matzah, dip them quickly into lukewarm water for about 30 seconds on each side). Keep them covered so they don't dry out.

To make the filling:

1. In a separate mortar, mash the pine nuts and fresh cilantro to create a homogeneous paste. Add honey and lime juice and stir well before setting aside. Whisk the 3 eggs with salt in a large bowl to make an omelet.

2. Pour 3 tsp olive oil in a skillet, making sure the entire surface of the skillet is oiled. With the heat on medium, pour the first half of the beaten egg-salt mixture to create an omelet shape. Cook for 1 minute, then flip and cook for another minute. Repeat this process with the remaining egg mixture before setting aside. (You can also cook both omelets at one time.)

To make the egg-matzah-tortas:

1. Place a soft square matzah onto a flat surface and spread a small spoonful of the pine nuts and fresh cilantro mixture over it. Lay a slice of cheese on top of this. Cut the flat omelet to match the dimensions of the matzah, add it on top of the cheese, and then spread another spoonful of the cilantro mixture over the top. Finally, cover this with another soft square matzah, creating a sandwich-like structure, and press down to ensure everything sticks together.

Final preparation:

1. Place the nigella seeds, cumin seeds, and the breadcrumbs on a large flat plate. In a separate deep plate, beat the 2 eggs. Heat 2 tablespoons of olive oil in a skillet over medium heat.

2. Take the matzah sandwich and dip it in the beaten eggs on all sides, making sure to remove any excess. Then, coat it with the seeds and breadcrumbs. You can use a spoon to coat the edges with the breadcrumb mixture, ensuring that they stick to the beaten eggs. You can do it on one side, or for both sides.

3. Add the matzah sandwich to the skillet. Do not move it for 15 seconds; cook over medium heat for approximately 3 minutes. Carefully, flip the sandwich and cook the other side for approximately 3 minutes until it is golden brown. Use kitchen tongs to pick up the sandwich to help fry the edges. If there is no olive oil left in the skillet, add a little more.

4. Transfer the egg-matzah-torta to a plate and decorate it with fresh edible flowers.

---

*See the photo on the next page.

CRISTÓBAL AND ANGELINA DE LEÓN'S ROUND TORTILLAS

SPAIN

Cristóbal and Angelina de León were new Christians living in the city of Almazán. They were denounced by María who testified against Angelina because "her mistress made with dough and eggs some round flat cakes [*tortillas redondas*] with [black] pepper and honey and [olive] oil, and she baked them in the oven; and she did this around the Holy Week [Semana Santa]." The trial dates to June 17th, 1505 in Almazan, Spain.

SERVES: 8 tortillas

TIME: 30 minutes

- 3 cups (450 g) wheat flour
- 2 tbsp (25 ml) virgin olive oil
- 1 cup (200 ml) warm water
- 1 tbsp (13 ml) olive oil for brushing
- 1 tbsp (21 ml) honey
- ½ tbsp black pepper
- ½ tbsp salt flakes

1. Preheat your oven to 536°F (280°C). Place aluminum foil in a baking tray and lightly flour it. Take a rolling pin and a fork, and keep them close to you.

2. In a large bowl, mix together the flour, olive oil, and water. Knead vigorously for five minutes; the dough should be supple.

3. Cover and refrigerate for thirty minutes. Then, divide the dough into 8 equally-sized balls (3½ oz/100 g each). Flour a work surface and place a ball of dough on it. Using a floured rolling pin, flatten the dough to obtain a 6-inch (15 cm) diameter disk. The dough should be thin. Prick the entire surface of the dough with a fork, and place it on the baking sheet.

4. In a small bowl, mix the olive oil, honey, and black pepper. Lightly brush the bread with the mixture and sprinkle with salt. You can bake the bread right away or wait to put several on the baking sheet.

5. Bake for 1 minute 30 seconds to 2 minutes on one side. Flip the bread and cook for 30 seconds on the other side. The bread should be golden. Remove from the oven and place on a wire rack to cool.

SPAIN

PESACH WINE FLAT CAKES
FROM JUANA DE LA FUENTE AND BEATRIZ DÍAS LAÍNEZ

Juana de la Fuente denounced Beatriz Díaz Laínez, Ruy Díaz Laínez's wife, for preparing (with Beatriz) unleavened wine cakes (*tortas de vino*). One can read in an Inquisition trial dated June 7, 1505 in Almazan (Spain) that "Before Pascua Florida [Passover, *Semana Santa]* . . . they [Juana and Beatriz] kneaded other flat cakes [*tortas*], apart [*aparte*], from another dough without yeast and kneaded with white wine and honey and cloves and [black] pepper, and kneaded from them up to twenty . . . and that they kept them with the *rollilos* in their chest; and that later she saw Ruy Díaz and his wife eating them."

SERVING: 8 matzot

TIME: 30 minutes

2¼ cup (340 g) wheat flour

½ cup (100 ml) water

¼ cup (50 ml) white wine

1 tsp salt

1 tbsp honey

2 ground cloves

½ tsp black pepper

1. Preheat your oven to 536°F (280°C). Put aluminum foil in a baking tray and lightly flour it. Take a rolling pin and a fork and keep them close to you.

2. Put all the ingredients in a large bowl and mix them with a spoon, then knead vigorously with your hands or a stand mixer for five minutes. The dough should be smooth. Cover and refrigerate for thirty minutes.

3. Then, divide the dough into 20 equal balls (⅞ oz/25 g each). Flour a work surface and place a ball of dough on it. Using a floured rolling pin, flatten the dough to make a 6-inch (15-centimeter) disk. The thickness of the dough should be relatively thin, about 0.2 inches (3 mm). Place the bread on the baking sheet and prick it across its surface with a fork. Do the same with the rest of the dough.

4. Bake for 1 minute on one side. Flip the bread and bake for another 30 seconds. The bread should be golden brown. Remove from the oven and place on a cooling rack.

CATALAN MATZAH "BRIE," FROM MOSSEN DALMAU OF TOLOSA

The following historical trial was conducted against Mossen Dalmau de Tolosa, in Tarragona, which dates back to the end of the 15th century. Mossen was the son of converso parents, and his mother, Isabel de Tolosa, was considered a heretic by the Inquisition. Mossen was denounced for celebrating "many Passovers and Jewish holidays, especially the Passover of the Jews, also called of the unleavened bread (moltes paschas e festes dels jueus en especial la pascha dels jueus quis diu del pa alis) eating "unleavened bread and other foods that the Jews usually eat at such festivals and Passovers" (pa alis e altres viandes que los jueus en les tals festes e paschas acostumen manjar).

Some details from the trial concern the way the *pa alis* was used in order to make the dish: "they made unleavened bread cakes [coques alises] and gave them to the old mother of the aforesaid Tholoses by which unleavened bread cakes [*pa alis*] were chopped in a mortar and cooked them with sauces with spices and eggs [*ous*] in a new casserole [*caçola nova*] [. . .] in the time of grapes and figs from Burgiçot."

A further record of the trial reads as follows:

"They make and serve and solemnize the above-mentioned Passover of the Jews in the form that follows: they purge the wheat that was to be used for the bread of said Passover very neatly in the house of the same Gabriel de Tolosa in the city of Tarragona. And then came a Jew who was a relative of the same Toloses named the Jew of the Vine carrying the wheat to the Jewish quarter. And after the wife of the same Jew kneaded it and she finished kneading it the Jew of the Vine took it to the house of Gabriel de Tolosa for the Jewish Passover, which was celebrated by making *coca alis* (unleavened *coca* breads) and giving them to the old mother of the above-mentioned Tholoses, who made them chopped with a mortar and made them cooked with sauces with spices and eggs in a new casserole and bought all new plates. And after the end of the Passover, which lasted over eight days, they kept the same plates and they were no longer useful, and during all this time the same Dalmau de Tolosa and all the above-mentioned ate from the bread. And to hide and disguise it, if someone came to the house in order that they wouldn't see that they ate this unleavened bread [*pa alis*] of Passover, they put on the table leavened bread, but they did not eat of that one. And to hide and disguise it better, Dalmau Lois and Gabriel Tolosa sometimes had their hands up under the hoods, and they took it by the tips of their finger. In this way they ate this bread, and in these days of the Passover they ate slaughtered chickens and meat from the butcher shop of the Jews."

SERVES: 2 people

TIME: 15 minutes

3 tbsp (40 g) butter

9 oz (250 g) matzah breads

2 cups (400 ml) cold water

4 eggs

½ cup (125 ml) whole milk

1 tsp salt

1 tsp ground nutmeg

1 tbsp brown sugar

2 tbsp neutral oil for frying

2 tbsp salted butter

1 tsp ground cinnamon (to sprinkle)

1 tsp sugar (optional)

1. Melt 3 tablespoons of butter in a saucepan over medium heat until it bubbles and turns golden with a hazelnut smell. Turn off the heat and let it cool until the sediment settles at the bottom.

2. Break matzah into medium-sized pieces and soak in cold water for 2 minutes.

3. In a separate bowl, whisk together eggs, whole milk, salt, ground nutmeg cinnamon, and brown sugar. Using a muslin or a fine colander, pour the browned butter over the egg mixture, avoiding the sediment, and stir until smooth. Drain the soaked matzah pieces and add them to the egg mixture, stirring gently.

4. Heat butter and neutral oil in a frying pan over medium heat until melted. Pour a layer of matzah pieces and cook for about 3 minutes until golden. Carefully flip the matzah brei with a spatula and cook for another 3 minutes.

5. Sprinkle ground cinnamon and sugar on the dish and serve hot. Repeat until all the mixture is used up.

*See the photo on the next page.

SPAIN

HORMIGUILLOS: MILK, HONEY AND ALMOND MATZAH SOUP

The breadcrumbs of *hormigos* were used to prepare dishes, often made for the Jewish Passover, because the dough does not contain yeast. *Hormigos* are made with the same dough as that used for unleavened bread.

Hormiguillo (or *hormigo*) refers both to the crumbs of unleavened bread rolled in oil, and to the name of the dish that uses them. For the Sephardic Jews of Spain, it is a soup consumed during Passover, made with milk, breadcrumbs of unleavened bread, honey, and crushed almonds.

The inquisition trials in northern Spain mention the consumption of this soup by the Sephardic Jews of Siguënza, Soria, and Almazán, as part of the dishes prepared during the Jewish Passover. For example, on March 3, 1486, a servant denounced the mistress of the house Elvira, because she "for the Passover of the unleavened bread [*pascuas del pan cençeño*] . . . saw unleavened bread [*pan cençeño*] being brought from the Jewish quarter [*judería*] to the house of the said Doña Elvira, and they made *hormigos* from it and ate them, as did many others in her household."

It is also recorded that "during a Passover of unleavened bread [*Pascua del pan cençeño*], which coincides with Holy Week, the mother of the protonotary ate hormiguillos instead of unleavened bread. Throughout the Passover, this witness did not see her eat any other bread, and believes that she ate hormiguillos in place of unleavened bread [*pan cençeño*]."

Another testimony includes "she made *rollillos* [*hormigos*], and from the same dough she made flat cakes [*tortas*]."

A cookbook written by Domingo Hernández de Maceras, published in 1607 in Salamanca (Spain), contains a recipe titled "hormigo de avellanas" (*hormigo* from hazelnut). Among the four definitions that the Spanish dictionary of the Real Academia Española proposes for "*hormigo*," one is a "dessert typically made of breadcrumbs, grilled and chopped almonds and hazelnuts, and honey."

Serves: 2 people

Time: 30 minutes

¼ cup (30 g) crushed almonds

¼ cup (30 g) crushed hazelnuts

2 large oil-based unleavened breads (see recipe p. 25)

2 cups (400 ml) milk

½ cup (170 ml) honey

1 tsp cinnamon

1. Preheat the oven to 350°F (175°C). Spread the whole almonds and hazelnuts on a baking sheet and toast in the oven for 5 minutes, being careful not to let them burn. Remove the baking sheet from the oven and let the nuts cool on a cutting board for 15 minutes.

2. Pour 1 cup of milk into a saucepan. Break the two matzot into small pieces, taking half of the breadcrumbs and adding them to the milk in the saucepan. Heat the milk and bread mixture over low heat, stirring regularly, and cook for 2 minutes until the bread crumbs have almost disintegrated into the milk. Add ¼ cup of honey to the mixture and stir well. If you prefer a smoother mixture, transfer it to a blender and blend until smooth before returning it to the saucepan.

3. Rub the cooled nuts with a paper towel to remove some of the skins (if they were not already peeled), and then chop them with a large knife and set them aside.

4. Heat the saucepan with the milk, bread, and honey mixture over low heat. Add the second cup of milk to the saucepan and stir for 2 minutes, then add the remaining half of the bread crumbs and cook for 2–3 minutes. Divide the mixture into two bowls.

5. Sprinkle the crushed almonds and hazelnuts and remaining ¼ cup of honey over the top. You can also sprinkle ground cinnamon if desired.

*See the photo on the next page.

GERONA RABBI'S LAMB AND *PA ALIS*

At the end of the 15th century, the Rabbi of Gerona brought a meal to Joan Çarriera, a converso living in the Spanish city of Gerona, in the Carrer de Sanet Lorenç. We learn that "They did it in this way: during the Holy Week [*Semana Sancta*], at the time of the Passover of the Jews [*la Pascha dels jueus*], the Rabbi of the Jews from Girona came there and brought unleavened bread [*pa alis*] and a pot of food in which there were pieces of goat or lamb and hard-boiled eggs. He also brought a bowl in which there was something that looked like mustard, and wine from the Jews. Before they ate . . . the Rabbi brought food and they cooked from it."

SERVES: 4 people

TIME: 30 minutes + 1 night for marinating

For the marinade:

3 cloves of garlic, chopped

Juice of 1 fresh lemon

1 tsp salt

1 tbsp chopped rosemary leaves

2 tbsp olive oil

1 tbsp mustard with seeds

Other ingredients:

8 lamb chops

2 tbsp olive oil (for cooking)

4 boiled eggs

8 matzot (see recipe p. 117)

1 tsp olive oil (for brushing)

1 tbsp mustard (with seeds, for spreading over the unleavened bread)

1. In a bowl, mix together all the ingredients for the marinade. Add the lamb chops and ensure that they are fully coated with the marinade. Cover the bowl with plastic wrap and refrigerate for at least 1 hour, or overnight for a stronger flavor.

2. Preheat the oven on the broil setting. Brush the matzot with 1 tsp olive oil and spread mustard seeds over them. Broil for 2 minutes or until golden brown, then remove from the oven.

3. Heat a skillet over medium heat and add 2 tbsp of olive oil. Add the lamb chops and cook for 2 minutes on each side. Increase the heat and grill each side for 1 additional minute.

4. Serve the lamb chops on a plate with broken pieces of the mustard-matzah and boiled eggs on the side. This dish pairs well with fried eggplants.

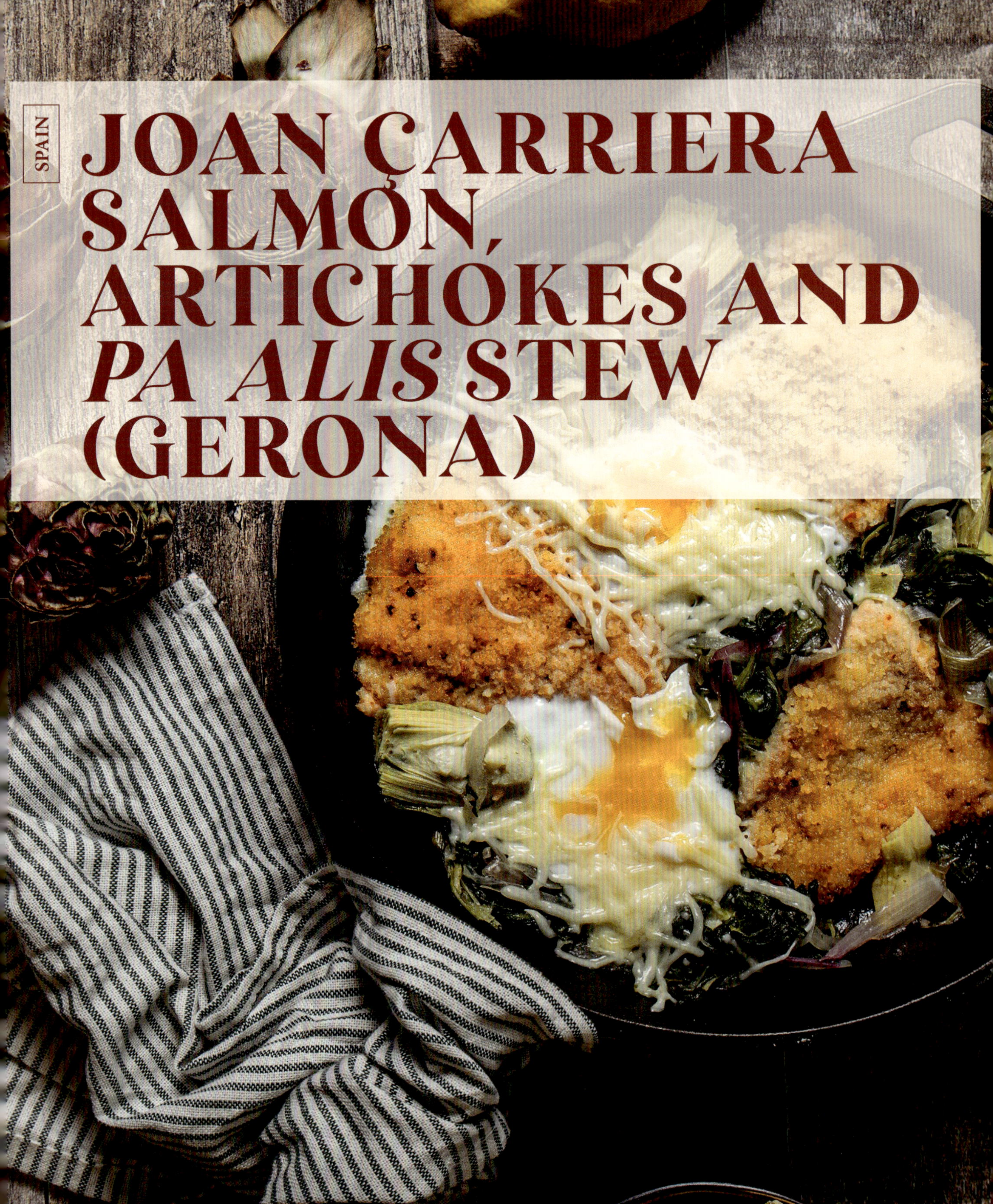

SPAIN

JOAN CARRIERA SALMON, ARTICHOKES AND *PA ALIS* STEW (GERONA)

Joan Çarriera, a Jewish convert, lived on the street of Sanet Lorenç in the Spanish city of Gerona, in the late 15th century. Court testimony about her reads as follows:

"And so it happened that, like Sanct-Jordi and Casafranca who had fled, they celebrated the aforementioned Passover of the Jews with unleavened bread (*pascua dels judeus del pa alis*) with other converts, eating unleavened bread for the eight days that the Passover lasted, and now they ate fish and eggs, and did not eat leavened bread but unleavened bread (*pa alis*)".

In 1505, the inquisitors declared Casafranca "Heretic, Judaizer, and Apostate". Nevertheless, they required to "moderate the punishment towards him, without death, shedding of blood, or mutilation of limbs."

SERVES: 4 people

TIME: 30 minutes

---

4 skinless salmon fillets

1 tsp salt

1 tsp black pepper

1 tbsp olive oil (for marinade)

1⅞ oz (50 g) matzah, crushed into breadcrumbs

2 tsp sumac flakes

4 tbsp olive oil

2 small red spring onions (with the green leaves), sliced

3 cloves garlic, crushed

2 tsp honey

4 cups fresh spinach

8 artichoke quarters, cooked (fresh or canned)

1 lemon, for juice

4 eggs

1 tsp salt

½ cup grated hard cheese (such as Manchego)

---

1. In a bowl, make the marinade by mixing 1 tbsp olive oil, salt, and black pepper. Coat the salmon fillets with the marinade. Mix the crushed matzot and sumac flakes on a plate. Coat each salmon fillet with the mixture and place on a plate. Chill in the refrigerator for about 1 hour.

2. In a skillet, heat 4 tbsp olive oil. Cook the salmon fillets for 3 minutes on each side. Remove from the skillet and put in a plate. Cover with aluminum foil to keep them warm.

3. In the same skillet, add sliced spring onions and crushed garlic. Cook for about 3 minutes over medium heat until the garlic is golden. Add the honey and stir. Add the spinach leaves and artichoke quarters. Cook for 5 minutes, adding olive oil if the mixture becomes too dry. Add the fresh lemon juice and stir.

4. Place the cooked salmon fillets back into the pan, in the middle of the sauce. Crack 4 eggs into the skillet. Cover and cook over medium heat for about 10 minutes until the eggs are cooked.

5. Sprinkle the dish with 1 tsp salt and grated cheese over the eggs. Serve with broken pieces of matzah.

SPAIN

ISABEL NÚÑEZ'S "DIRTY" BREAD

WITH PASSOVER SALAD (SALAMANCA, 1620)

Originally from the city of Ciudad Rodrigo, in the Spanish province of Salamanca, Isabel Nuñez was accused in 1620 of making "Passover bread [Pan de Pascua] that they kneaded without leaven or salt, reciting certain prayers, and they baked it in an oven that was in another prisoner's house on the top of his house, and they set this table for 'The Big Day of Pesach' (*Pascua del día grande*). And they kneaded it with finely sifted soil [*tierra muy cernida*], and they ate that bread on the night following the fast with salad, oil, and vinegar."

What is surprising in this trial, is what resembles a mix of ritual dietary practices. The term "Great Day" [*Pascua del día grande*] is regularly used in Inquisition trials to refer to the feast before Yom Kippur. As for the bread soaked in ash, it refers to the ritual practice during Tisha B'Av (See "Shulchan Arukh"). Professor David Gitlitz explains in his book *A Drizzle of Honey* that these confusions reflect, in the 17th century, a loss of knowledge of the normative specificities linked to the practice of Judaism.

Isabel Nuñez's friend, Ana López, was accused in 1622 of preparing the same bread with the same ingredients "A Passover bread [*un pan de Pasqua*] which they knead with very finely sifted earth without adding leavening or salt."

SERVES: 10 pieces/4 people

TIME: 40 minutes

For the matzot:

⅔ cup (200 g) flour + extra if needed

1 tbsp (10 g) activated charcoal powder

1 tsp olive oil

½ cup (100 ml) hot water

For the salad:

2 cups fresh arugula leaves

2 radishes, finely sliced

¼ cup parsley

1 tbsp neutral oil

1 tsp salt

2 tsp vinegar

1. Preheat your oven to 536°F (280°C). Put aluminum foil in a baking tray and lightly flour it.

2. In a large bowl, mix flour and charcoal together with a spoon. Add olive oil and hot water, and combine with a spoon; then mix by hand for about 1 minute until the dough is homogeneous. Wrap the dough in plastic film and refrigerate for about 30 minutes.

3. Once chilled, divide the dough into 5 equally-sized balls, each about the size of a ping-pong ball (1⅜ oz/38 g each). Flour a work surface and your hands, and place one ball of dough on it.

4. Using a floured rolling pin, flatten the dough to obtain a 6-inch (15-centimeter) disk. The dough should be relatively thin, about ¼ of an inch (3 mm).

5. Place the flattened dough on the prepared baking sheet, and repeat this process with the remaining dough balls. Bake the bread for 30 seconds on one side, then flip it and bake for another 30 seconds. The matzot should brown. Remove the bread from the oven and place it on a cooling rack.

6. Wash the arugula leaves and drain them. Wash the radishes, peel them, and slice them very thinly. Arrange a bed of arugula leaves on individual plates. Place the thinly sliced radishes on top of the arugula leaves. Sprinkle chopped parsley over the radishes and arugula, and season with olive oil, salt, and vinegar. Serve and eat with the matzot.

GABRIEL AND GRAÇIANA'S MATZAH AND LAMB PIES
FOR PASSOVER

On June 18, 1505, a neighbor from the Spanish town of Almazán reported Gabriel and Graçiana for preparing unleavened bread and meat pies using sheep. The witness claimed that "it has been seen that sometimes, around Christmas (*Navidad*; perhaps for the 10th of Tevet) and after the last Easter celebration (*Pascua de Resurrección*) . . . Graçiana kneads dough without yeast, with cold water and makes cakes with Lamb (*pasteles de carnero*), spices, and some cakes. She eats these on meat days and the cakes [*tortas*] on any day. And other times she does this with yeast and cold water."

SERVES: 4 people

TIME: 1 hour + the day before

For the matzah

SERVES: 4 pieces

TIME: 18 minutes

1⅛ cup (170 g) flour

½ cup (100 ml) cold water

1. Preheat your oven to 536°F (280°C), and line a baking tray with aluminum foil. Take a rolling pin and a fork, and keep them handy.

2. Mix together the water and the flour, and knead the dough for 5 minutes. Cut the dough into 4 pieces and roll them into balls. Each ball should fit in the palm of your hand. Take the rolling pin (or your hands) and spread each ball into a very thin layer of dough (6 inches diameter).

3. Put the matzah on the prepared baking sheet, and prick it with a fork across its surface.

4. Bake for 30 seconds on one side and 30 seconds on the other side.

For the lamb pie crust (for a 9 inch/23 cm pie):

1½ cup (220 g) flour (or matzo meal)

1 tsp ground allspice

1 tsp salt

½ cup (100 g) neutral oil

¼ cup (50 g) cold water

To make the quince puree:

3 medium quinces, boiled and mashed (Or 2⅛ oz/65 g of ready-to-use quince paste)

1 lemon's juice

1 tsp salt

1 short cinnamon stick

To make the spice paste:

2 garlic cloves, peeled

2 medium-sized scallions, peeled and diced

2 teaspoons honey

1 tablespoon vinegar

¼ tsp teaspoon cinnamon

½ teaspoon cumin

1 teaspoon ginger powder

¼ tsp salt

To make the lamb:

2 tbsp olive oil

1 pound (450 g) ground lamb

5 onions, peeled and diced

1 teaspoon salt

¼ teaspoon black pepper

5 leaves chopped mint

⅓ cup chopped parsley

2 tablespoons lemon juice

2 teaspoons vinegar

1 tablespoon mustard with seeds

1 egg, beaten (to brush)

1. For the crust of a 9-inch pie, combine oil and water in a small bowl. Combine flour, allspice and salt in a separate bowl. Stir with a spoon, make a hole in the center and pour the oil/water mixture into it. Mix together from the middle to the edges. Finish by kneading by hand until the dough is smooth, wrap in a plastic bag, and cool in the fridge for about 30 minutes.

2. Separate the dough in two parts: ⅔ + ⅓. Lightly flour a parchment paper and a rolling pin.

3. Put the bigger piece of dough in the middle of the parchment paper. Cover it with another parchment paper and roll the dough out until it is about ¼ inch thick.

4. Remove the parchment paper of the top and transfer the dough to a greased pie plate, spreading it up onto the edges. Prick with a fork. Cover with a towel and cool it in the fridge for about 30 minutes.

5. Take the smaller piece of dough, and put it in the middle of new parchment paper. Cover it with another parchment paper and roll the dough out until it is about ¼ inch thick. Cool it in the fridge for about 30 minutes.

6. To prepare the quince puree, begin by filling a pan with water and adding the lemon juice, salt and the short cinnamon stick. Next, peel three medium quinces, cut them into quarters, and remove the pits and hard parts. Place the prepared quince pieces into the pan and cover them, allowing them to boil over medium heat for 30 minutes. The water level should remain just above the quince pieces. Afterward, transfer the cooked quince pieces to a mixer and blend them until you achieve a smooth texture, with some small chunks remaining for added texture. Drain.

7. To create the spiced paste, use a mortar and pestle to combine cloves of garlic, 2 onions, honey, and vinegar. Then, add cinnamon, cumin, and ginger powder to the mixture.

8. Heat a medium skillet over medium heat and add 2 tbsp of olive oil, 5 sliced onions, and salt. Cook for approximately 5 minutes or until the onions become translucent.

9. Add the ground lamb into the skillet, along with the spiced paste, and cook while stirring for approximately 5 minutes until it thickens. Once thickened, remove it from the heat and add chopped mint, parsley, lemon juice, vinegar, mustard seeds, and quince puree. Let the mixture cool.

10. Remove the pie dough from the fridge and preheat the oven to 425°F (220°C). Fill the pie with the lamb mixture, lightly water the edges of the bottom crust, and cover it with the top part of the crust. Gently press the top crust and edges of the bottom crust together, making a roll with the excess dough to seal the pie. Brush the pie with the beaten egg and make a hole in the middle to allow vapor to escape and avoid unsealing the pie. Cover the pie with parchment paper to prevent the crust from browning too quickly. Cool in the refrigerator for 20 minutes.

11. Bake the pie for approximately 40 minutes at 425°F (220°C), then remove the parchment paper and bake for an additional 10 minutes until the crust is golden-brown.

12. Remove the pie from the oven and let it cool at room temperature. Serve lukewarm with salad, matzah and pomegranate molasses.

ANDALUSIAN SOUP
FROM MARÍA DÍAS'S PASSOVER SEDER

María Días, a wax worker from the Andalusian town of Palma near Cordova, was not present during the trial against her that started on January 12, 1484; she had fled when the court of the Inquisition moved to the city of Ciudad Real. The account of this trial recounts in detail the dishes that María Días had prepared for the two Seders of Passover. In the record of the trial, the use of a particular herb called "sow-thistle" is noteworthy (*Sonchus oleraceus* L. 1753). This herbaceous plant has long leaves in rosettes, with winged and slightly spiny petioles as well as yellow ligules. The herb has the characteristics of a thistle which make it, among other properties, taste bitter. In his work *Kitāb al-Jāmiʿ li-Mufradāt al-Adwiya wa-l-Aghdhiya* (Compendium on Simple Medicaments and Foods), a pharmaceutical encyclopedia, the 12th–13th century Andalusian botanist Ibn al-Bayṭār cites the sow-thistle under the Berber name of *tifāf* and under the Arabic name *ẖas al-ḥamār* (donkey lettuce). He also mentions it as one of the "vegetables of the Jews" (*Bakla yehoudiya*). This leads at least to two conclusions. The first is that the Jews were already identified by a diet different from that of others (and in particular the Muslims who reigned in the 13th century in the south of Spain). The second is that in the 13th century the sow-thistle must have already been used by the Jews of Spain for the Passover ceremony.

Two centuries later, the Andalusian María Días was denounced for having used it for the Seder meals. The account of the trial includes the following: "thus the Passover of the unleavened bread [*Pascua del Pan Cenceño*], eating it, like another ceremony that they [the Jews] do on Passover on the first two nights, in which they eat lettuce and celery and sow thistle and vinegar [*lechugas y apio y çerrajas y vinagre*], and another ceremony that they do with *maror*, which means bitter, and with certain small unleavened breads [*tortillas de pan cenceño pequeñas*]. She [the witness] saw her [María Días] doing everything and keeping and celebrating no less than the Jews do and keeping [Jewish practices], wearing clean clothes as well as eating in new vessels that no leavened bread [*pan libdo*] had come near to, and if they ate in some of them, they were of copper or wood or other metals, and those being very well scalded with boiling water and then with cold water." María Días was condemned and burned to death on February 24th, 1484.

In today's Andalusia, there is a plant that grows in March (sometimes the beginning of April, when Passover is usually celebrated) which is very similar to the sow-thistle. It is called *tagarninas* (*Scolymus Hispanicus* L.). Andalusians use it in stew and soups that they cook during Easter.

Serves: 4

Time: 30 minutes

For the broth:

2 carrots, peeled, washed and cut into chucks

1 medium onion, peeled and sliced

2 stalks of celery, peeled, washed and cut into chucks

1 clove garlic, mashed

4 cups (1L) water

1 tbsp salt

For the soup:

4 cups (800 ml) vegetable broth

9 oz (250 g) cleaned and rinsed *tagarninas*, cut to 1.2 in/3 cm (use asparagus as a substitute)

5 small cloves of garlic, sliced

4 tsp olive oil

1 bay leaf

2 tsp salt

1 tsp black pepper

3 strands saffron, crushed in a mortar with one ice cube

2 eggs, beaten

1 shallot, thinly sliced

4 unleavened breads (see recipes p. 145, or p. 130)

1 tsp smoked paprika (optional)

To make the broth:

1. Take a pan and pour in 4 cups of water and salt, and bring it to a boil.

2. Add the chopped vegetables, and cover and cook for about 10–15 minutes, until tender.

To make the soup:

1. In a pan, pour olive oil. Add the thin slices of garlic and a bay leaf. Sauté over medium heat for 2–3 minutes, making sure not to burn the garlic. It should be golden.

2. Add the cut *tagarninas* (or asparagus), salt, pepper, and the saffron previously crushed in a mortar with 1 ice cube. Mix gently for about 2 minutes and add 4 cups of vegetable broth. And the cooked vegetables as well. Cook covered over medium heat for approximatively 15 minutes. Then, turn off the heat.

3. In a bowl, beat the eggs. Pour them into the soup and gently move to cook them.

4. Prepare the bowls, and add finely chopped scallions. Then add 5 pieces of broken matzah, and pour the soup on top. Sprinkle with smoked paprika if desired. Serve hot without waiting.

*See the photo on the next page.

ANA CORTES' *COCAS* AND ROASTED LAMB
FROM THE JEWISH GHETTO OF MAJORCA

Information regarding food preparation for the Passover Seder is mentioned in sources dealing with the general practices of conversos. The custom of burning a lamb bone—in order to place it in the Seder dish—is a common but not a universal practice among Sephardic Jews. Some sources do not mention any meat (or any bones) in the Seder dish, at least in the 15th–16th century. It seems that this practice was observed later among Iberian and American Sephardim. The testimony from 1678, against Ana Cortes, fits this pattern. It reveals the custom of crypto-Jews living in the Spanish island of Majorca regarding the consumption of roasted lamb and the burning of the bone to be placed in the Seder dish. We read the following:

"We had to observe a fast called the Passover of the Lamb [*Pascua del Cordero*], not eating or drinking throughout the day. And after this fast, the Passover was to be celebrated, which lasted for seven days; and during this time, a lamb was killed and roasted whole, with which a feast was made for all the relatives. The bones were to be burned [*los huesos se habían de quemar*], which signified the sacrifice of the law of Moses. And during these seven days, unleavened bread [*pan sin levadura*] had to be eaten, and no yeast could be kept in the house. They had to make some cakes [*cocas*, a typical bread from the Balear Islands and the Eastern coast of Spain] on a new brick and cook them over the fire, and these had to be distributed among the relatives."

As David Gitlitz says in *Secrecy and Deceit*, eating the Paschal lamb was also a custom among crypto-Jews from Mexico, as Juan de Leon told the inquisitors in 1642.

SERVES: 6 people

TIME: 2 hours 30 minutes + 1 night for marinating

For the roasted lamb cooked on a barbecue or in a smoker (you can cook it in a pressure cooker as well, for about 45 minutes):

1 medium lamb shoulder (about 1.8–2.2 kg), bone-in

2 tsp sea salt

1 tbsp coriander seeds

1 tbsp cumin seeds

½ tbsp fennel seeds

½ tbsp caraway seeds
5 big garlic cloves, mashed
2 tbsp dried thyme
2 tsp ground black pepper
½ tbsp turmeric powder
1 tsp sumac
1 fresh lemon juice
4 tbsp olive oil

1. Remove any fat excess from the lamb. Score the top of the meat (the fat white part) with a sharp knife in a grid at 2 cm intervals. Rub the whole shoulder with the salt, and set aside.

2. In the meantime, prepare the marinade. In a mortar, put all the seeds, and grind them for 3 minutes. Add the mashed garlic cloves, the thyme, and the black pepper. Grind for an additional 2 minutes. Add the turmeric powder, sumac, lemon juice and olive oil. The result should look like a thick marinade.

3. Rub the marinade all over the lamb shoulder, cover with plastic wrap, and put it in the fridge overnight.

4. Heat the barbecue or smoker using enough charcoal to burn for two hours. Wrap the lamb shoulder with aluminum foil, and put it on the grill to roast, turning it over every 30 minutes. Repeat 3 times.

5. On the fourth flip, remove the aluminum paper and roast uncovered. (Alternatively, you can cook it in a pressure cooker, for about 45 minutes.)

Serves: 4 individual cocas

Time: 1 hour

For the *cocas*:

⅔ cup (150 ml) water
⅓ cup (90 ml) sunflower oil
2½ cups (370 g) flour
2 tsp salt

1. Preheat the oven at 380°F (200°C), and mix all the ingredients in a large bowl. Knead for about 5 minutes, then cover the dough and cool it in the fridge for about 20 minutes.

2. Roll the dough out into a thin rectangle, about 0.2-inch/ 0.5 cm thick and 8 inches by 12 inches (20 cm by 30 cm). Cut it into 4 rectangles; each one should be about 4 inches by 6 inches (15 cm by 10 cm).

3. Put parchment paper in a baking tray. Flour it lightly and place the cocas on it.

4. Pinch the edges of the dough up to form a short ledge; this will prevent the filling from spilling out. Prick the dough with a fork over its surface.

5. Bake in a wood-fired oven at the highest temperature for 5 minutes, or in an oven at 380°F (200°C) for 15 minutes. Remove from the oven.

6. You can eat the lamb with *cocas* as a side, or you can fill the baked *cocas* with roasted lamb pieces.

*See the photo on the next page.

UNLEAVENED FLAT SNOW CAKES OF MARÍA GONZÁLES

In 1513, María Gonzáles, a conversa from Ciudad Real, was accused of eating matzah cakes, "*tortas* as white as snow [*tortas blancas como la nieve*], tasteless, with a slight flavor of olive."

This accusation suggests that the accuser not only saw María Gonzales prepare the unleavened bread cakes—which would have been made with very white wheat flour, probably wheat flour—but also ate and enjoyed them to the point of being able to make an informed judgment about their taste.

SERVES: 20 pieces

TIME: 45 minutes

- 1 cup (150 g) wheat flour
- ⅛ cup (20 g) rice flour
- ¼ cup (50 ml) milk
- ¼ cup (50 ml) water
- 1 tbsp olive oil (to brush)
- ½ cup black olives, pit less
- ½ cup green olives, pit less
- 2 salted anchovy fillets
- 1 tbsp fresh oregano leaves

1. Mix together the two flours. Add the milk and water little by little, and then knead the dough for 3 minutes. Wrap the dough in a plastic bag and cool it in the fridge for about 20 minutes.

2. Take the rolling pin and roll out the dough over a floured surface until you get it 0.15-inch (3 mm) thick. Use a round cookie cutter to shape the small breads or a knife if you would like them squared.

3. Heat an iron skillet over low-medium heat. You do not want the bread to be golden. It needs to be as white as possible. Cook for 20 seconds on one side and 20 seconds on the other side. You can cover the skillet during baking.

4. Remove from the skillet, brush it lightly with olive oil, and place on a cooling rack. Chop very thinly together the two kinds of olives and the salted anchovy fillets, using a knife or a mincer. It should be like a puree. Spread the olive puree on the white matzah and sprinkle with fresh oregano leaves.

ICA ELA ENR
MEXICO HIJA
HEREGE HECH
IADA

Micaela Enríquez, a native of Mexico and Sebastian Cardoso's wife, was considered a heretic, a witch, and a practitioner of Judaism. She was punished with a solemn abjuration *de vehementi* and a confiscation of her assets, but she relapsed. It was in the year 1648. Because she confessed her Judaizing practices and promised to "be a Christian," the inquisitors said:

"Wishing to show mercy towards her, we must admit her and we do admit her to reconciliation, and we command that as a penalty and penance for what she has done, said, and committed, on the day of the *auto* she shall go to the house balcony with the other penitents in her bare body, holding a green wax candle in her hands, and wearing a penitential habit of yellow cloth with two red St. Andrew's crosses. There, the pronounced sentence shall be read aloud to her, and she shall publicly abjure the aforementioned errors that she has confessed in front of us, as well as any other form of heresy and apostasy. We hereby absolve the said Micaela Enríquez from any sentence of excommunication incurred by reason of the aforesaid acts, and we unite and reincorporate her into the fold and union of our holy mother Catholic Church, restoring her to the participation in the holy sacraments and communion of the faithful Christians. We condemn her to perpetual and irremissible imprisonment, and she shall publicly wear the aforementioned habit over her garments and maintain her character in the perpetual prison of the city [. . .]. And likewise, we condemn her to perpetual banishment from all these West Indies and from the cities of Seville and Madrid, the Court of His Majesty. She shall embark to fulfill this sentence on the first fleet departing from the port of San Juan de Ulua, bound for Spain. And once she arrives in the said Kingdoms, within one month, she shall present herself before the tribunal of the Holy Office of the Inquisition in Seville to be recognized and registered, and her place and location of imprisonment and habitation shall be designated. And in the event of non-compliance, action may be taken against the aforementioned Micaela Enríquez as an impenitent [. . .]. And before the tribunals of the aforementioned Inquisition in Seville, Lima, and Cartagena in these said West Indies. And we declare the same Micaela Enríquez to be incapacitated and we incapacitate her and her descendants so that they may not hold or obtain any ecclesiastical or secular dignities, benefits, or offices that are public or honorable, nor may they wear gold, silver, pearls, precious stones, silk or damask, fine cloth, or ride on horseback, nor engage in or use other things that, according to common law, the laws and pragmatics of these Kingdoms, and the instructions of the said office of the Inquisition, are prohibited to similar incapacitated individuals and their descendants in the designated degrees. All of which we command to be done and fulfilled as the penalty for her impenitent relapse. [. . .] Monday, the thirtieth of March of the year one thousand six hundred and forty-eight."

Here is the abjuration:

Porque Micaela Enríquez, hereje, reincidente, apostata, ha confesado sus prácticas judaizantes y ha prometido «ser cristiana,» los inquisidores dijeron: «Queriendo usar con ella de misericordia: la debemos admitir y admitimos a reconciliación, y mandamos que en pena y penitencia de lo por ella hecho, dicho y cometido, el día del auto salga al casa balcón con los otros penitentes en cuerpo con una vela verde de cera en las manos y un habito penitencial de paño amarillo con dos aspas coloradas de la cruz de San Andrés, donde se le sea leída alta viva sentencia y allí públicamente abjure los dichos sus errores que ante nos tiene confesados, y otra cualquier especie de herejía y apostasías y esta la dicha abjuración mandamos absolver y absolvemos a la dicha Micaela Enriquez de cualquier sentencia de la excomunión en que por razón del susdicho sacaido; lincurrido, y la unimos y reincorporamos al gremio y unión de nuestra santa madre iglesia católica y la restituimos a la participación de los santos sacramentos y comunión de los fieles cristianos de ella y la condenamos a cárcel y habito perpetuo irremisible y que el dicho habito lo traiga públicamente encima de su vestiduras y tenga y guarde carateria en la cárcel perpetua de la ciudad [. . .].Y así mismo la condenamos a destierro perpetuo preciso de todas estas Indias Occidentales y de la ciudad de Sevilla y de Madrid Corte de su Majestad. Y que se embarque a cumplirlo en la primera flota que del puerto de San Juan de Vlva?? Saliere, de vuelta para España. Y que luego que a los dichos Reinos llegue dentro de un mes se presente en el tribunal de dicho Santo Oficio de la Inquisición de Sevilla para que sea reconocida y se tome razón de su persona y se le señale la parte y lugar en que se ha de cumplir su carcelería y habito. Y para que en caso de contravención se pueda proceder contra la dicha Micaela Enríquez como contra impenitente. [. . .] Y a los tribunales de la dicha Inquisición de Sevilla y de las ciudades de Lima y Cartagena en estas dichas Indias Occidentales. Y declaramos la dicha Micaela Enríquez ser inb/havil y la inb/havilitamos y a su descendencia para que no puedan tener ni obtener dignidades, beneficios, ni oficios eclesiásticos ni segulares que sean públicos ni de honra ni traer sobre sí ni en su persona oro, plata, perlas, ni piedras preciosas, ni seda o hamelote, ni paño fino, ni andar a caballo, ni ejercer ni usar de las otras cosas que por derecho común, leyes y pragmáticas de estos Reinos e instrucciones del dicho oficio de la inquisición a los semejantes inhbiles y a su descendencia en los grados que están señalados les son prohibido/as. Lo cual todo la mandamos así haga y cumpla su pena de impenitente Relapsa. Y por esta nuestra sentencia [. . .]

Lunes a treinta de marzo de mil y seiscientos y cuarenta y ocho años.

Aquí la abjuración

(Archivo General de la Nación,
Gobierno de Mexico, Inquisición, 1642)

The two Judaizing sisters, Rafaela and Micaela Enríquez (daughters of the dogmatist Blanca Enríquez), were friends of the inquisitorial notary, Don Eugenio de Saravia, and the inquisitor Don Francisco de Estrada y Escobedo. The first even became the mistress of the notary, Eugenio de Saravia. Once again, these relationships had significant consequences for the smooth progress of the inquisitorial proceedings: the "wise" advice to make "spontaneous" confessions, without waiting for an imminent arrest, was given to Micaela Enríquez by her friends in the tribunal. The purpose was to gain future indulgence from these judges. Micaela Enríquez's confessions, contrary to all norms, were received by the notary Saravia in his own residence. We can thus read that Micaela Enríquez "threw herself at the feet of Mr. Francisco de Estrada, shedding abundant tears." Once her statements were received, she was able to return to her residence, around 11 o'clock at night.

(AGN, Inquisición,
Proceso contra Micaela Enríquez, 1642).

MEXICO

BLANCA ENRÍQUEZ'S MEXICAN SMALL CAKES

In Mexico in 1642, Beatriz Enríquez, although herself a conversa, described to the inquisitors how her mother Blanca took great care in preparing matzah, with the same simple ingredients as were used among Jews in Spain in other trial records: flour, water, no salt, no yeast.

"Three days before Easter . . . having sent the house slaves to see the processions, her [Beatriz] mother laid on the table new tablecloths or towels, and then the new knife, and in the new bowl put the flour, and from the new pitcher poured some cold water, and mixed and kneaded the flour with both hands, with a fire already kindled in the new brazier; and after having blessed each separate thing, and having kneaded the flour, she broke three small pieces off of the dough, reciting certain prayers over each one . . . of which she only remembers the following: 'Blessed are You Adonai, and You gave us your commandments [*encomendanzas*], holy and blessed, blessed and holy.' Then she gathered [*juntaba*] the three pieces [*tres pedacitos*] in one, and threw into the fire [*la lumbre*] which was under this said brazier [*brasero*], reciting the same prayers, and if this dough [*la dicha masa*] popped when she threw it into the fire, her mother said that that was a sign that the God of Israel [*el Dios de Israel*] had approved this feast [*la dicha Pascua*], and that He had accepted the sacrifice of the challah [*hala*] [. . .] and from this dough she made three flat small cakes [*tres tortitas*], but she could have make five or seven or as many as she wanted if it was nona time [*como fuesen nonas*]. She baked these [*Las cuales coció*] on the fire [*encima de la dicha lumbre*], and she shared the three small pieces of the bread [*y repartió todas tresberes pedacitos del dicho pan con*] with Juana Enriquez [. . .]."

SERVES: 7 pieces

TIME: 18 minutes

1 cup (150 g) white wheat flour

1½ cup (180 g) corn flour/masa harina, nixtamalized

1½ cup (300 ml) + 2 tbsp cold water

1. Preheat your nonstick iron skillet to medium-high heat. Prepare 2 sheets of plastic wrap that are a little bit larger than the tortilla press. They will be used for the tortilla press to avoid the dough sticking to the tortilla press sides.

2. Mix together the two flours. Progressively add the cold water to the flour and stir constantly until the flours absorbs all the water. Knead the dough for about 5 minutes. The dough should be moist to the touch.

3. Cut the dough into 7 pieces and roll into balls (each one should be 3½ oz or 100 g).

4. Open the tortilla press, place a plastic sheet (or parchment paper) on the bottom, a ball of dough in the middle, and cover with the other plastic sheet. Close the tortilla press and press down to flatten the dough, until it is 0.16 inches (2 mm) thick. Open the tortilla press. Remove the plastic sheet from the top of the dough, and flip the dough from the bottom plastic sheet onto the palm of your other hand. Then, lay it carefully on the hot skillet. Cook for 20 seconds, and then flip it and cook for another 20 seconds. Keep them hot.

SALOMÓN DE MACHORRO'S FISH TACOS

MEXICO

Corn tortillas are undeniably linked to the culinary heritage of Mexico, since they were already prepared in pre-Columbian times. As we know, adaptability is inherent to Jewish culture, both for the survival of its culture and its people.

In 1642 in Mexico, Salomón de Machorro (aka Juan de León, famous for his travels and knowledge of Judaism) was denounced by Catalina de Rivera for having consumed corn tortillas with fish and vegetables with his friends for Passover. She also noticed that because the corn tortillas dried, they ate regular bread.

Serves: 4

Time: 1 hour

For the dough:

2 cups (300 g) corn flour/ masa harina, nixtamalized

1½ tsp salt

1⅓ cup (260 ml) hot water

1 tsp olive oil

For the fish and sauce:

¼ cup (50 g) olive oil

2 chopped cloves of garlic

½ lb (220 g) fresh white fish

2 very thinly sliced red onions

2 tbsp chopped fresh cilantro

½ tsp black pepper

2 tbsp finely chopped chives

juice of 1 lime

1 tsp salt

1. To make the dough, mix together corn flour and salt in a large bowl. Add the olive oil and the hot water, and mix the preparation with a spoon until all the water is absorbed. Make balls of dough the size of a golf ball (1⅛ oz or 30 g). Let them rest on a plate for 20 minutes, covered so they do not dry.

2. To flatten and cook the tortillas, you can use a tortilla press if you have one: remember to put the dough ball between two pieces of parchment paper so it does not stick to the press. Place it in the center of the bottom part of the press, then open it and carefully, and with the palm of your hand remove the tortilla from the parchment sheet. If you don't have a tortilla press, you can use the bottom of a heavy saucepan and press down hard. Again, do not forget the parchment paper!

3. Cook in a preheated (medium-high heat) nonstick skillet for 20 seconds. Then flip the tortilla over and cook the other side for 20 more seconds. Repeat the operation once more until the tortilla has golden-brown marks. Keep the tortillas in a plastic bag, not completely closed, while you make the filling.

4. Put the olive oil, red onions, and garlic in a frying pan. Cook for 5 minutes on medium heat until golden. Add the fresh fish cut into pieces and pour in the fresh lime juice. Add salt and black pepper. Cover the frying pan and cook on a low heat for 5 minutes.

5. Then, sprinkle with the chopped fresh cilantro and chives.

6. Fill the corn tortillas with the delicious fish and its lime juice, and enjoy.

> "Without it, Mexicans don't feel like they are eating"
> Fray Bartolomé de Las Casas, on chile and its importance in the Mexican diet, 15th century.

PASSOVER INDIAN WHEAT AND HERBS CRACKERS

Another proof of Marranism—the combination of Jewish and Christian practices in the Americas—consisted of preparing small bites of bread for Passover in the image of the host offered to Christians during the act of communion in church. This is how Pedro de Tinoco told the inquisitors of Mexico (1649) that he learned from his grandmother the customs of Passover, including the preparation of unleavened bread. The trial revealed that he said he would put a small piece of this bread in his mouth, with herbs and parsley."

I propose to link the consumption of these crackers to salsa verde. A reference to the main ingredient of this sauce, the tomatillo, is found in a botanical text written by the Spanish converso, doctor, physician and botanist Francisco Hernández born in La Puebla de Montalbán (Toledo) in 1517, thus one century before Pedro de Tinoco's life. He travelled throughout Latin America, and spent most of his time in Mexico. He wrote "History of the Plants of New Spain," in which he mentions maize (corn), which he calls "Indian wheat," and tortillas, which he calls "Pan de Indias," (Indian bread). He mentioned the process of nixtamalization (corn soaked in an alkaline solution, cooked, and hulled, in order to increase its nutritional value), a process already used in the 16th century in Mexico to get the best tortillas: "It's not too surprising because nowadays Mexicans mix cal [with maize] so that it cooks and softens more easily and better, and when ground, they make their tortillas from it." (No es mucho de espantar, pues mezclan hoy los mexicanos yeso para que mas facilmente y mejor se cueza y se ablande, y molido se hagan dello sus tortillas).

Salsa verde is a hot sauce made with tomatillos, green tomatoes (*Physalis philadephica*), and green chiles. This salsa was already consumed before the arrival of the Spanish conquistadores in the 15th century, and the Jewish converso Francisco Hernández used to consume it with its tortillas.

*See the photo on the next page.

Serves: 4

Time: 1 hour

Herb crackers:

½ cup flat-leaf parsley

1 tbsp celery leaves

½ cup arugula leaves

½ cup (60 g) yellow corn flour, nixtamalized

⅓ cup (66 ml) water

1 tbsp olive oil

1 tsp salt

1 tsp coarse salt (to sprinkle)

1 tsp chili flakes (to sprinkle)

¼ cup corn flour (to flour the parchment paper)

Salsa Verde:

5 Mexican green *tomatillos*

5 green chiles *Serrano* or *Jalapeño* (use regular hot green chili for substitution)

2 tsp salt

3 garlic cloves, unpeeled

¼ cup fresh cilantro and/or parsley

1. For the crackers, preheat the oven to 310°F (100°C). Combine all ingredients except for the coarse salt and the chili flakes, and put the ball of dough in a plastic bag and freeze for 10 minutes. Flour a parchment paper with corn flour, place the dough in the middle, and flour the top of the dough. Place another parchment paper over the dough.

2. Roll the dough out between the two sheets of parchment paper until the dough is thin (about a tenth of an inch), and chill in the refrigerator for 20 minutes.

3. Place the parchment paper with dough on top of a baking tray. Remove the top parchment paper and sprinkle the dough with the chili flakes. Press carefully with a rolling pin or with your hands so the flakes stick to the dough.

4. Use a cookie cutter to cut the dough into cracker shapes. They can be round or squared. Do not remove them from the parchment paper. Sprinkle with coarse salt.

5. Bake for 30 minutes, and then broil for 3 minutes. Be careful not to burn them.

6. Let cool for 10 minutes before separating the crackers.

For the salsa verde:

1. Heat an iron skillet to medium-high heat and sear the chiles, garlic cloves and *tomatillos* with their husks for about 4 minutes. Set aside.

2. Take a pan and boil water. Remove the husks from the tomatillos, boil them for about ten minutes, and drain. Take a blender or, better, a molcajete (or a mortar), and grind the cloves of garlic (without their peel) with the chiles until it they make a paste. Add the salt and half of the chopped cilantro (and parsley) and half of the boiled tomatillos. Grind for about two more minutes. Add the other half of the tomatillos and keep grinding, but not too much; you do not want a homogeneous paste. Add the other chopped cilantro and stir.

3. Pour in a bowl if ready to use, or in a sealed jar to keep in the fridge.

4. The crackers are great to dip in the salsa verde, which also tastes wonderful with fried eggs.

CHESTNUT AND DATE HAROSET BALLS
FROM FERRARA

Díaz Nieto's Portuguese converso family is one of the more important Sephardi families. Their customs reflect much of the Sephardi diaspora culture and carry knowledge of many of the practices of Judaism they gathered along their journey through Portugal, Italy and Mexico.

In 1594, Diego Diaz Nieto and his father Ruy arrived in Mexico, hoping to prosper in their business and live more comfortably. However, this hope was short-lived, as the Inquisition tribunal installed in Mexico caught up with them. In an inquisitorial trial dating back to 1601, when Diego was 27 years old, he explained to the inquisitors that when he lived in Italy, in Ferrara, Portuguese Jews from that city prepared "balls [*albóndigas*] made of sweet, ground apples and chestnuts and other things that he doesn't particularly remember. And these balls dissolve [*se deshacen*] in vinegar, and lettuce and celery are dipped in this vinegar, and they eat them."

In Moroccan Amazigh culture, nearly identical balls are made for many festivals and rituals. The Amazigh are a people which were present in Morocco long before the arrival of Muslims. They have a unique culture and celebrate many festivals that are different from those of Muslims, and some of which are similar to Sephardic Jewish holidays. In Moroccan Amazigh culture there is also an edible ball similar to the *haroset* of the Sephardic Jewish tradition (also spelled *charoset*), and which is consumed during the holiday of Passover (Pesach). Both dishes are made with similar ingredients, such as dried fruits, honey, spices, and sometimes sesame seeds. They also have a similar texture, with finely chopped ingredients mixed to form a dense paste. However, the recipes vary according to regions and families, and the two dishes have a different meaning and use in their respective cultural contexts.

The use of vinegar in the haroset recipe recalls the writings of the Babylonian Talmud regarding the preparation of this deliberately thick paste that resembles the mortar, or clay of Hebrew slaves, but should also contain spices such as nard and cinnamon. Moses Maimonides, in his "Commentary on the Mishneh" (1145–1168) and later in his "Mishneh Torah" (Repetition of the Torah, 1170–1180), proposes two different recipes for haroset. In Commentary on the Mishneh, he states that haroset should be acidic since it is related to mud or clay. It should be made from figs or dates soaked in water and then cooked and mashed until they are soft. Then they should be kneaded with vinegar and nard or thyme or hyssop, but these herbs should not be chopped. The use of hyssop is interesting and shows the importance that Maimonides places on the use of certain foods to remember the history of the Jews (hyssop is the herb that, when dipped in blood, was used to mark the doors to identify the houses of the Hebrews and prevent the firstborn Hebrews from being killed during the 10th plague of Egypt). However, in the Mishneh Torah, he proposes a slightly different recipe. He still uses figs or dates but suggests adding grapes or other similar fruits. This time, the fruits are not cooked beforehand but are directly mashed and mixed with vinegar. Spices are added, but they do not seem to be ground into powder, as Rambam specifies that this preparation should resemble mud mixed with straw. As a scientist, physician, and dietitian, Maimonides proposes a haroset that respects the human constitution, allows for good health, and respects Jewish principles of life. In his haroset, Moses Maimonides says that dates should be cooked to reduce their acidity, which will be compensated for by the use of vinegar, but fresh figs and grapes should be used (along with almonds) which are beneficial if consumed dried or fresh. Therefore, it is a sweet and sour haroset.

This recipe for haroset is notable for its use of chestnuts. A manuscript dating back to the 12th century and written in Hebrew, the *Teshuvot HaGeonim HaḤadashot* (The New Responsa of Geonim), proposes a completely unique recipe for haroset. This recipe was prepared in the south of France, in the city of Lunel, which housed a significant community of Sephardic Jews, as well as Ashkenazim.

Professor Susan Weingarten proposes the following translation of the recipe from the manuscript in *Haroset: A Taste of Jewish History*:

"A reminder of how we make haroset on Passover:

To a third of a *hin* (biblical measure of volume) of strong vinegar we add fruit:

2 liters of white chestnuts, which should be cooked before grinding,

2 liters of almonds, which should not be peeled,

30 small dates or 10 large ones.

800 nuts,

50 medium apples or 30 large ones.

And if you reduce the chestnuts and almonds and add [wal]nuts it will be better and nicer.
Of spices:

Half an ounce of ginger (*yeni bar*)
Half an ounce of spikenard (*sanbal*), which is called *ashpik*,
Half an ounce of *kaneh*, which is called *canella*,
Half an ounce of *teven mika*, which is called *ashkinant* (*Cymbopogon schoenanthus*),
Half an ounce of pepper.

And this amount is barely sufficient for us."

Serves: 7 balls

Time: 30 minutes

4 Medjool dates

½ green apple, grated

2 large dried figs

1 tbsp large Malaga raisins

1 tsp vinegar

4 cooked chestnuts, ground

½ tsp ground ginger

20 almonds with peel

30 pistachios

1 short cinnamon stick

5 dried hyssop leaves

1. In a skillet, toast the almonds and pistachios over medium heat for about 3 minutes. Let them cool for 10 minutes and chop them coarsely. Place them on plates and set aside.

2. Remove the pits from the dates and set the dates aside. Peel and remove the core of a green apple, and grate it using a vegetable grater to shred it. Place the shredded apple on paper towels, cover with another paper towel, and set aside.

3. In a mortar, crush the figs, raisins, and dates together until you obtain a paste. Add the vinegar and crush again for 30 seconds. Transfer this paste to a small bowl.

4. In the same mortar, place the cooked chestnuts (see recipe of Felipa Cardosa's Chestnut Matzah for Passover) and crush them. It doesn't have to be ground to a powder; you can keep some small chunks.

5. Mix the ground chestnuts, ground ginger, the fig-raisin-date paste, and the grated apples.

6. Prepare a serving plate or an airtight container.

7. Grate or very finely dice the stick of cinnamon and do the same with the hyssop leaves. Pour into the fruit paste and mix gently.

8. Lightly oil your hands. Take the equivalent of a heaped tablespoon of the fruit paste and roll it between your palms to form a ball, and then roll the ball in the chopped almonds and pistachios. Do the same with the rest of the paste.

9. Enjoy immediately or store in an airtight container in the refrigerator.

MEXICO

THE CASTELLANOS' LAMB AND LETTUCE STEW WITH UNSALTED BREAD

The Castellanos family lived in Mexico City in the 16th century, and observed Passover more than other Jewish holidays. Christian Holy Week and Passover always fall very close to one another, so the crypto-Jewish traditions of the Americas are the reflection of a mix between Jewish practices and Christian ones. For example, Passover in the Americas used to begin on Holy Thursday, which is the most important day of the Christian Holy Week, which allowed the conversos to hide their practices. Gabriel de Castellanos used to buy a lamb in the market and then slaughter it saying a prayer in Hebrew on the patio of his house where nobody could see him. Julian, his son, saw how he cut it and how his mother Blanca stewed it in a new pot. They used lettuce instead of the chard she used to put in the pot when they lived in Portugal. Julian also saw his mother preparing unleavened and unsalted bread for this meal while his father was telling the story of Passover.

In *Secrecy and Deceit*, David Gitlitz provides us with information regarding the shape of unleavened bread prepared for Passover in a nearby town of Albuquerque, New Mexico. In "The International Review of Jewish Genealogy" Edwin Berry explains that he "recalls his mother making what he says resembled unleavened bread once a year around Lent. It was like a long biscuit, and it was eaten only a few days of the year."

SERVES: 4 people

TIME: 1 hour 30 minutes

- 1 lb (450 g) boneless lamb shoulder or leg, cut into 1-inch cubes
- 1 onion, finely chopped
- 2 garlic cloves, minced
- 1 teaspoon ground ginger
- 1 teaspoon ground cumin
- ½ teaspoon ground cinnamon
- ¼ teaspoon cayenne pepper
- 2 tsp salt
- 2 tsp black pepper
- 1 tablespoon olive oil
- 1 head of lettuce (butter or green leaf), washed and chopped
- ½ cup (120 ml) chicken broth
- 2 tablespoons honey
- ½ cup raisins

For toppings:

2 tablespoons chopped fresh parsley

2 tablespoons chopped fresh cilantro

Instructions for the lamb:

1. In a large bowl, combine the cubed lamb, onion, garlic, ginger, cumin, cinnamon, cayenne pepper, salt and black pepper. Heat the olive oil in a large skillet over medium-high heat. Add the lamb mixture and cook, stirring occasionally, until all sides are browned. Add the chopped lettuce to the skillet and stir to combine with the lamb mixture.

2. Pour in the chicken broth and bring to a simmer. Cover the skillet and reduce the heat to low. Cook for 30–40 minutes, until the lamb is tender and the lettuce is wilted. Add the raisins, and stir in the honey.

3. Shred the lamb meat, and cook for another 5–10 minutes, until the sauce has slightly thickened. Sprinkle with chopped parsley and cilantro.

4. Serve hot with strips of matzah.

SERVES: 3 pieces

TIME: 18 minutes

1 cup (150 g) white wheat flour

1½ cup (180 g) corn flour/masa harina, nixtamalized

½ cup (100 ml) + 2 tbsp cold water

(For instructions for the matzah, see Blanca Enríquez's Mexican small cakes, p. 150)

1. Preheat your nonstick iron skillet to medium-high heat. Prepare 2 sheets of plastic wrap that are a little bit larger than the tortilla press. They will be used for the tortilla press to avoid the dough sticking to the tortilla press sides.

2. Mix together the two flours. Progressively add the cold water to the flour and stir constantly until the flours absorbs all the water. Knead the dough for about 5 minutes. The dough should be moist to the touch.

3. Cut the dough into 3 pieces and roll into balls the size of ping pong balls.

4. Open the tortilla press, place a plastic sheet (or parchment paper) on the bottom, a ball of dough in the middle, and cover with the other plastic sheet. Close the tortilla press and press down to flatten the dough, until it is 0.16 inches (2 mm) thick. Open the tortilla press and carefully remove the dough from the plastic wrap.

5. Cut the dough into strips about ½ inch wide, and lay the strips carefully onto the hot skillet with a small amount of oil. Fry the strips for about 15 seconds on each side; you want them to be lightly golden.

*See the photo on the next page.

SHMIRA MATZAH FREEKEH BREAD

MEXICO

In the 17th century, the Jewish population in New Spain used the early-harvest wheat to make bread. As Liebman says, it is possible that this information refers to the use of freekeh grains.

Studying the fragments of manuscripts found in the Cairo Genizah provides insights into the food habits and practices of 12th-century Jews. However, these manuscripts do not seem to mention specific dish names or meals. The most abundant information regarding food concerns the pricing and quantities of wheat, indicating that it played a central role in the diet of Egyptian Jews in the 12th century. For example, one letter reads: "I have no more urgent request than the [purchase of] wheat and grapes."

In *A Mediterranean Society*, Goiten explains that in the 12th century, the weekly bread ration distributed by the Jewish community of Fustat to a destitute person consisted of four loaves, each weighing approximately a pound, for a total of about 1750 grams. The shopping lists and account registers from the Genizah also provide information about the food habits of Jewish communities, both for daily needs and for the preparation of festive meals, such as Shabbat and Pentecost (Shavuot). Goiten states that "a large portion of the population bought flour because they did not have the means to purchase wheat during harvest time but still preferred to make their bread dough at home. Others were too poor to buy any wheat at all, so they had to rely on flour dealers." In the 13th century, Jewish families in Egypt, specifically in Cairo, required 12 *irdabbs* (1 *irdabb* corresponds to 90 liters and 70 kilograms) of wheat, which equates to 840 kilograms.

SERVES: 3 flatbreads

TIME: 20 minutes

- 1 cup (180 g) freekeh flour
- ¼ tsp salt
- ¼ cup + 3 tbsp (100 ml) water
- 1 tbsp olive oil
- 2 tbsp neutral oil

1. In a mixing bowl, combine the freekeh flour and salt. Add the water and olive oil, and mix until a dough forms. Knead the dough on a floured surface for about 5 minutes. Be careful because it will be very crumbly!

2. Divide the dough into 3 equal portions (each one should be 3¾ oz or 100 g) and roll each portion into a ball. Flatten each ball into a disc shape, about ¼ inch (6 mm) thick, using a tortilla press, or by hand.

3. Heat an iron skillet over medium-high heat. Cook each disc for about 2 minutes on one side, until the edges are brown. Flip it very carefully (it is very crumbly) and bake for another 1 minute. Serve warm.

MURAKKABA
MOROCCAN MUFLETA FOR MIMOUNA

The Andalusian *Kitāb al-ṭabīẖ* contains two recipes that resemble the well-known mufleta, still prepared today in the same way by Moroccan Sephardic Jews. These recipes are called "Murakkaba" and "Murakkaba Layered with Dates." The dish is a sweet one that is made by "composing" (*murakkaba* in Arabic) alternating layers of dough that are stuck together and then turned upside down. Although the recipe titles may have changed over time and the ingredients may have been modified, the culinary techniques have remained the same.

SERVES: 4

TIME: 40 minutes

For the dough:

2¾ cup (430 g) flour

1 cup (150 g) extra fine semolina

½ tbsp fresh yeast, crushed (or ½ tbsp active dry yeast, or 1 tbsp sourdough starter)

1 tsp salt

1 egg

⅛ cup (13 g) sugar

1⅓ cup (266 ml) water

neutral oil for frying

sugar to sprinkle

For the toppings:

1 cup (340 g) honey

½ cup (100 g) melted butter

10 dates chopped into small pieces

1. Mix the flour, the salt, the semolina, the yeast, and the lukewarm water in a bowl. Knead for 10 minutes, and then form 8 small balls, brush them with oil and set aside for 15 minutes.

2. Take one ball and flatten it out to form a very thin disc. Put it in a hot, greased pan for about 10 seconds, then turn it over. Flatten a second ball and put this new disc on top of the first one. After 10 seconds, turn the two layers upside down. Flatten a third ball and place it on top, and keep going until you have no more disks left, turning the stack upside down each time you add a new layer.

3. Place the tower on a serving plate, and pour melted butter and drizzle the honey over it. Chop the dates into small pieces and sprinkle them over the dish.

SEFFA
SWEET FIDEOS FOR MIMOUNA

MOROCCO

Vermicelli dishes, called "fideos" in Spain, are part of the culinary heritage of Sephardic Jews. The 18th century records of the Inquisition in the Canary Islands attest to a regular supply of this product from the Mediterranean basin. The "fideos" (*fidāwīsh* in Arabic) (see "Sephardi" recipe for "Short Vermicelli Noodles" on page 96) were already consumed by Jewish families in Morocco in the 15th century, and were prepared for festivals, especially for Shavuot. To this day in Morocco there is a dish called "seffa," eaten by both Jews and Muslims, which is usually made from short, steamed angel hair pasta noodles. There is also a savory version of this dish that is prepared with chicken. However, the sweet version, flavored with cinnamon, is often consumed by Jews during the celebration of Mimouna, which marks the end of the Jewish Passover.

SERVES: 2 people

TIME: 30 minutes

- 1 cup (100 g) short vermicelli noodles
- 1 tbsp neutral oil
- 1 tsp salt
- 1 tbsp (15 ml) water
- 2 tbsp (15 g) raisins
- 1 tsp (5 ml) olive oil
- ¼ cup icing sugar, to taste
- 1 tbsp ground cinnamon
- ¼ almonds, chopped

1. Boil water in a pot with a steam basket. Place the short vermicelli in a large bowl and pour the 1 tbsp neutral oil into it. Mix well with your hands and then place the vermicelli in the steam basket. Cover the pot, reduce heat to medium, and steam for about 15 minutes.

2. Then, carefully remove the steam basket from the pot and flip it upside down to pour the vermicelli into a large flat dish. Sprinkle the salt over the noodles.

3. Take a bowl with very cold water. Dip your hands quickly into the cold water and then separate the vermicelli with your fingers, making sure there are no clumps.

4. Add the raisins into the boiling water, and return the noodles to the steamer to steam for an additional ten minutes. When the ten minutes are up, carefully remove the steam basket from the pot again, and flip it upside down into your large flat dish. With a skimmer, remove the raisins from the pot and add them to the cooked vermicelli noodles. Separate the noodles again with your fingers. If they are dry, add 1 tsp oil and 1 tbsp water, and mix.

5. Return it to the steamer for a final ten minutes. Then, carefully remove the steam basket from the pot and pour the noodles into the large flat dish for a third time. Add 1 tsp (5 ml) of olive oil and separate the short vermicelli noodle using your fingers.

6. Pile the vermicelli like a cone into a large dish.

7. Sprinkle it with cinnamon, icing sugar, and chopped almonds.

SWEET COUSCOUS

MOROCCO

Meat and vegetable couscous is just as much a part of the culinary habits of Muslims in Morocco and North Africa as it is for the Jews of these territories and their diaspora (see recipe p. 281). The same goes for sweet couscous that is cooked in milk, which Moroccan Sephardic Jews mainly consume to celebrate Mimouna, but also for Purim. Shavuot would also be a good time to eat it.

SERVES: 4 people

TIME: 20 minutes

1 cup ¼ (240 ml) water

Pinch of salt

1 cup (130 g) couscous

1 cup (200 ml) whole milk

¼ cup (80 g) honey

2 tbsp salted butter

1 tsp ground cinnamon

Pinch of ground cardamom

¼ cup (40 g) raisins

¼ cup (35 g) chopped almonds

Raisins, to sprinkle (optional)

1. In a saucepan, bring 240 ml water to a boil. Add a pinch of salt and the couscous to the water, stir, and remove from heat. Cover and let sit for 8 minutes until the water is fully absorbed.

2. In a separate saucepan, heat the whole milk over medium heat, along with the honey and butter. Stir. Add the cinnamon and cardamom and stir some more, and then add the raisins.

3. Add the cooked couscous to the saucepan with the honey mixture and stir until fully combined. Cook the couscous mixture over low heat for 5 minutes, stirring.

4. Place the sweet couscous in a dish and sprinkle with the chopped almonds and raisins to taste.

5. Serve warm.

SHAVUOT

"Shavuot, also known as the Feast of Weeks, is a Jewish holiday that occurs seven weeks (or 50 days) after the second day of Passover (Pesach). It falls on the sixth day of the Hebrew month of Sivan. Shavuot has several significant themes and observances:

Harvest Festival: Historically, Shavuot was an agricultural festival marking the wheat harvest in ancient Israel. It was a time for offering the first fruits (bikkurim) of the harvest at the Temple in Jerusalem.

Giving of the Torah: Shavuot is often associated with the giving of the Torah (a sacred Jewish text) to the Israelites at Mount Sinai. According to Jewish tradition, it was on this day that God revealed the Ten Commandments and the entire Torah to Moses.

Customs and Traditions: On Shavuot, it is customary to stay up all night studying Torah in a practice known as "Tikkun Leil Shavuot." Many synagogues hold special study sessions and readings from the Book of Ruth, which is traditionally read during this holiday. Dairy foods, such as cheesecakes and blintzes, are also commonly consumed on Shavuot.

Synagogue Services: Special synagogue services are held on Shavuot, including the reading of the Ten Commandments from the Torah scroll. Many Jewish communities also decorate synagogues and homes with flowers and greenery to symbolize the beauty and fertility of the land of Israel.

Confirmation and Conversion: In some Jewish denominations, Shavuot is a time for the confirmation of Jewish youth who have completed their religious studies. It is also considered a meaningful time for those undergoing the conversion process to formally become Jewish.

Modern Observance: While the agricultural aspects of Shavuot have diminished in importance with urbanization, the holiday's focus on the giving of the Torah and the study of Jewish texts remains central. It is a time for Jews to renew their commitment to the study and observance of Jewish law and tradition.

Overall, Shavuot is a holiday that celebrates both the agricultural bounty of the land of Israel and the spiritual significance of the Torah in Jewish life and history.

ITALY

MONTE SINAI
THE JEWISH MARZIPAN PASTRY

The name of this dish is enough to catch our attention. It obviously refers, in Judaism, to Mount Sinai on which Moses received the Tablets of the Law. Sephardic Jews, to commemorate this event which is part of the celebration of the holiday of Shavuot, used to prepare a cake made of almond paste, marzipan, which had the particularity of being conical in shape to recall the shape of the mountain.

Italian Sephardic Jews have continued to prepare and consume *marzapane* primarily during marriages, circumcisions, and other celebrations. This goes for Monte Sinai pastry too. The pastry, defined by the *Guide to Italian Gastronomy* as a "Jewish marzipan cake," is also called *sinaini* in Venetian documents, as the historian Dr. Ariel Toaff notes. Just like *marzapane di martorana*, the existence of a Jewish dish and the integration of Jewish culinary practices into Italian food heritage is mentioned in the "Guide." Furthermore, sinaini is included in *piyyut* (a liturgical poem for the Jewish holidays) written in Judeo-Livornese from 1750 onwards, which is riddled with terms in Spanish, Portuguese, Venetian, and Hebrew. The "Guide" refers explicitly to "Mount Sinai."

In *Le Livre de la cuisine juive*, Claudia Roden includes a recipe for *Monte Sinai con uovo late*, which she describes as "typically Portuguese, almost identical to a dessert called 'bola de amor' in the *Jewish Manual* published in 1846 in London, likely by Judith Montefiore." Ariel Toaff establishes a link between *marzapane* and the dish *marzapane a uova late*, which dates back to the second half of the eighteenth century. It was "a cake made of almond paste, very widespread among Italian and Sephardic Jews, kneaded in the shape of a twist or in small pies shaped like chestnuts, and cooked in the oven in a few minutes; it was coated in egg yolk, the peel of *melarancia* and a candied citron. In Livorno, it was considered to be a typical cake of Iberian Jewish cuisine, and was shaped into small conical mounds and eggs strands, placed on top of pastry wafers, and coated in icing and colored sprinkles." The fact that the Iberian origin of *marzapane* is mentioned is significant, as is the use of citron in the preparation of the dish, given the importance of this fruit in Jewish culture.

I've recreated the recipe below for Monte Sinai with the help of the French pastry chef Julien Ruffin from Valantin, in Bordeaux, solely based on the information mentioned above.

SERVES: 20 pieces

TIME: 30 minutes

For the sablés (shortbread cookies):

2¼ cup (450 g) salted butter, softened

1¼ cup (240 g) sugar

½ tsp salt

½ tsp vanilla powder

4¼ cups (630 g) flour

½ cup + 2 tbsp (90 g) whole wheat flour

¼ cup (30 g) baking powder

---

1. Preheat the oven to 150°C (300°F). In a bowl, cream the butter, then incorporate the sugar, salt, vanilla powder, and finish with the sifted flours mixed with baking powder. Roll the dough out to a thickness of 3.5 mm using a rolling pin, and cut out long diamond-shaped forms, measuring 3 inches (7 cm) long by 0.8 inches (2 cm) wide.

2. Bake at 150°C (300°F) for approximately 20 minutes, and set aside to cool.

Marzipan with Candied Orange Peel:

500 g Marzipan (70% almond paste)

100 g candied orange peel

1. Dice the candied orange peel into very small cubes of 0.5 cm (0.2 inches).

2. Incorporate the candied orange peel into the marzipan, mixing until you get a homogeneous mixture. Wrap the marzipan mixture with plastic wrap and refrigerate it for a while to firm up.

Italian Meringue:

¾ cup + 1 tbsp (160 g) water

2½ cups (500 g) sugar

250 g egg whites (from about 7–8 eggs)

1. Pour the egg whites into the mixing bowl of a stand mixer. Use the wire whip attachment. Start beating the egg whites at medium speed until they become frothy.

2. Meanwhile, in a saucepan, pour the water and add the sugar. Mix them together. Cook the mixture until it reaches 121°C (250°F). Use a sugar thermometer to check the temperature.

3. While the egg whites are still being whipped, slowly pour the cooked sugar syrup (at 121°C) onto the egg whites in a thin stream. Increase the mixer speed to maximum and continue beating for about 4 minutes. The whipped egg whites should turn creamy and silky.

4. The Italian meringue is now ready to be used as a topping or filling for various desserts. It is commonly used in cakes, pies, and other sweet treats. Make sure to use it while it's still fresh for the best results.

To make the egg yolks strands:

¾ cup (150 g) sugar

¼ cup (50 g) water

2 egg yolks

1. Mix the egg yolks gently, without beating them. Pour the yolks into a piping bag and seal it.

2. Prepare a bowl with very cold water, preferably iced water.

3. In a saucepan, boil the sugar and water over medium heat until it forms large bubbles (the syrup will reach 118°C or 244°F). Cut just the tip of the piping bag. The hole should be very small to create thin filaments.

4. Pipe spiral shaped threads of egg yolk into the boiling syrup. This should be done quickly, in no more than 10 seconds. Use a slotted spoon to remove the cooked egg yolk filaments from the syrup and immediately transfer them into the bowl of very cold water to stop the cooking process.

5. After 5 minutes, take the filaments out of the water and place them on absorbent paper, then transfer them to a plate. Be careful not to leave them on the absorbent paper for too long or they will stick to it. These sugar-cooked egg yolk filaments can be used as a delicate and decorative addition to various desserts, providing a unique and sweet touch.

To assemble the Mont Sinai pastry:

1. Take a Marzipan-orange ball (each one should be 1 oz/30 g), shape it into a small cone (like a mountain) and place it on top of a sablé, leaving a bit of space on the edge of the cookie.

2. Take a spoonful of meringue and spread it over the marzipan to cover it. It should look like the Mount Sinai; you can use two spoons to help shape it.

3. Decorate with candied egg yolks strands and candied citron and candied orange peel. Repeat with all the sablés.

BREAD
OF THE SEVEN HEAVENS

This dish lacks any medieval written sources, which is not surprising due to the absence of specific and open references to Jewish culinary practices in books during that time, likely stemming from fears of religious persecution. Its origins can be traced to the Iberian Peninsula; it later made its way to Salonika when Jews migrated there following their official expulsion from Spain in 1492. This dish holds traditional significance as it is prepared for Shavuot, also known as the "Feast of Weeks" or "Pentecost," a Jewish holiday that marks the beginning of the wheat harvest and commemorates the sacred giving of the Torah to Moses and the people of Israel on Mount Sinai. It is known as "Pascua de la Cincuesma" (Passover of the Fifty days), or "Pascua de la dada de la Ley" (Passover of the Giving of the Law) in "procesos." The Torah itself draws a connection between bread and Heaven, as seen in Exodus 16:4 where God tells Moses, "I will rain down bread for you from the sky." Even in the detailed Inquisition records of Spain, no specific information regarding foods for Shavuot was found. However, an intriguing discovery comes from a trial in 1484 in the northern part of the country. The records mention that conversos (Jewish converts to Christianity) were seen observing a fifty-day feast they referred to as "the giving of the Law." Another trial record from 1501 references a converso man who was reported for spending "the entire night cooking" to celebrate "Pascua del Espíritu Santo" (Shavuot or Pentecost). This Christian holiday is celebrated seven weeks after Easter, while for Jews, Shavuot is observed seven weeks after Passover. A further notable reference to Jewish practices can be found in a trial record from seventeenth-century Mexico, which was then a Spanish colonial territory. In this instance, conversos were accused of celebrating Shavuot fifty days after Passover, indicating their continued adherence to Jewish customs despite external pressures.

The significance of the seven rings in this bread is quite intriguing, with various interpretations proposed by different sources. Some suggest that the rings may represent the seven stages of holiness through which the soul passes when the body dies. Another possibility is that they symbolize the traditional seven-week waiting period after Passover, during which Jews eagerly anticipate the celebration of Shavuot and the momentous event of the giving of the Torah on Mount Sinai. Additionally, it's plausible that the rings could represent the seven days of Passover when leavened bread is forbidden, adding another layer of symbolic meaning to the bread.

Moreover, the bread's shape likely serves as a representation of Mount Sinai, the sacred mountain where Moses received the divine revelation of the Torah.

Even though there is no official historical documentation for this particular dish, I have made the decision to recreate it, incorporating cheese as a filling. This choice aligns with the traditional consumption of dairy products during Shavuot. By reviving this dish and adding your own touch, you are participating in the celebration of Shavuot and connecting to the rich customs and symbolism of the holiday.

Serves: 6 people

Time: 1 hour

For the stuffing:

1⅓ cup (200 g) cheese (like feta)

¼ cup (60 g) olive oil

½ tsp salt

1 clove of garlic

5 leaves mint

1 sprig of thyme

For the dough:

1⅓ cup (200 g) flour

1⅓ cup (200 g) semolina

1½ tsp salt

1 tbsp fresh yeast +
3 tbsp lukewarm water

1 cup (200 ml) lukewarm water

To decorate:

pomegranate seeds

honey

1. Begin by preparing the filling: lightly mash the cheese in a bowl using a fork. Mix in the olive oil, crushed mint, garlic, thyme, and salt. Set the mixture aside in the fridge while you move on to making the dough.

2. Line a roasting pan or a baking tray with parchment paper. To make the dough, dissolve the yeast in 3 generous tablespoons of lukewarm water. In a separate bowl, combine the flour, semolina, and salt. Add the water and yeast mixture to the dry ingredients and knead the dough for 10 to 15 minutes. Cover the dough with a towel and let it rise for an hour.

3. Next, flour lightly the working surface. Use a rolling pin to roll out the dough into a rectangle shape that is 6 inches (15 cm) wide and 28 inches (70 cm) long. Spread the filling along the long edge of the dough and then roll up the dough.

4. Stretch the roll into a cylinder that is 1 inch (2 cm) in diameter. Grease your hands with olive oil and shape the dough into a tall spiral to resemble Mount Sinai. Do not squeeze the dough too much as it needs to rise. Brush the bread with olive oil.

5. Pre heat the oven at 375°F (190°C), and place the bread on the baking tray and let it rise for about 30 minutes.

6. Bake for 30 minutes, then lightly brush it one more time with olive oil and sprinkle with thyme and mint on top. Add pomegranate seeds and/or honey, if desired.

7. Serve hot or lukewarm accompanied with a fresh salad with a honey dressing.

MOROCCO

BARKOUKCH
SWEET AND CREAMY COUSCOUS PORRIDGE

Barkoukch is a Moroccan soup made with milk semolina flour which has been rolled into tiny pellets. It's a traditional dish mainly consumed by Berbers, whether they are Jewish or Muslim. Moroccan Sephardic Jews usually eat it to celebrate Shavuot since milk is a main ingredient, but it can also be prepared for Purim.

Purim is a Jewish holiday commemorates the rescue of the Persian Jews in the 5th century BCE from a genocidal plot against them by King Ahasueros's vizier, Haman, as recounted in the Book of Esther (Megillah Esther). During the 15th and 16th centuries, it was referred to as "The Feast of the Stars," but for crypto-Jews, observing the Fast of Esther held more significance than hosting elaborate celebrations. Today, it is joyfully celebrated as "The Feast of Lots" and falls on the 13th day of the Jewish month of Adar (usually on mid-March).

SERVES: 4

TIME: 40 minutes

1 cup (190 g/6⅞ oz) barkoukch (or alternatively, use large-grained couscous)

1.5 cup (300 ml) water

2 tsp salt

1 cup (200 ml) whole milk

¼ cup (50 g) butter, diced

1. If preparing with small barkoukch: in a pot, add the water and salt, and bring it to a boil.

2. Add the barkoukch and cover the pot. Cover and cook on low heat for about 5 minutes until they become tender and have absorbed most of the water.

3. If you are preparing the recipe with large-grain couscous, the preparation process is different: put the couscous in a large bowl, and add the salt. Moisten the grains with ½ cup (100 ml) of water (taken from the 1.5 cups/300 ml). Mix with your hands to ensure that all the grains are moistened. Pour the remaining 1 cups (200 ml) of water into a couscous steamer and heat, with the steamer basket in place.

4. When the water boils, add the couscous to the basket. Steam for 15 minutes, then pour the couscous out onto a very large plate and separate any clumps. You can break them up with your hands, but be careful as they will be very hot. Let them cool. Then, put them in a saucepan.

5. Meanwhile, in another saucepan, heat the milk to a gentle boil. Pour the hot milk over the cooked barkoukch or large couscous grains in the first saucepan. Gently stir and cook for another 3 to 4 minutes.

6. Take some ramekins or small bowls and pour the *barkoukch* into them. Sprinkle with small pieces of butter and serve hot.

Genesis 2:2-3: In the creation narrative, it is said that God created the world in six days and rested on the seventh day. This seventh day, the day of rest, is the prototype for Shabbat. While the text in Genesis doesn't explicitly mention food, it sets the precedent for the idea of ceasing from work and dedicating the day to rest and holiness.

Exodus 16:22-30: In the story of the manna in the wilderness, God provides the Israelites with a double portion of manna on the sixth day of the week (Friday) to sustain them for both Friday and Shabbat (Saturday). This demonstrates the importance of preparing food in advance for Shabbat, as cooking is prohibited on the day of rest.

Exodus 20:8-11: The fourth of the Ten Commandments instructs the observance of Shabbat. It emphasizes not only rest for humans but also the rest of domestic animals and even the land itself. This rest extends to abstaining from work, which includes cooking, baking, and kindling fires. Consequently, preparation of food for Shabbat is done on the day preceding it, which is usually Friday.

Leviticus 24:5-9: In the context of the Tabernacle, the Bible mentions the "showbread" or "bread of the Presence" (*Lechem HaPanim*). Twelve loaves of bread were placed in the Tabernacle each week, representing the twelve tribes of Israel. These loaves were baked on Friday and were replaced every Shabbat, emphasizing the sanctity of the day and the importance of special food offerings.

SHABBAT

Shabbat, also known as the Sabbath, is a central concept in the Bible and Jewish tradition. In the Bible, particularly in the Old Testament (Tanakh), Shabbat is introduced in the Book of Genesis, specifically in the story of the creation of the world. The connection between Shabbat and food in the Bible is significant and is primarily related to the observance of Shabbat as a day of rest and sanctification. Below is an overview of Shabbat in the Bible and its connection to food.

In Jewish tradition, the observance of Shabbat involves special rituals and blessings related to food. Traditional Shabbat meals typically include challah (a braided bread), wine, candles, and a festive meal with various dishes. The blessings recited over the wine (Kiddush) and the bread (*HaMotzi*) are central to the Shabbat meals. There are typically three main meals associated with Shabbat:

Friday Night Dinner (*Erev Shabbat*): This is the most elaborate meal of the week for many Jewish families. It often begins with the lighting of Shabbat candles and the recitation of blessings over wine (Kiddush) and bread (Challah). Traditional foods like challah bread, chicken, soup, and various side dishes are enjoyed during this meal.

Shabbat Morning Lunch: This meal is usually less elaborate than Friday night dinner but still special. Challah bread, fish, salads, and other dishes are common during this meal.

Se'udah Shlishit (Third Meal): This meal is eaten in the late afternoon on Shabbat and typically includes lighter fare, such as bread, fish, and salads.

The connection between Shabbat and food in the Bible underscores the idea that Shabbat is a day of physical and spiritual nourishment, a time for rest, reflection, and gratitude. It is a day when Jewish families gather to share meals and celebrate the holiness of the day.

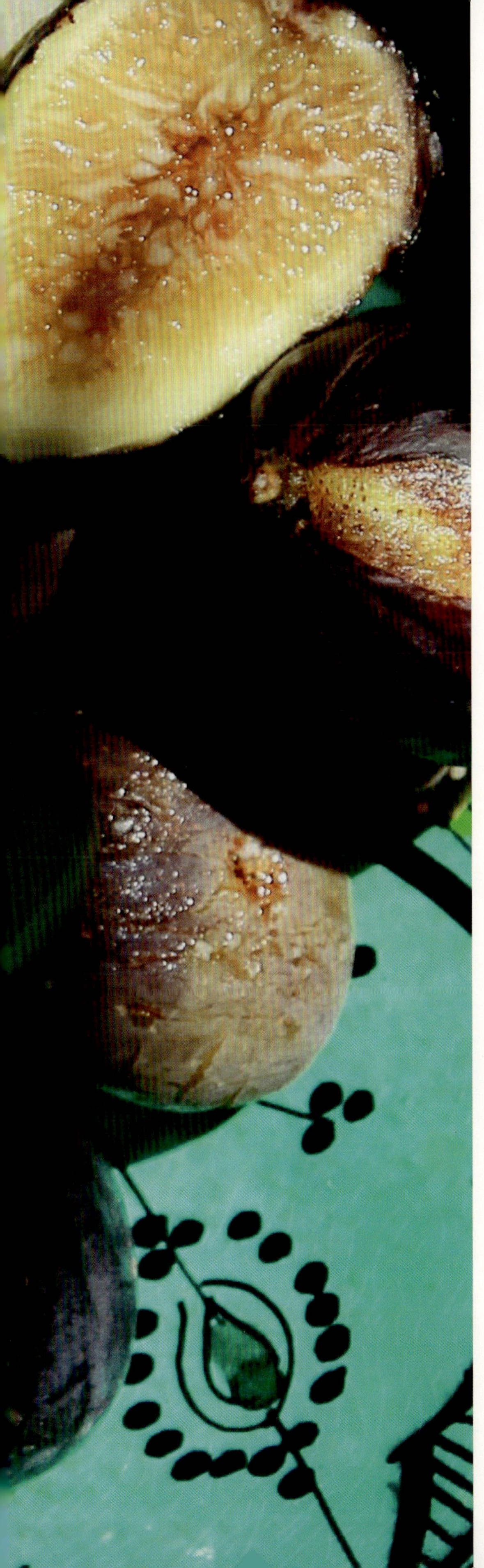

Ki Eshm'rah Shabbat/כִּי אֶשְׁמְרָה שַׁבָּת

Ki Eshm'rah Shabbat, which means "Because I shall keep the Sabbath," is a traditional Shabbat Afternoon Zemer, composed by Rabbi Avraham ibn Ezra.

If I keep Sabbath day, God safe will keep me,
From Him to me 'twas given, a sign for aye to be,
No toil, no traveler's staff my rest profaning,
All gain, all statecraft's thoughts and cares disdaining,
All cares disdaining,
His Law shall make me wise, His Law of Liberty,
From Him to me 'twas given, a sign for aye to be.

Wearied and careworn, there let me always rest.
Thou did'st ordain this day my doubting sires to test.
Thy hand with twofold food each sixth day blest.
Lord, so for me each week my Sabbath food decree,
From Him to me 'twas given, a sign for aye to be.

Priests laid before Him bread of the Presence divine
Commanded in His Law, each Sabbath to deck
His Shrine.
"This day thou shalt not fast full joy be thine
Save it be Kippur's fast to purge thine iniquity,"
From Him to me 'twas given, a sign for aye to be.

O day renowned, O day of my soul's delight!
For thee I quaff red wine, for thee my bread is white.
O shed thy rays of hope o'er sorrow's night,
Cheer my sad heart, thou day of sacred gaiety.
From Him to me 'twas given, a sign for aye to be.

He who profanes thee sells his dead soul in vain.
From greed, Lord, set me free, O purge me pure from
stain, And let my fourfold prayers acceptance gain,
Help me this day, Lord, to serve Thee in sincerity.
From Him to me 'twas given, a sign for aye to be

Translation by Herbert Loewe, *Medieval Hebrew Minstrelsy, Songs for the Bride Queen's Feast*, published by James Clark & Co., 1926.

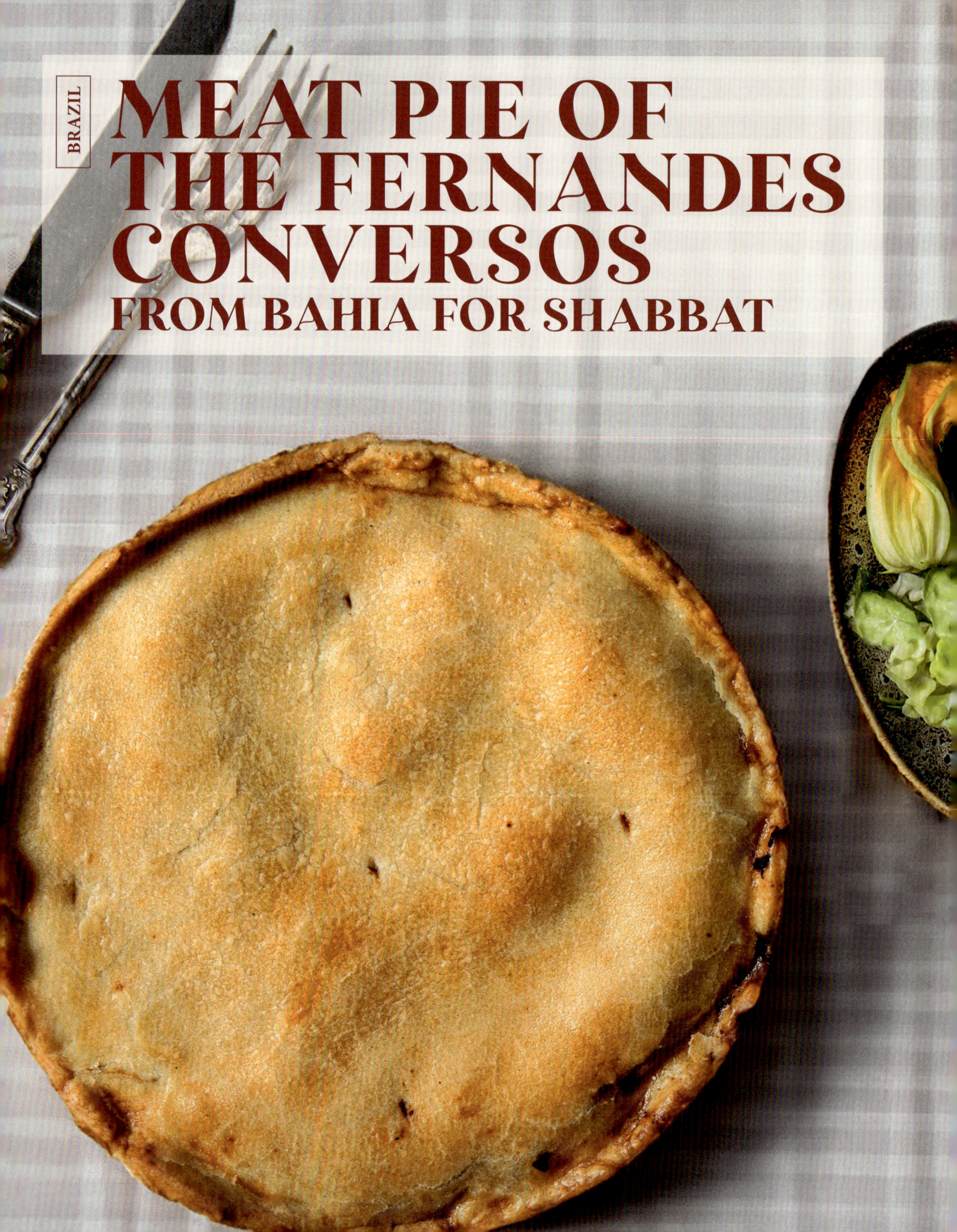

BRAZIL

MEAT PIE OF THE FERNANDES CONVERSOS

FROM BAHIA FOR SHABBAT

Pies were a favorite dish of conversos. This recipe is based on a 1590 Inquisition trial record, which explains how the Fernandes family from Bahia, Brazil, were reported for their Shabbat cooking: preparing a baked dish of meat with onion, olive oil, seeds, spices and other ingredients, sealed with dough all around.

SERVES: 6 people

TIME: 1 hour

For the dough:

2 eggs

1¾ cup (280 g) flour

½ tsp salt

⅓ cup (75 g) soft butter or margarine

egg wash

For the filling:

¼ cup (50 g) olive oil

2 cloves of garlic, chopped

2 onions, sliced

½ pound (220 g) ground meat

3 eggs, beaten

¼ cup (15 g) fresh coriander

2 tsp ground cumin

1 tsp salt

1 tsp black pepper

egg wash

1 tbsp oregano

1. To make the dough, beat the eggs, and add the flour and salt. Add the soft margarine (or oil). Mix all the ingredients together, and knead the dough for 5 minutes until even and smooth. Split the dough in 2 balls, cover, and cool them in the fridge for 30 minutes.

2. For the filling, pour the olive oil into a frying pan, add the garlic and onions. Fry for 3 minutes until golden. Add the ground meat and cook for 5 minutes at medium-high heat. Then place the mixture in a big bowl to cool.

3. In another bowl, beat the 3 eggs. Add the salt, black pepper, fresh coriander, and cumin, and mix. Then, add the cooked ground meat (drained of its liquid) to the mixture.

4. Turn on the oven at 375°F (190°C). Roll out the first ball of dough between two pieces of parchment paper, until it is a tenth of an inch thick (a couple of millimeters). Do the same with the second ball.

5. Lay the first disk of dough in a pie dish, and add the filling until just before it reaches the top of the dish. Cover with the second disk of dough, pinching and flattening the edges. Refrigerate for at least 30 minutes.

6. Brush the pie with egg wash and sprinkle with oregano. Prick the dough in the middle with the tip of a knife. Bake for 40 minutes, and let it cool for 15 minutes before serving.

MEXICAN SHABBAT FRIED FISH

The Shabbat meal was more consistent than usual during colonial times (16th–19th centuries), and the Friday night meal of the Sephardim of Mexico commonly consisted of fish (salted or not), small breads with salt sprinkled on top, meat, wine and halvah made with ground nuts.

Serves: 4 people

Time: 30 minutes

2 whole fish (such as red snapper), cleaned and scaled

1 cup (150 g) flour

1 teaspoon salt

½ teaspoon ground black pepper

½ teaspoon paprika

Vegetable oil, for frying

For the sauce:

2 limes (for fresh juice)

1 green jalapeño chili pepper, diced

1 tsp salt

1. Rinse the fish under cold water and pat them dry with paper towels. In a shallow dish, combine the flour, salt, black pepper, and paprika. Mix well. Heat vegetable oil in a large skillet or deep fryer until it reaches a temperature of around 350°F (175°C).

2. Dredge each fish in the flour mixture, shaking off any excess. Carefully place the fish in the hot oil and fry for about 5–7 minutes per side, or until the fish is golden brown and crispy. Fry one fish at a time or as many as can comfortably fit in the pan without overcrowding.

3. Once cooked, transfer the fried fish to a plate lined with paper towels to drain excess oil.

4. Prepare a sauce mixing the juice of the limes, the salt and add the diced green jalapeño.

5. Serve the fried fish hot, using the lime-jalapeño sauce as a dip. You can serve this fried fish with a side of beans for a complete meal.

SALTED FLATBREADS

SERVES: 12 small flatbreads

TIME: 30 minutes + 30 minutes + 30 minutes

2 cups (300 g) flour (you can also use corn flour instead of flour)

2 cups (260 g) corn flour

1 tbsp salt

1 tbsp (35 g) fresh yeast (or ½ tbsp active dry yeast, or 1 tbsp sourdough starter)

3⅓ +½ cup (440 ml) lukewarm water

2 tsp salt flakes

1. In the bowl of a stand mixer, add the flour, corn flour, and salt. Mix with the hook attachment for 1 minute. Add the crumbled fresh yeast, and gradually add the lukewarm water (in 4 batches). The dough will be a bit sticky but that is normal. Continue to mix at least for 10 minutes. If you do not have a stand mixer, knead by hand for at least 20 minutes.

2. Line a baking tray with parchment paper, sprinkling with a little flour. Divide the dough into 12 equal parts (each one should be 2⅞ oz or 80 g) and knead them again until they are very smooth. On a lightly floured surface, flatten the balls with a rolling pin to form round disks around 6 inches/15 cm in diameter. (You can use a tortilla press as well, placing a ball of dough in the middle and between two sheets of plastic, and pressing.) Place the discs on the tray, sprinkle with a little flour, and cover with a kitchen towel. Let them rest at room temperature for 30 minutes.

3. Heat a skillet (cast iron is ideal) over medium-high heat. Gently, take a flatbread and place it in the skillet. Wet your fingertips and gently moisten the top of the bread as it cooks, and sprinkle it with salt flakes. After 1 minute, gently turn the bread over and cook the other side for about 30 seconds. It should be a light golden color. Remove from the skillet and let cool on a tray.

CARNE ASADA
GRILLED MARINATED BEEF

SERVES: 6–8 people

TIME: 4 hours

4 dried Pulla chili pepper, dry and toasted

4 dried Guajillo chili pepper, dry and toasted

1 dried Chipotle chili pepper, dry and toasted

1 dried Espelette chili pepper, dry and toasted (optional)

1 small canned Chipotle chili, (in adobo sauce)

¾ cup (180 ml) fresh lime juice (5 medium limes)

¼ cup (60 ml) fresh orange juice (1 medium orange)

¼ cup (60 ml) sunflower oil

4 tsps ground cumin

1 teaspoon paprika

2 teaspoon dried coriander, crushed

4 tbsp sugar cane (preferably liquid)

2 tsp salt

1 tsp bl ack pepper

1 bunch fresh cilantro

2 tsp fresh oregano leaves

6 cloves of garlic, minced

2 pounds (900 g) flank steak or skirt steak

1. Remove the stems from the chilies and discard the seed pods and seeds. Toast them in a hot skillet for about 3 minutes, and cut them into small pieces.

2. Put the peppers in a food processor and add the canned chipotle pepper and 1 tbsp adobo sauce. Add the fresh lime and orange juices, sunflower oil, ground cumin, paprika, dried crushed coriander, sugar cane, salt and black pepper, and blend well.

3. Chop the fresh cilantro and oregano and crushed the garlic. Add them to the blended mixture and stir. The marinade is ready.

4. Place the flank steak or skirt steak in a resealable plastic bag or a shallow dish. Pour the marinade over the steak, ensuring it is coated evenly. Seal the bag or cover the dish and refrigerate for at least 2 hours, or preferably overnight to allow the flavors to develop.

5. Preheat your grill or barbecue to medium-high heat. Remove the marinated steak from the refrigerator and let it come to room temperature for about 30 minutes. Remove the steak from the marinade, allowing any excess marinade to drip off. Reserve the marinade for basting.

6. Grill the steak for about 4–6 minutes per side, or until it reaches your desired level of doneness. Baste the steak occasionally with the reserved marinade while grilling. (Alternatively, you can cook the steak in the oven at 375°F (180°C) for about 15 minutes on one side and 10 minutes on the other side.)

7. Once cooked, transfer the steak to a cutting board and let it rest for a few minutes.

8. Slice the carne asada across the grain into thin strips. This carne asada is delicious with warm tortillas and salted breads.

GROUND NUT HALVAH

- ¼ cup (35 g) sesame seeds
- 2 tbsp pistachios or pecans, chopped
- 1 cup tehina (sesame paste)
- ½ tsp salt
- ½ vanilla extract
- ⅓ cup (66 g) water
- 1 cup (200 g) sugar
- 3 tbsp candied pomegranate or hibiscus (optional)

1. Line a medium rectangular or square baking pan (7 or 8 inch) with parchment paper, making sure the paper comes up the interior edges of the pan. Spread the sesame seeds and chopped nuts on the parchment paper and set aside.

2. Take 2 sauce pans. In the first one, pour the tehina, salt and vanilla extract. Heat the mixture over low-medium heat, stirring with a spoon.

3. Meanwhile, in the second sauce pan, put the water and sugar. Stir with a wooden spatula until you have an homogeneous liquid. Take a candy thermometer and place it into the water-sugar. Bring the mixture to a boil until you reach 248°F (118°C). The temperature is very important because it will determine the texture of the final product. Once the sugar-water reaches 248°F, turn off the heat for both pans, and little by little pour the sugar water over the hot tehina paste, stirring slowly for 30–45 seconds. Do not over stir!

4. Carefully pour the mixture into the pan on top of the sesame and nuts, and smooth quickly with a spatula. You can sprinkle the top with candied pomegranate or hibiscus flowers.

5. Let the halvah cool at room temperature. Once it has cooled completely, cut it into large slices or squares.

AVRAHAM IBN EZRA (c. 1093–c. 1167)

"One of the most important transmitters of the Andalusian heritage was Avraham Ibn Ezra, who is sometimes considered a fifth major poet of the Spanish-Hebrew Golden Age. [. . .] He was born sometime between 1090 and 1093, in Tudela—then a border town of Muslim Spain with a large Christian population—and he passed most of the next fifty years in the south and Toledo. [. . .] It is the work of this post-Spanish period that made Ibn Ezra's reputation. [. . .] By 1140, he was in Rome, where in a foreword to his commentary on Ecclesiastes he wrote: 'And from his home / in Spain he fled / descending to Rome / his soul afraid.' In another commentary he noted the persecution that he'd faced in Spain, most likely under the Almoravids: 'Oppressors have driven me out of Spain.' And in response to the Almohad invasion of the mid-1140s—word of which reached him in France—he wrote one of the most explicit elegies in the literature for the lost communities of Andalusia and North Africa. [. . .] Over the next twenty-seven years Avraham HaSefaradi (the Spaniard), as he usually called himself, earned his living by writing for the edification of Jewish communities in North Africa, Italy, Provence, northern France, and even England, where some scholars believe he died in either 1164 or 1167. [. . .] In addition to his elegy on the lost Andalusian communities, his newly diverse subjects include chess, flies, his torn coat, his rotten luck, his offended honor, and the presence of God in the world [. . .]. Perhaps the most philosophical of all the Hebrew liturgical poets, he merged meditation and devotion."

(Pete Cole, *The Dream of the Poem: Hebrew Poetry from Muslim and Christian Spain 950–1492*, Princeton, NJ: Princeton University Press, 2007, p. 176)

A CLOAK

I have a cloak that's a lot like a sieve
for sifting **wheat** and **barley**:
at night I stretch it taut like a tent,
and light from the stars shines on me.
Through it I see the crescent moon,
Orion and the Pleiades.
I weary, though, of counting its holes,
which look like a saw's sharp teeth,
and dreaming they might be mended with thread
drawn back and forth's no use.
If a fly land there with force like a fool,
at once it regrets what it's done:
Replace it, Lord, with a mantle of glory—
and one that's properly sewn.

THE FLIES

Who could I turn to in my distress?
The flies have plundered my home;
they will not leave me a minute of peace,
attacking me fiercely like foes.
Across my eyelids and eyes they race;
in my ears they recite their poems;
like a pack of hungry wolves they devour
my **bread** when I'm eating alone,
and as though I'd asked them over like friends,
they take what they want on their own.
It seems they're only seeking their share
when I offer them **lamb** and **wine**—
but that, it turns out, isn't enough:
they also covet what's mine.
If I summon guests to come and dine,
at the head of the table they swarm,
and so I long for winter lest
I starve because of them.
Its cold and rain will wipe them out—
thank God, who dwells with the cherubim.

SPAIN

BEEF EMPANADA

Empanadas are mentioned in the "Shulchan Arukh" (Set Table), which is the most widely accepted code of Jewish law ever written. This text was compiled in 1543, in Safed (Tzfat), by Yosef Karo, a Spanish Rabbi. It is written in the Spanish language but spelled out in Hebrew characters.

The Shulhan Arukh is a condensed and simplified version of the *Beit Yosef*, a commentary that on the Tur that Rabbi Karo had written earlier. It has been written in accordance with Sephardic traditions; in the Shulhan Arukh 318:16 Rabbi Yosef Karo uses the Spanish term "empanada," as one can see below:

מותר ליתן אינפאנדה כנגד האש במקום שהיד סולדת ואף ע"פ שהשומן שבה שנקרש חוזר ונימוח

"It is permitted to place an empanada close to fire in a place where one's hand is repelled [from the heat], and the congealed fat within it will soften."

SERVES: 25 pieces

TIME: 45 minutes

For the dough:

3 cups (450 g) flour

1 tsp (5 g) baking powder

½ tsp salt

½ cup (100 g) neutral oil

¾ cup (180 g) water

In a large bowl, combine quickly flour, baking powder, salt and margarine. Then, add little by little the water. Knead by hand for about five minutes, until you have a smooth and homogeneous dough. Form the dough into a ball and put it in a plastic bag. Cool it in the fridge for about 30 minutes, or overnight.

For the beef filling:

1 tbsp olive oil + ¼ cup olive oil

1 medium onion, diced

2 cloves garlic, diced fine

½ lb (250 g) ground beef

½ teaspoon salt

1 tsp ground cinnamon

1 tsp ground nutmeg

¼ cup fresh cilantro

1 cup (200 g) spinach leaves, cooked

1 eggplant, sliced and fried

1 egg, beaten (for egg wash)

¼ cup (35 g) sesame seeds, to sprinkle (optional)

1. In a frying pan, pour 1 tbsp olive oil, and add the onion and garlic. Cook for about one minute, and then add the cooked spinach.

2. In the same frying pan, pour the ¼ cup olive oil and add the ground meat. Cook it for only about one minute, and remove from the heat. Add the salt, cinnamon, nutmeg and the ¼ cup fresh cilantro, and mix with a spoon.

Making the empanada:

1. Preheat the oven to 350°F (180°C), and prepare two parchment papers on your work surface. Take the dough and cut it in two parts (one should be a little bigger) to make two balls.

2. Place the smaller of the two balls on one piece parchment paper, cover it with the second paper, and roll it between the two pieces of parchment paper until it is ⅛ inch thick. Remove the top sheet of paper, and using a pizza cutter, cut the sheet of dough to produce a rectangle of about 12 by 8 inches (30 by 20 cm). Place the dough (along with the parchment paper on the bottom) onto a baking sheet.

3. Spoon the beef filling onto the rectangle of dough, smoothing it until you have a flat layer, with an exposed border of dough on all sides. Brush the edges of the dough very lightly with water.

4. Roll out the bigger ball of dough in the same way, remove the top sheet of parchment paper, and cut it to the same size as the first layer of dough. Flip the dough and parchment over (so that the bottom piece of parchment paper is now on the top), and carefully place the dough on top of the filling, lining up the edges of both pieces of dough. Carefully smooth the top layer of dough down against the filling, remove the parchment paper, and then press the edges of the dough all around the rectangular in order to close the empanada. You can use a fork to ensure a good seal, or for a more aesthetic look, roll the edges with your fingers. Make sure to remove any jagged edges of dough.

5. Whisk an egg to use as egg wash, brush it over the surface of the empanada, and sprinkle sesame seeds onto the egg wash. Using a knife, make two holes on the top of the dough so the steam can escape. Bake at 350°F (180°C) for about 45 minutes until it turns golden. Allow to cool slightly before eating.

*See the photo on the next page.

SPAIN

MARÍA GARCIA'S YOUNG PIGEON PIE FOR SHABBAT

In 1505, the Inquisition tribunal of Almazán declared that the converted María García, wife of Martín García, had been denounced for preparing a dish made of pigeon meat in a crust for Shabbat. The trial transcript reads: "this witness saw her [María García] eating some young pigeon put in bread crust [*palominos puestos en pan*] one Saturday. And they have said that she [this witness] saw the aforementioned remove the fat [*el sebo*] from the meat with her nails, and that she never saw her [María García] eating bacon [*tocino*] or putting it in the pot."

SERVES: 4–6 people

TIME: Approximately 5–6 hours (excluding overnight refrigeration):

Deboning and preparation of pigeon braising base: 1 hour (plus overnight refrigeration)

Recipe for the pie crust: 30 minutes (plus 2 hours refrigeration)

Chickpea cooking: 2 hours (plus overnight refrigeration)

Assembling the pie and baking: 2 hours (including chilling time)

Deboning and Preparation of Pigeon Braising Base (prepared the day before):

1 whole pigeon (approximately 300 g). If you cannot find pigeon, you can make the recipe with duck breast fillet.

½ onion

3 cloves garlic

1 carrot

Vegetable broth

Salt and pepper

1. For this recipe, buy a beautiful pigeon. Trim the legs using sharp scissors, burn off any excess feathers, and ensure it is properly cleaned. Remove the thighs, the breasts, and the wings. Cut the carcass into several pieces. In a hot cast iron pot, brown the carcass, wings, and thighs. Add half an onion, 3 cloves of garlic, and a carrot. Once caramelized, add enough vegetable broth to cover the pieces (see recipe below). When it boils, skim off impurities using a skimmer, cover, and place in the oven at 270°F (130°C) for 2 hours.

2. Remove the pigeon meat from the bones, keeping only the flesh, and place in the refrigerator. Strain the braising liquid through a fine mesh strainer into a saucepan. Reduce the liquid by ¾ to obtain a divine braising jus to accompany the pie. Chill in the fridge.

Recipe for the Pie Crust (prepared the day before):

⅓ cup + ½ cup + 2 tbsp flour (135 g total)

2½ tbsp (34 g) duck fat

2½ tablespoons (37 g) butter (or oil)

1 small egg

½ cup (60 g) potato starch

¾ tsp salt

2 tbsp (32 g) water

Using a pastry blender, mix ⅓ cup flour, duck fat, butter (or oil), and the egg to create a crumbly dough. Transfer everything to a mixer or a bowl and add ½ cup + 2 tbsp (90 g) flour, potato starch, salt, and water. Knead until you have a homogeneous dough. Shape the dough into a rectangular block, wrap it in plastic film, and refrigerate for 2 hours.

Chickpea Cooking (prepared the day before):

¼ cup (50 g) chickpeas

1 tsp salt

1 clove of garlic

3 sprigs thyme

2 bay leaves

Soak the chickpeas in lukewarm water for 1 hour, then simmer them for 1 hour with a pinch of salt, a clove of garlic, thyme, and bay leaf. Chill in the fridge.

Assembling the Pie and Baking:

4 small Swiss chard leaves

1 green spring onion

Pigeon meat (reserved after deboning)

Cooked chickpeas (prepared the day before)

Fennel, stalk or powdered seeds

Red pepper flakes, chili flakes

Swiss chard leaves

Brown eau-de-vie (a type of brandy)

1 egg yolk

Grilled or roasted vegetables, or salad (for serving)

1. Take the dough out 20 minutes before using.

2. Finely chop 4 small Swiss chard leaves and 1 green onion. Blanch them in boiling salted water, then immediately cool them in ice water. Drain well and add to the shredded pigeon meat. Add the cooked chickpeas, fennel, and a bit of red pepper flakes to spice up the filling.

3. Roll out the dough to obtain two small rounds with different diameters, and place the larger one on the bottom of a pie pan. On the bottom of the pie, arrange oiled and lightly salted Swiss chard leaves, then place the pigeon meat on top, adding salt and pepper and drizzling with brown eau-de-vie. Cover the pigeon meat with another layer of Swiss chard leaves.

4. Take the smaller round and delicately place it on top of the pie. Press around the edges to seal the dough. Brush the entire pie with salted egg yolk and refrigerate for 1 hour and 30 minutes.

5. Preheat the oven to 390°F (200°C), and score the top of the pie. Place it in the oven, then reduce the temperature to 350°F (180°C) for 15 minutes, and further reduce to 320°F (160°C) for 30 minutes.

6. Reheat the jus in a saucepan. Let the pigeon pie cool completely on a wire rack before slicing and serving. Serve with grilled or roasted vegetables or a salad.

*See the photo on the next page.

LODGE

BERNAL AND MARIA ALVARES' BREADCRUMB AND SWISS CHARD FRITTATA

SPAIN

The Inquisition court of the Spanish town of Almazán recorded a trial on June 4, 1505, during which Francisca, wife of Pedro the blacksmith, denounced Maestre Bernal and María Alvares. Francisca declares that "on Fridays [for Shabbat], she saw her mistress cooking Swiss chards in water until partially cooked [*acelgas sancochadas*], and then frying them in olive oil with onions. She would add breadcrumbs [*pan rallado*], spices, and egg yolks, and cook it until it became very thick." This dish sounds remarkably similar to what is known today as a frittata.

2 cups chopped Swiss chard (only the green leaves; use spinach leaves as a substitute)

½ cup (60 g) breadcrumbs

4 tablespoons olive oil

1 small spring onion (green and white parts), diced

2 cloves garlic, minced

½ teaspoon salt

¼ teaspoon black pepper

2 tablespoons flour

3 large eggs

¼ cup (15 g) cilantro, chopped

2 tbsp olive oil

1 tbsp olive oil, to pour over the dish once it is done

1. Wash the green leaves of the Swiss chard, dry them, and chop them finely. In a large bowl, combine the chopped Swiss chard and breadcrumbs. Set aside.

2. Heat olive oil in an oven-safe skillet over low-medium heat. Add the diced onion and minced garlic. Sauté until the onion becomes translucent and the garlic is fragrant, about 5 minutes. Add the Swiss chard and breadcrumb mixture to the skillet with the onions and garlic. Stir well to combine, and add the 2 tbsp olive oil.

3. Preheat your broiler. In a small bowl, whisk together the salt, black pepper, flour and egg until smooth. Pour this mixture over the Swiss chard mixture in the skillet. Stir as you pour it in to ensure everything is evenly coated. Cook on the stovetop until the egg thickens.

4. Transfer the skillet to the preheated oven and broil for about 3 minutes, or until it is set and the top is golden brown.

5. Remove from the oven and let it cool for a few minutes. Sprinkle with the diced spring onion and the chopped cilantro, and slice into wedges or squares and serve warm. You can leave it in the skillet as well.

6. You can eat it with a green arugula salad as a side.

CILANTRO AND GARLIC
ON UNLEAVENED BREAD WITH CHEESE

SPAIN

The Bernal family (mentioned above) was denounced on several occasions for their culinary practices, particularly those related to dishes made with bread to celebrate Shabbat. On July 4, 1505 Maestre Bernal and his wife were denounced by Madalena, the wife of Pedro the carpenter, because when she was living with them and their children twelve years prior, she saw them preparing beef sausages that they would eat on Saturdays. What is even more surprising is the precision of Madalena's memory when she describes the unleavened bread (*pan cuez*) that her mistress made for Shabbat. She explains that Maestre Bernal and his wife "took cilantro and put it in a skillet with garlic, ground spices, water, oil, and added bread crumbs [*pan desmenuzado*], and green cilantro and they stirred everything together. They did such unleavened bread [*pan cuez*], for Saturdays and Fridays, and they used to eat it."

Serves: 2 flatbreads

Time: 20 minutes

- ½ cup (100 g) breadcrumbs
- 5 tbsp water
- 2 tbsp olive oil
- ½ tsp salt
- 2 tbsp cilantro, freshly chopped
- 2 spring onions (both the green and white parts), diced
- 1 clove garlic, diced
- 1 tsp ground ginger
- 1 tsp black pepper
- 1 tbsp olive oil
- 1 tsp ground nutmeg
- 2 tsp olive oil to grease the skillet (1 tbsp per flatbread)

1. Mix together the breadcrumbs, water, olive oil, and salt.

2. In a pan, sauté the sliced garlic and the spring onions for about 1 minute over medium heat, then set aside.

3. In a mortar, mash the fresh chopped cilantro, ground ginger, black pepper, olive oil, salt and ground nutmeg to produce a coarse puree.

4. Add the puree and half of the onions and garlic to the breadcrumb dough. Mix for about 2 minutes and divide the dough into 2 halves.

5. Heat a small cast iron skillet over medium-high heat. Pour in 1 tsp of olive oil and put the first portion of dough into the pan, flattening it into a thin layer. Cook only on one side for about 30 seconds.

6. Remove the flatbread from the skillet and put it on a plate. Sprinkle ½ of the remaining onions and garlic over the bread. You can also sprinkle fresh goat cheese on top of the flatbread. Repeat with the remaining breadcrumb dough and onions and garlic.

SPAIN

DIEGO GARCÍA COSTELLO'S FISH EMPANADAS FOR SHABBAT

Diego García Costello—a tailor who became then a surgeon—lived in Palenzuela, where he was well known among the Jewish community. Several trials prove that he usually ate adafina for Shabbat, lit candles on Friday nights, read books written in Hebrew, went to the synagogue, prepared the table for Saturday on Friday night, and so on. He was also known for celebrating the Jewish holidays, and Passover in particular. In an Inquisition trial from December 22, 1488, he was denounced by Jamila, Simón ben Fara's wife, because "[. . .] as a witness she [Jamila] saw Diego García Costello and his wife [. . .] made fish empanadas on Friday for Saturday."

SERVES: 15 empanadas

TIME: 1 hour 30 minutes

For the dough:

3 cups (450 g) flour

1 teaspoon salt

½ cup (115 g) unsalted butter, cold and cut into small cubes (or neutral oil)

¾ cup (180 ml) cold water

For the filling:

1 tablespoon olive oil

1 small onion, finely chopped

2 cloves garlic, minced

½ pound (250 g) white fish fillets, such as cod or tilapia, cooked and flaked

4–6 anchovy fillets, finely chopped

¼ cup (15 g) chopped fresh parsley

1 teaspoon ground cumin

1 tsp salt

1 tsp pepper

Egg wash (1 egg beaten with 1 tablespoon water), for brushing

1. In a large bowl, mix together the flour and salt. Add the cold butter cubes and use a pastry cutter or your fingers to cut the butter into the flour until the mixture resembles coarse crumbs. Gradually add the cold water, a little at a time, and mix until the dough comes together. Form the dough into a ball, wrap it in plastic wrap, and refrigerate for at least 30 minutes.

2. While the dough chills, preheat your oven to 375°F (190°C) and line a baking tray with parchment paper.

3. In a skillet, heat the olive oil over medium heat. Add the chopped onion and minced garlic, and sauté until softened. Add the flaked fish and cook for about 5 minutes. Add the chopped anchovy fillets, chopped parsley, ground cumin, salt, and pepper to the skillet. Stir well to combine and cook for another 2–3 minutes. Remove from heat and let the filling cool.

4. On a lightly floured surface, roll out the chilled dough to a thickness of about ⅛ inch (3–4 mm). Use a round cutter or a small bowl to cut out circles of about 4–5 inches (10–12 cm) in diameter. Lightly wet half of the edge of the circle, and place a spoonful of the filling in the center of each dough circle. Fold the wet part of the dough over the dry one to enclose the filling, and seal the edges by pressing them together with a fork.

5. Place the empanadas on the parchment paper in the baking tray. Brush the tops with the egg wash, poke a small hole in the middle on the top of the empanada, and bake for about 20–25 minutes or until golden brown.

6. Remove from the oven and let the empanadas cool on the baking tray for a few minutes before serving. They can be enjoyed warm or at room temperature with the cold tomato soup *salmorejo* (see the recipe on p. 383).

---

*See the photo on the next page.

GOAT MEAT STEW AND UNSALTED BARLEY CAKES

FOR SABBATH IN THE CANARY ISLANDS

The Canary Islands constituted an important stop in maritime trade between the Americas and the Old Continent since the discovery of America. Just as in the Azores, Madeira, and also in coastal ports like Genoa or Livorno, many Jewish families of conversos settled there. The purpose was to facilitate and develop maritime commerce, but it also allowed the conversos to be surrounded by other members of the Jewish community. The increasing presence of converso Jews on the islands, including Jewish butchers and Jewish gathering places, went hand in hand with the growth of their activities. Because these activities were known and recognized by the institutions of the Spanish crown, an Inquisition court was established in Las Palmas in 1502.

The climate and geography of the Canary Islands favored goat farming and lead to the production of goat cheese, meat, and milk. One of the Shabbat dishes prepared by the conversos of the Canary Islands was a goat meat stew made with plenty of onions and olive oil. This stew was consumed with unsalted barley bread, as David Gitlitz mentions in his book "A Drizzle of Honey."

SERVES: 10 people

TIME: 1 hour 20 minutes

4.4 pounds (2 kg) goat meat

1 goat liver

1 cup (120 g) bread crumbs

6 cloves of garlic

½ cup (100 ml) vinegar

2 cups (400 ml) olive oil

2 cups (500 ml) white wine

10 peeled and sliced onions

4 cups (800 ml) vegetable broth (made with boiling 2 carrots, 2 onions, 2 bay leaves, thyme, and salt for about 30 minutes)

2 bay leaves

2 small sprigs of thyme

1 bunch parsley

1 tsp black pepper

2 tsp salt

1. Pour 6 cups (1.2 L) of water in a pot and add 2 peeled carrots, 2 onions (whole), 2 bay leaves, thyme, and salt. Bring to a boil and then cook uncovered for 30 minutes. Strain out the vegetables and set the broth aside.

2. Wash and cut the goat meat into small pieces. Season with salt, pepper, and thyme. In a large pot on medium-low heat, add the olive oil and the pieces of goat meat and sliced onions. Fry and turn the pieces for 20 minutes. Remove the meat and onions from the pot and set aside.

3. Take some oil from the pot in which the meat cooked and put it into a skillet. Add the peeled garlic cloves (whole) and the liver, cut into large pieces. Cook for 5 minutes over low heat. Add the vinegar and bread crumbs. Fry for 5 minutes and crush the mixture with a fork.

4. Put the goat meat back into the pot used at the beginning and add the crushed stuffing. Fry everything for 5 minutes. Pour the white wine over it and cook for 5 additional minutes over medium heat. Add the broth, bay leaves, the bunch of parsley, and thyme.

5. Cook covered for an hour until the meat is tender. Remove the meat from the pot and roast it in a hot oven at 425°F (220°C) for about ten minutes. Meanwhile, strain the sauce to remove the chunks. Reduce the sauce for ten minutes over high heat.

5. Place the meat on a dish, arrange the fried onions around and on top of the meat, and pour the sauce over it. Serve with barley bread.

Barley is not a cereal that is prominently featured in documents related to breadmaking by Jews. This includes sources from the Cairo Geniza, which testify to the habits of Sephardic and Mizrahi Jews throughout the Mediterranean basin for hundreds of years. Therefore, it can be safely assumed that the majority of the flour used to make bread was wheat flour, not barley flour. However, there are a few references to the making of barley bread in the sources. For instance, Paulus Aegineta—a Greek physician from Aegina who lived in Alexandria—mentions it in his 7th century medical encyclopedia *The Seven Books of Paulus Aegineta* (Book VII, Chapter XX, Section 1). He describes various types of bread, including "azyma" or unleavened bread, which is likely a reference to matzah: "The matzah, as Zeunius explains it, consisted of the flour of toasted barley pounded with some liquid, such as water, oil, milk, oxycrate, oxymel, or honied water."

For the barley bread:

3 cups (450 g) barley flour, toasted

1 tsp salt

1 tbsp olive oil

1 tbsp honey

1 tbsp vinegar

1 tbsp white wine

1 cup (240 ml) of lukewarm water

1. In a large bowl, combine the toasted barley flour, salt, and olive oil. Add the honey, vinegar, and white wine, and mix everything together with a large spoon. Add the lukewarm water little by little and knead the dough with your hands for about 5 minutes. Place the dough in a plastic bag and cool in the fridge for about 30 minutes.

2. Turn on the oven to 400°F (200°C), put some parchment paper in a baking tray, and divide the dough into 4 balls. With a rolling pin, flatten each ball of dough over a floured (barley or wheat flour) working surface until it is less than a tenth of an inch thick (about 2 mm).

3. Place the dough on the parchment-lined tray.

4. Take a ball and, with your hands, flatten it into a circle about ½ inch thick. Put it on a baking tray with parchment paper. Baked for 20 minutes, on one side.

5. Remove the baking tray from the oven and let the breads cool in the baking tray before eating.

13TH CENTURY ANDALUSIAN CHALLAH

Challah is a term that has attracted a lot of interest from biblical times to the present day. Many scholars and lovers of Jewish cuisine have ventured into historical and culinary research—not always with sound findings—on the term's origins and on the dish itself. Stories of challah's history abound online and in cookbooks, but there is little information actually drawn from historical sources.

I looked into what information Iberian sources can offer us, such as the *Kitāb al-ṭabīẖ*, from Al-Andalus (southern Spain). In the manuscript challah bears the name عمل الضفاير, which means "the making [عمل] of braids." The term "braids" [الضفاير] corresponds to the word ḍafair in Arabic, which no other source or recipe from the same period mentions. What is interesting is that the Spanish translation of this recipe has the word "guedejas" for "braids," and the closest translation of guedejas in Hebrew is the term "peot" (i.e. side curls). This recipe entitled "The making of braids" matches very closely with the preparation of braided challah bread. Nonetheless, no inquisition trials mention this braided loaf.

Braided challah bread, an icon of today's Ashkenazi Jewish cuisine, could have its first recorded recipe in Spain's first cookbook in the thirteenth century. Accompanying the Sephardic Jews who were expelled from the Iberian Peninsula in the fifteenth century, challah began its long journey north and eastward, passing through Italy, to Eastern Europe. There it was blended with the culinary practices of Ashkenazi Jews, who adopted it and gave it a permanent home, affording its survival not only at home but throughout the world.

This is the original recipe from the *Kitāb al-ṭabīẖ* (in Arabic, translated into English by David Friedman): "Take what you will of white flour or of semolina, which is better in these things. Moisten it with hot water after sifting, and knead well, after adding some fine flour, leavening, and salt. Moisten it again and again until it has middling consistency. Then break into it, for each *ratl* of semolina, five eggs and a *dirham* of saffron, and beat all this very well, and put the dough in a dish, cover it and leave it to rise [. . .]. When it has risen, clean a frying pan and fill it with fresh oil, then put it on the fire. When it starts to boil, make braids of the leavened dough like hair-braids, of a handspan or less in size. Coat them with oil and throw them in the oil and fry them until they brown. When their cooking is done, arrange them on an earthenware plate and pour over them skimmed honey spiced with pepper, cinnamon, Chinese cinnamon, and lavender. Sprinkle it with ground sugar and present it."

In the original recipe, the challah is fried. Using the same recipe, I tried two cooking methods: fried and baked in the oven. Both crumbs are very similar, but my preference is for the baked version. I also find that preparing the dough only with flour works well (rather than with both flour and semolina), but I shall leave this up to your preference in my version of the *Kitāb al-ṭabīẖ* recipe below.

SERVES: 4

TIME: 2 hours 25 minutes

5 eggs

3 cups (460 g) flour

¼ cup (87 g) extra fine semolina (or the same amount of flour if not using semolina)

2 tbsp fresh yeast crushed (or 1½ tbsp active dry yeast, or 3 tbsp sourdough starter)

1 cup (200 ml) lukewarm water

2 saffron strands, mashed in 2 tsp hot water

¼ cup (60 g) olive oil

½ tsp salt

1 tsp orange blossom water

3 tbsp sugar (optional, for a sweeter flavor)

egg wash (1 beaten egg)

To drizzle:

⅛ cup (13 g) sugar

⅛ cup (20 g) honey

½ tsp pepper

1 tsp ground cinnamon

⅛ cup (25 g) butter (optional)

dried lavender flowers

1. In the bowl of a stand mixer, put the eggs, flour, semolina, saffron, olive oil, salt, orange blossom water, and sugar (if using). Mix slowly with the hook attachment for 30 seconds. If you are using fresh yeast or active dry yeast, dissolve it in a small bowl with the lukewarm water for about 2 minutes first, then add it to the bowl of the stand mixer with the other ingredients. If you are using a sourdough starter, put it directly in the bowl of the stand mixer with the other ingredients, and add the lukewarm water.

2. Mix all for at least 15 minutes on a medium speed. Grease another bowl lightly with oil. Transfer the dough out of the mixer bowl into the greased one, cover it with a plastic wrap and let the dough rise in a warm place for 1 hour.

3. Uncover the bowl. Grease your hands lightly and punch down the dough, to get some of the air out. Stir it in the stand mixer again for 5 minutes. Afterwards, put it back in the bowl, cover it again with plastic wrap and let it rise for another 30 minutes. Then, punch the air out of the dough once again, before moving on to braiding.

4. You can braid your challah in a lot of different ways, but the easiest way is with three braids. Divide the dough in three balls of equal weight and diameter. Roll them into 3 equally sized strands about 11 inches (30 cm) long. Their surface should be smooth, without grooves. Lay the strands side by side and pinch the tops together. Start braiding as if you were braiding hair, placing the strands at each side alternately in the middle between the other two strands. So, start with the right strand and put it between the middle and the left strands. Then, take the left strand put in between the middle and right strands, and so on. When you finish braiding, pinch the ends and fold under the loaf.

5. Place the braid on a lined tray and leave to rise in a warm place for 1 hour, covered with a kitchen towel. Preheat the oven to 330°F (170°C).

6. Lightly brush the challah dough with the egg wash and bake for 35 minutes until golden brown.

7. Meanwhile prepare the drizzle: melt the sugar, honey, and ground cinnamon (with the pepper and butter, if using) in a saucepan over medium heat. When the challah is baked, brush it with the syrup and let it cool. Decorate with the dried lavender flowers.

You can also make parsley and garlic croutons with leftover challah with the recipe below.

GARLIC AND PARSLEY CHALLAH CROUTONS

SPAIN

Serves: 6–8

Time: 35–50 minutes

Leftover challah bread (preferably a day or two old)

2–3 cloves of garlic, minced

2–3 tablespoons olive oil

2 tablespoons fresh parsley, chopped

Salt and pepper to taste

1. Preheat your oven to 350°F (175°C), and cut the leftover challah into bite-sized cubes or pieces. You can remove the crust if you prefer, but leaving it on will add extra texture to the croutons.

2. In a small saucepan, heat the olive oil over low to medium heat. Add the minced garlic to the oil and sauté for 1–2 minutes, or until the garlic becomes fragrant. Be careful not to let it brown; you just want to infuse the oil with garlic flavor. Remove the garlic oil from the heat and set it aside.

3. In a large bowl, place the challah cubes, and pour the garlic-infused olive oil over the challah cubes and toss them to coat evenly. Make sure the cubes are well-coated but not soggy. You can drizzle more olive oil if needed.

4. Sprinkle the chopped fresh parsley over the challah cubes and season with a pinch of salt and a bit of black pepper. Toss everything together to distribute the seasonings evenly.

5. Spread the seasoned challah cubes in a single layer on a baking sheet. Bake in the preheated oven for about 15–20 minutes or until the croutons are golden brown and crisp. Be sure to check them and give them a stir halfway through for even browning.

6. Once the croutons are done, remove them from the oven and allow them to cool on the baking sheet. They will become even crunchier as they cool. These delicious croutons are perfect as a side for any poultry dish.

THE GENIZA HUMMUS

EGYPT

A shopping list found in the Geniza of Fustat appears to list the ingredients for making hummus. The list is so similar to the ingredients required that there is little doubt about the identity of the dish being prepared, even though hummus is not explicitly mentioned:

Sumac ⅜ (dirhem)
Tahina ¼
Olive and sesame oil ¾
Salt ¼
Sesame oil 1⅝
Wood for fuel ¼

(Goiten, vol. 4, 440. See: TS NS Box 320, f.19)

My recipe for hummus:

SERVES: 4 people

TIME: 15 minutes

- 1½ cups (300 g) chickpeas, cooked
- 1 tbsp extra virgin olive oil
- 1 tsp salt
- ⅓ cup (80 g) tehina (sesame paste)
- 1 tbsp fresh lemon juice
- ¼ cup ice, crushed
- 1 tsp sesame oil, to pour over
- 1 tsp olive oil, to pour over
- 2 tsp sumac, to sprinkle
- 1 tsp sesame seeds, to sprinkle

1. In a blender or food processor, add the cooked chickpeas, olive oil, and salt. Mix for about 30 seconds. Then, add the tehina. (Do not forget to stir the tehina before adding it to the chickpeas; tehina tends to settle and you do not want to use only the oily liquid on top, but all of the mixed golden tehina). Mix for another 30 seconds.

2. Add the fresh lemon juice and the crushed ice. Mix for another 30 seconds or until the hummus is creamy and buttery.

3. Take a plate, place the hummus in the middle, and spread it out to the edges.

4. Drizzle with olive and sesame oil and sprinkle with sumac and sesame seeds.

HARĪSA WHEAT GRAIN AND CHICKEN STEW

This is a story about the renowned Sabbath dish of the Jews in pre-Islamic Arabia, including Yemen, called *harīsa*. According to Geniza fragments, harīsa is made of semolina dough that is stuffed with meat, fat, and spices. The dough is cooked overnight, allowing it to absorb all the flavors of the meat and spices. Goiten's work mentions *that* during a party, the caliph and gastronome Mu'āwiya from Syria (661–680) asked a Jew to recite a poem, but the Jew explained that his father would be better at reciting it. The caliph's companions did not approve of the Jew's deferral, as they believed the caliph, as the more important person, should be obeyed. They reprimanded the Jew for being impudent. To change the subject, the caliph asked the Jew if his family still prepared harīsa as well as they did in pre-Islamic times. The Jew replied that his family's harīsa was even better, and the caliph requested that some be prepared for him to taste. He ate the harīsa, and he enjoyed it.

In the third chapter of his book *On Asthma*, Maimonides writes that "Anything made from wheat [prepared] in a different way is bad and harmful for people in general and for my honorable Master in particular, such as that [food] prepared from wheat itself (as, for instance, harīsa, or ḥarīra)." Harīsa was one of the most popular dishes in al-Andalus as well. It could be made at home or bought at the market. The name comes from the Arabic "harīs" (هريس) meaning "ground" or "pounded." The Andalusian *Kitāb al-ṭabīẖ* cookbook includes harīsa recipes, and it states that they should be made with ⅔ wheat and ⅓ meat. The meat used can be breast or thighs of chicken or goose, but also lamb or veal. The dish is cooked in the oven, overnight, similar to dishes made for Shabbat. A very similar dish is still prepared today by Sephardic Jews, mainly from Morocco. Even the name has hardly changed: it is called *oriza* (or *adafina de trigo*, i.e. adafina made from wheat).

The following recipe is the Andalusian version.

SERVES: 4–6 people

TIME: 30 minutes + overnight

2 cups (300 g) wheat grain (whole if possible)

½ cup (100 g) olive oil

2 onions, sliced

3 garlic cloves, crushed

2 tbsp sugar

½ lb (or less, 220 g) chicken breasts

1 tsp salt

½ tsp black pepper

3 strands of saffron (or ¼ tsp food coloring)

4 hard-boiled eggs, peeled (optional)

2 potatoes and 2 sweet potatoes (optional, as they were unknown to thirteenth-century Europe)

1. Leave the wheat grains to soak in water for a whole day. The next day, drain the wheat and rub it dry. In an oven-safe pot, pour the olive oil, the onion, garlic, and sugar. Add the wheat and brown it for 5 minutes.

2. Add the chicken breasts, sprinkling with salt, black pepper, and saffron. Pour in 1 cup of water, mix, and cook for 5 minutes, stirring.

3. Take the pot off of the stove and cover completely with water (about 3 cups) and add the hard-boiled eggs, as well as the potatoes and sweet potatoes, cut into large pieces (if using).

4. At the end of the day, cover the pot with a lid, and put it in the oven at 150°F (70°C) until noon the next day.

MARZIPAN

THE ICONIC SEPHARDIC ALMOND SWEET

Rarely have the origins and etymology of a dish been shrouded in so much mystery. *Mazapán*, *marzipan*, *massapan*, *massepain*, *mauthabān*, *marzabān*, *maçapães*, and so on: the plethora of different names for this dish reflect the diversity of the populations that have prepared and eaten it. A sweet almond paste, which the Spanish today call *mazapán*, is among the foods that are considered an integral part of the culinary heritage of modern Spain. This specialty is of utmost importance for measuring the significance of the Jewish legacy in Iberian culinary heritage.

This almond sweet is regularly used in the *Kitāb al-ṭabīẖ* cookbook and is paired with drinks. Preparations are sometimes shaped in the form of flowers, oranges, or pears. All the recipes mentioned in it use sweet almond paste as a stuffing to fill pastries made from flour, semolina, and oil. Sometimes baked in the oven, but usually fried, the aesthetics of the food are important since it can be molded into different shapes.

However, sweet almond paste is called something else when another ingredient is added: starch. The difference is considerable. In this case, marzipan is no longer used as a filling, but is a pastry on its own, whose unique quality is that it is dried. Adding starch creates what is called in the Andalusian *Kitāb al-ṭabīẖ*—which contains explicitly Jewish recipes—*qāhirīya* (قاهرية). The cookbook contains five such recipes. The first is called "Preparation of *Cairotes*." It is made of sugar that is cooked until it turns into syrup. Then peeled and grounded almonds are added. Once the pastry is oily, nard, cloves, rose water, and a little camphor are added. The mix must be dry in order to form small piles, which are left to solidify.

The way in which this method differs from the previous preparations is that the sweets have to be soaked in a thick starch-based liquid and left to dry. They are then fried and coated in rose syrup, julep syrup, or honey. The recipe "Cairotes in the Oven" is made from marzipan, to which flour and starch are added in order to make it more solid. After adding spices, camphor, and rose water, small piles of paste are made and placed on a plate to be put in the oven. The "Sunny *Cairotes*" recipe also uses marzipan with spices. After shaping them into little mounds, they are placed in liquid starch and left to dry in the sun until the coating of starch dries. Finally, the last recipe is "*Cairotes* Called *Ṣābūniya*," which are shaped like little pieces of soap (*ṣābūn*). According to the *Kitāb al-ṭabīẖ* this preparation was known in Marrakesh and is almost identical to the previous one. However, the coating, made from a thick sweet rose and julep syrup, forms three layers around the *cairote*.

These four marzipan recipes, which incorporate starch to enable the consumption of sweet almond paste on its own rather than as a filling, closely resemble modern marzipan, with a single distinguishing feature. While the shaping of marzipan into fruit-like forms is a common practice today, it was not always the prevailing tradition. However, this is done in the case of the last sweet almond paste recipe in the *Kitāb al-ṭabīẖ*, listed under the name *sanbūsak* (سنبوسك), the recipe that most closely resembles today's *mazapán*. Particular attention must be paid to the shape. The sweets are to be molded into the form of mini loaves or balls representing oranges, pears, or apples. These round shapes are very important. The *Kitāb al-ṭabīẖ*'s recipe states that these sweets are to be served with drinks and that they are, in the East, called *sanbūsak*.

The creation of marzipan in diverse forms, coupled with its Eastern name (*sanbūsak*), may suggest the multicultural nature of Spain during the late Middle Ages. The confection's inclusion in the *Kitāb al-ṭabīḫ* suggests that both Jews and Muslims in al-Andalus shared this culinary tradition.

Apart from culinary sources, the term "marzipan" makes multiple appearances in early sources which link it to Jews specifically. For instance, in a letter penned by Jacob di Consiglio da Toscanella, a prominent Jewish banker from Siena, dated May 5, 1463. In the letter, addressed to Giovanni di Cosimo de' Medici in Florence, marzipan and other sweets are referred to as "fatte all'hebrea," signifying their Jewish connection. This association between marzipan and Jews is further documented in the records of the sixteenth-century "Processi del Santo Uffizio di Venezia contro ebrei e giudaizzanti" (1579–1586). The consistent presence of marzipan in these trials suggests that it was not merely an occasional treat but a part of Jewish culinary traditions, enjoyed on various occasions, including celebrations like circumcisions. The inclusion of citron/etrog among the ingredients allowed for the fusion of the delightful flavor of the citrus fruit with its significance in Jewish liturgy, particularly during the observance of Sukkot. For instance, in 1568, Leone da Montesanto, a banker in Mantua, presented city officials with "Jewish marzipan and Malvasia from Candia." Furthermore, the existence of a dish called "braciadelli de marzapano all'hebrea" made from marzipan paste serves as additional evidence of the deep-rooted link between Jewish culture and marzipan.

What adds to the intrigue is the tangible connection between marzipan and Italian Jews. In this case, it is important to grasp the connotation of "fatte all'hebrea," which means "Jewish made." Marzipan had become a vital component of the Italian upper class's culinary repertoire as early as the Renaissance, and the delicacy found its way onto tables in countless variations. Ariel Toaff, in his work "Mangiare alla giudia" points out that during the sixteenth century in the Venetian ghetto, guests were not only presented with fresh seasonal fruits like pears and cherries but also with marzipan, a bit of malvasia, and perennial Jewish-style treats like *frittole*, *rafioli*, and *pignoccata*. These confections, crafted from sugar and featuring marzipan centers, took on round shapes resembling nuts and fruits.

The meticulous attention to the precise shaping of marzipan should not be underestimated. This particular aesthetic detail was instrumental in identifying marzipan as a creation of Jewish origin, resulting in accusations against its makers. Indeed, records from the Holy Office mention round-shaped confections (*son cose tonde*) resembling nuts and fruits (*in foza de nose e de fruti*) and filled with marzipan paste (*che dentro ve è pasta de marzapane*). In essence, the Inquisition trials in Venice during the sixteenth century unmistakably associate marzipan and similar sweets with the practices of the Mosaic religion. And these ties to Jewish traditions endure. A multitude of diverse sources attests to this, and marzipan continues to be a part of contemporary celebrations among Sephardic Jews hailing from the Iberian Peninsula. Whether it's marriages, circumcisions, or other festivities, marzipan remains a cherished component of these Jewish celebrations.

RUPERTO DE NOLA'S MARZIPAN, 1529

SPAIN

This recipe is an adaption from a Spanish cookbook from 1529 (Logroño). The *maçapanes* are vegan and baked in the oven. You can also make this recipe raw, without baking the marzipan. It will remain dense and will not spread while baking in the oven. The colored marzipan in the photo is the raw variety.

SERVES: 18 figurines

TIME: 1 hour

7 oz (200 g) almonds, peeled

½ + ⅛ cup (120 g) icing sugar

12 tbsp light syrup (2¾ cup [540 g] water + ¾ cup [144 g] sugar + 1 teaspoon rose extract)

2 tsp flour

Food coloring gel (optional)

1. Pour the water and rose extract into a pan and add the sugar. Boil on high heat for 5 minutes and 30 seconds, then set aside.

2. Using a grinder, grind together the whole almonds and the icing sugar for about 10 seconds. You want a fine mixture, but do not over grind! Put this mixture in a blender or food processer and add 10 tbsp of syrup little by little. The remain 2 tbsp syrup will be used to brush the marzipan ones they are baked. Mix slowly for 15 seconds. (You can also do it by hand.) Do not grind the marzipan too much because you do not want it to be oily. You can add food coloring gel and mix by hand until you have a homogeneous color of marzipan dough.

For Nola's baked marzipan:

1. Heat the oven to 400°F (200°C) and place a baking sheet in the oven to heat it.

2. Remove a piece of marzipan about ⅞ oz (30 g). This amount of dough will allow you to make about 18 small figurines, braids, fruits, etc. Shape them quickly and place them on a plate. Keep the plate covered with plastic wrap while you work to keep the figurines from drying out.

3. When you finish shaping all the marzipan and when the oven is ready, carefully remove the very hot baking tray and place it on a working surface. Place parchment on it and flour it. The flour needs to be spread all over the parchment paper. Place the marzipan figurines on it, leaving about an inch of space between each one.

4. Bake them for about 5 minutes. Carefully take the baking tray out of the oven and lightly brush the figurines with the last 2 tbsp of rose water syrup. Let them cool on the tray without removing them for at least 15 minutes.

For raw marzipan:

1. Shape the marzipan, as above, being careful not over mix. Place them on a plate and cover them with plastic wrap to keep them from drying out.

UNBAKED MARZIPAN WITH EGG WHITES

SERVES: 15 figurines

TIME: 1 hour

8 oz (225 g) whole almonds

1 tsp water (or more if needed)

16 oz (450 g) icing sugar (fine or extra fine)

2 egg whites, beaten

½ cup (100 ml) rose water

food coloring gel (optional)

1 tsp starch + 2 tsp water + 1 tsp fresh lemon juice

1. Soak the almonds in a bowl of water overnight, then remove the skins. In a food processor, add 1 tsp water and grind the peeled almonds for about 2 minutes at very high speed, until you have a very fine paste.

2. In a bowl, combine the egg whites, the fine sugar and the ground almond paste. Stir and add the rose water. Pour the mixture into a sauce pan and cook over low heat while stirring with a spatula until the paste does not stick to the edges of the sauce pan.

3. Take the spatula and carefully pour the mixture into a lightly-greased pan, and let it cool at room temperature.

4. If desired, you can add food coloring gel to suit the shapes you want to make. Shape the marzipan into the form of fruits, vegetables, animals, braids, etc. You can also lightly grease small molds and fill them with the almond paste. Once shaped, put them on a plate and brush them very lightly with a mixture made by beating 1 tsp starch, 2 tsp water, and 1tsp fresh lemon juice. Keep the marzipan covered so it doesn't dry out.

ORIGINAL MARZIPAN

SPAIN

This is my favorite recipe for marzipan. The almond flavor is intense, the texture is consistent and smooth, and it melts in your mouth.

SERVES: 10 figurines

TIME: 40 minutes

⅞ oz (25 g) bitter almonds, peeled

2⅝ oz (75 g) almonds, peeled

2 oz (57 g) icing sugar

Light syrup (1⅓ cup [270 g] water, and ¼ + ⅛ cup [72 g] sugar)

Food coloring gel (optional)

Fruit flavor extract (optional)

1. Prepare a sugar syrup. In a pan (preferably a copper pan), pour the water and add the sugar, and boil while stirring. Once the syrup reaches 248°F (120°C), which is called "gros boulé," set it aside.

2. In a blender or food processor, grind together the two kinds of almonds and the icing sugar for about 10 seconds. You want an extra fine mixture. Add 10 tbsp of syrup little by little.

3. Remove the marzipan from the blender (ideally onto a marble working surface to cool it down) and work gently with your hands until the mixture becomes pale and forms a paste, for about one minute and thirty seconds. Do not grind the marzipan too much because you do not want it to be oily.

4. After it has cooled down, pass it through a grinder several times until it becomes a smooth paste, but do not over mix it (not more than 30 seconds).

5. Bring it all together into a ball. If it seems too dry, add one or two tablespoons of sugar syrup. Lightly knead on a work surface until you have a smooth ball. Do not over knead it (no more than 30 seconds). Wrap in plastic wrap and put it in the fridge for at least 30 minutes.

6. Remove about ⅞ oz (30 g) of the dough and shape it the way you want. If desired, you can add food coloring gel and/or fruit flavor extract. When finished, keep them in a plastic bag in the refrigerator.

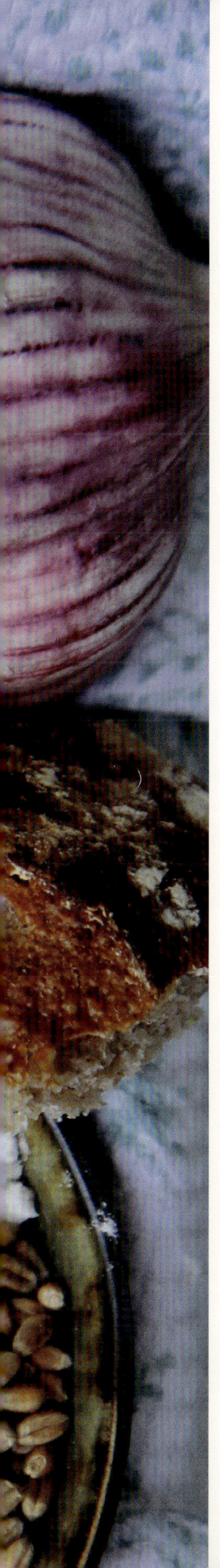

EVERY OCCASION

YITZHAQ ALAHDAB

(mid-fourteenth century to early fifteenth century)

"Conversion or hardship weren't the only options for Jews after the disturbances of 1391; large-scale emigration also followed. Some of the refugees headed for Muslim North Africa, some for the Land of Israel, and some for Sicily, which at the time belonged to the crown of Aragon and had a substantial Jewish population. Among the immigrants who settled in Sicily was Yitzhaq Alahdab, who had been raised in Castile and acquired considerable learning in the fields of astronomy, mathematics, Scripture, translation, and—to an extent—poetry. Between the years 1391 and 1426, Alahdab lived in Syracuse and Palermo, where he wrote books in all the aforementioned fields, and also invented what seems to have been an upgraded astrolabe."

Pete Cole, *The Dream of the Poem: Hebrew Poetry from Muslim and Christian Spain 950–1492*, p. 320

RENAISSANCE MAN

I'm skillful as skillful ever comes
and so I've mastered numerous trades
I know about spinning and weaving on looms

and how, with warp, the weft is made.

When I was a boy, I dreamed of becoming

a soldier on horseback, a man of war
and with my helmet charging on stallions
whose snorting terrified all who saw—

wearing a coat of armor and mail

bearing a bow, bringing down walls.

But when I beheld what the battle entailed—
how soldiers pursuing became the pursued
and fled at the sound of a wind-driven leaf—

I settled down to till the soil.

I planted gardens and tended vines

and plowed my fields with pairs of oxen;
beans, garlic, pumpkin, and squash . . .
I sowed all sorts of **greens** and **onions**.

But then the rains stopped in the heavens

and from my labor I earned not a thing.

And so I decided to take up construction
and build myself magnificent homes—
towers filled with wondrous paintings

high on hills, set in stone . . .

I also knew the secrets of numbers
and the work of observing and charting the skies:

I counted the grains of sand and dust
and accurately measured the waters' rise.

With ease I fathomed the new moon's phase

whether it lasted a day or two days.
I saw when I put the scope to my eye
the stars in their orbits, moving on high:

their zenith and nadir, ascent and decline

and when they'd cast an eclipse with their line . . .

To sell **fruit** and **bread** in the market,

and dry goods, too, I opened a store—

garlic, scallions, melons, legumes, herbs, greens, and beans galore.

To help out my brothers I went back to school

and learned how to weave blankets for mules.

In time, though, I became a cantor
for my voice is good and I can sing:
I chanted prayers and recited psalms

the Song of the Sea and all the hymns . . .

And I can translate from every tongue,

and swiftly turn the wheels at the mill:
I know how to properly sift the **flour**
and winnow **wheat** with tremendous skill.

I toiled to learn the secrets of glass—

through which sunlight would perfectly pass.

I laundered, bleached, and traded wares,
and also in Scripture instructed boys.
Better than all, I could cut hair

and knew how to press and filter **oil** . . .

PIGNOLATA AL MIELE
FRIED AND HONEYED ITALIAN PASTRIES

ITALY

During my PhD studies I worked on an Italian text of the very late 15th century (1497) written in Terracina, which bears the title of *Stanze di Lorenzo de' Medici*. It may have been written by several authors who, one by one, used their own culture to write an anti-Jewish satire. The goal of the text was to mock Jewish rituals (foods on Sukkot, Purim, etc.) and practices (culinary, professional, liturgical, etc.). In the text there is a pun between the word *pignorati* (a sweet pastry made with pine nuts), *pignolata (a sweet dish from Sicily)* and the verb *pignorare* (an allusion to a pawnbroker's activities of foreclosing and seizing). *Pignolata* are also called *Pignoccata* in Sicily and in Palermo. The *pignoccata* is also mentioned in the sixteenth century *Processi del Santo Uffizio di Venezia contro ebrei e giudaizzanti* (1579–1586) so we understand that the *pignocata* also bore this name in Venice. *Pignoccata and pignolata* bear also the name *struffoli* (and could be made with etrog) in the Campania region of Italy, mainly in Naples. *Pignolata al miele* is similar to a Spanish fried and honeyed pastry mentioned in Spanish inquisition trials of the 15th and 16th centuries and called *nuegados*.

SERVES: 4–6 people

TIME: 40 minutes

3 tsp (13 g) olive oil

1 lemon (for ½ of its peel)

1 orange (for its peel)

2 cups (300 g) flour

¼ cup (36 g) ground almonds

¼ cup (36 g) ground walnuts

3 eggs

1 tsp white wine (optional)

1 tsp sugar

¼ tsp baking powder

Neutral oil for frying

For topping:

1 cup (340 g) of honey

1 tsp orange blossom water (optional)

1. With a knife, peel the zest from a whole orange and half lemon (avoid including the white pith). Add both kinds of peel to a frying pan with the olive oil. Fry over low heat, without burning the peel, for 3 minutes, and then let it cool.

2. Remove the orange and lemon peel from the oil and dice them. Keep the flavored oil.

3. Put the flour, ground almonds and walnuts into a large bowl, and make a hole in the center. Add the eggs, white wine (if using), sugar, and the flavored oil that you fried the zest in. Mix with a spoon starting from the center outward. Add the baking powder and the diced peels.

4. Put in a stand mixer with the hook attachment for 5 minutes, or knead by hand for 10 minutes. You can add more flour if the dough is too sticky, but it must remain elastic, so do not add too much. With this dough, form long thin sausages, roughly a quarter of an inch (0.5 cm) thick. Shape all the dough in this way. It will dry out a bit and will be easier to handle.

5. Cut each strand into small chunks about half an inch (1 cm) long with a sharp knife or a pair of scissors. Heat up neutral oil in a frying pan or in a fryer at medium temperature.

6. Fry all the pieces until they are golden. Be careful, they cook very quickly! Take them out of the oil and put them on a paper towel.

7. Heat the honey and orange blossom water in a saucepan over low heat; do not let it boil.

8. Prepare a large plate in which to put the pignolata. You can also arrange them in portions using small cupcake or muffin liners.

9. In batches, stir the small fried pieces in the hot honey for 1 minute, and take them out with a skimmer. Put the fried pieces on the plate or in the paper liners and let them cool before eating.

FRITTOLE

ITALY

SWEET ORANGE AND RAISIN ITALIAN DONUTS

Today, *frittole* are traditionally eaten on Venice during the Carnevale period, at the end of February, just before the start of the Christian Lent. But their origin goes back to at least 500 years ago. In the sixteenth century "Processi del Santo Uffizio di Venezia contro ebrei e giudaizzanti (1579–1586)" (Trials of the Holy Office of the Inquisition in Venice against Jews and Judaizers), *frittole* are mentioned on several occasions: "Alle volte me ha anche mandato de le frittole fatte in foza de nose" (Sometimes he even sent me fritole made in the shape of a nose); or "che ghe le mandava deta Alumbra, [. . .] alcune cose come rafioli, fritole [. . .] che stava in geto dove stava li Hebrei" (she sent them, called Alumbra, [. . .] some things like ravioli, fritole [. . .] that were in the place where the Jews lived); or "Greco portava in nome di deta dona cose de magnar in casa cioè frittole, pasteli et anco [. . .]" (Greco carried in the name of the said woman things to eat at home, namely fritole, pastries, and also [. . .]). These references prove that in the sixteenth century, frittole were prepared and eaten in the houses of the ghetto of Venice and that this culinary tradition survives until today. Frittole are also known in the city of Trieste which is located 2 hours (driving) from Venice. They usually contain apples, orange and lemon zest and raisins.

Serves: 30 donuts

Time: 1 hour 30 minutes

Tea bag (fruity taste) + 2 cups boiling water

2 apples + 2 tsp sugar + 2 tsp water + 2 tsp rum (optional)

½ cup (120 ml) whole milk

2 eggs

¼ cup (50 g) butter, unsalted and melted

1½ cup (240 g) flour

½ tbsp (10 g) tsp fresh yeast (or ½ active dry yeast)

½ cup (100 g) sugar

½ tsp salt

6 tbsp raisins (sultana or muscatel)

½ orange (for the zest only)

sugar (to decorate)

Neutral oil for frying

(The recipe continues on the next page).

1. Boil the 2 cups of water, pour it in a bowl, and add the tea bag. After about 5 minutes, remove the tea bag and add the raisins; let them soak for about 30 minutes. Then, remove them from the water and put them on a paper towel to drain.

2. Peel the apples and remove the cores, and cut them into small chucks. Take a sauce pan and put the chucks of apple in, and add the 2 tsp of sugar, 2 tsp of water and 2 tsp rum (optional).

3. Cover and cook over medium heat for about 10 minutes. Uncover and cook for 5 more minutes. Mash the chunks until it looks like more or less like apple purée. Set aside and let it cool.

4. Take a bowl and beat the milk and egg together. In a separate bowl, mix the flour, sugar and salt. Then add the milk and egg mixture and the melted butter to the flour mixture. Stir well until homogeneous.

5. Next add the drained raisins, orange zest, and the apple purée. Mix well. The mixture should look like a thick cake batter. If it doesn't, add milk little by little to thin it out, or add flour to thicken it. Cover the batter and cool it in the fridge for at least 1 hour.

6. Take a frying pan and pour in some neutral oil. You should put enough oil to prevent the frittole from touching the bottom of the frying pan, or they will lose their shape. Heat the oil over medium-high heat, to around 338°F (170°C).

7. Take two large spoons and quickly stir the mixture. Take a spoonful (about the size of a ping-pong ball) of the mixture and, using the other spoon, drop it into the hot oil. You can do 3 or 4 at the same time.

8. Do not touch the frittole for 5 seconds, and then move the frying pan a little or use a skimmer to move it around in the oil so that it cooks evenly. Cook for about 1 minute, moving the ball. It could take a bit more time if the frittole is big, but they should develop a deep golden color. Then, with a skimmer, take the frittole out of the oil and allow it to drain and cool on a plate lined with paper towels. One minute after draining, roll the frittole in sugar.

9. Repeat until you've used all of the batter; serve hot with hot chocolate or tea.

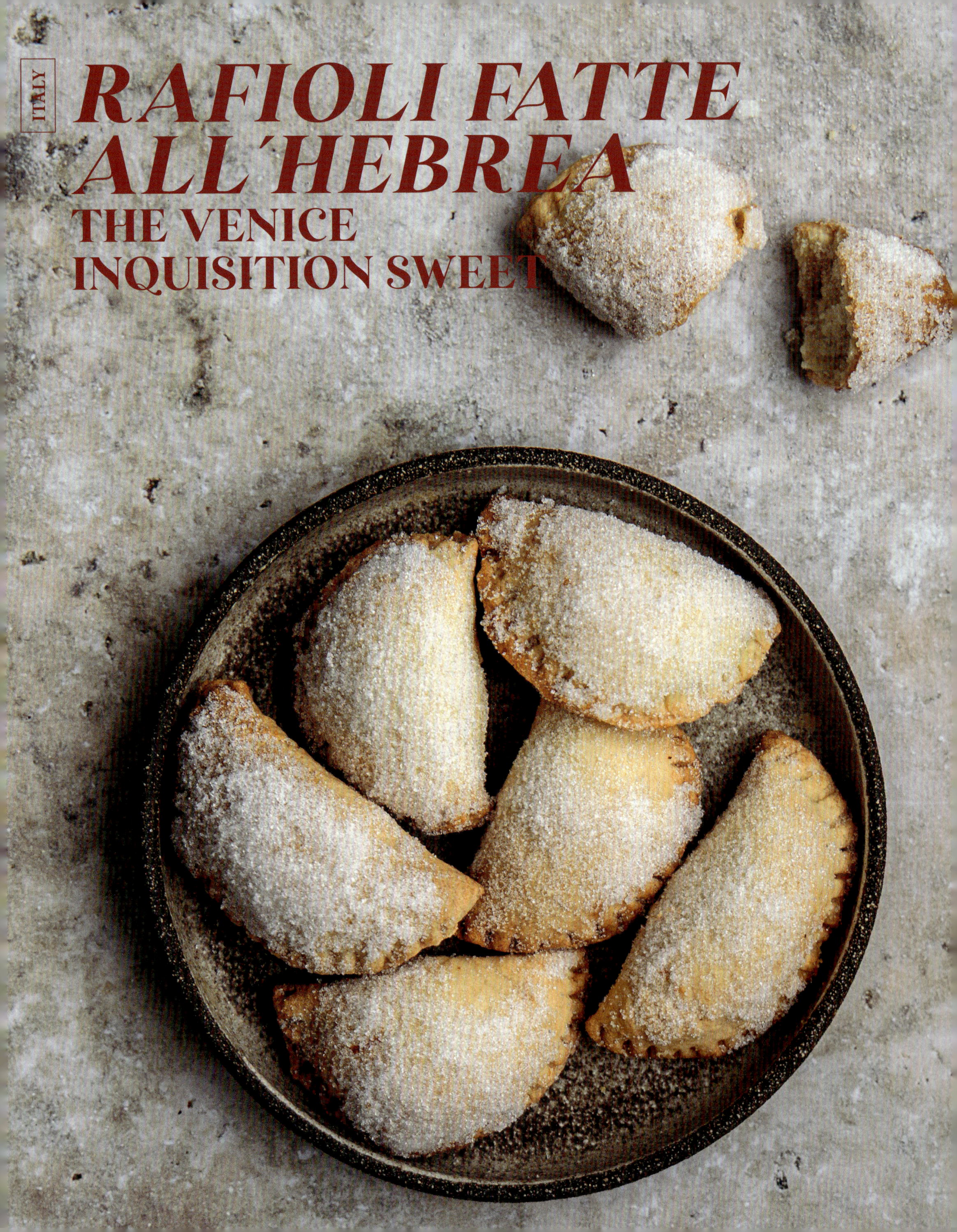

ITALY

RAFIOLI FATTE ALL'HEBREA

THE VENICE INQUISITION SWEET

Along with frittole, rafioli also appear among the sweets consumed by Sephardic Jews in Italy, particularly in Venice. Therefore, it's not surprising that rafioli are mentioned in the 16th-century "Processi del Santo Uffizio di Venezia contro ebrei e giudaizzanti (1579–1586)," from which we read: "that they sent her things like *rafioli*, *fritole* [. . .] that were in the ghetto where the Jews lived"; "things they sent her were *frittole*, *rafioli*, and other things to eat, made in the Jewish way with sugar and honey" (che ghe le mandava deta Alumbra, [. . .] alcune cose come rafioli, fritole [. . .] che stava in geto dove stava li Hebrei; cose che la mandavano erano frittole, rafioli et altrecose da manzar, fatte all'hebrea et cose di zuchero et di miel).

Rafioli are always mentioned alongside other sweets, indicating that they are not savory. Today, rafioli cookies are part of the culinary heritage of the Balkans, and are known as *trogirski rafioli* in Croatia.

SERVES: 12 pieces

TIME: 1 hour 30 minutes

For the dough:

- 2 cups (290 g) flour
- ½ cup (100 g) softened butter
- 2 egg yolks (40 g)
- 2 tbsp (28 g) sugar
- 1 split vanilla pod with scraped seeds
- ¼ cup (52 ml) milk
- 5 tsp (25 ml) rum (optional)
- 2 tbsp (20 ml) oil
- Zest of half an orange
- Zest of half a lemon

For the filling:

- 1 cup + 2 tbsp (130 g) almond flour
- 1 tbsp (20 g) softened butter
- ¼ cup + 1 tbsp (63 g) sugar
- ½ tsp cinnamon
- Zest of half an orange
- Zest of half a lemon
- 3 egg whites (3⅝ oz or 100 g)

Sugar (for dusting)

For the dough:

1. Mix the dry ingredients for the dough in a large bowl. In another bowl, mix the liquids and then add the eggs. Combine the two bowls and add the softened butter, and then the orange and lemon zest. Knead until a dough forms, and let it rest in the refrigerator for 30 minutes.

For the filling:

1. Put all the ingredients, except the egg whites, in a bowl and mix. Separately, whip the egg whites until stiff peaks form, then fold them into the filling mixture. Cover and let it cool in the fridge for about 20 minutes.

2. Preheat the oven to 350°F (180°C).

Assembly:

1. Take the dough out of the refrigerator and roll it out very thin (around 2 mm) on a floured surface. Cut out dough circles using a cookie cutter about 2.5 to 3 inches (6 to 8 cm) in diameter. Place parchment paper on a baking sheet and arrange the dough rounds on the paper.

2. Take a ⅜ oz (10 g) spoonful of filling, place it in the middle of the dough circle, and very lightly moisten the edge of one half of the circles with water. Close it with the other half and press the edges with a fork to seal the rafioli.

3. Bake for about 15 to 17 minutes. Once the cookies have cooled on a rack, take a brush and lightly dip it in water. Quickly moisten the *rafioli* before dusting them with sugar.

PIGNORATI: DE' MEDICI ITALIAN COOKIES
WITH PINE NUTS AND ALMOND PASTE

The text "Stanze di Lorenzo de' Medici" from 1497 contains descriptions of Jewish communities residing in different cities in Italy. It refers to a general gathering of Jews led by their rabbis upon hearing the announcement of the Messiah's arrival within the next twenty years. It emphasizes that Jews do not have their own "territories," and is an anti-Jewish satire that depicts an extravagant banquet (either real or imaginary, or a blend of both) held in honor of the coming Messiah. Among the numerous dishes, as well as orange blossom and rose water, there is mention of "pignorati," also known as "pinochiati"—a sweet pastry made of almond paste and pine nuts, discussed in this context because Jews consumed it. Indeed, there is an ironic play on the verb "pignorare," which means "moneylending" or "to seize," clearly alluding to Jewish professions that were despised by the rest of the population. It further implies the way Jews were perceived by others (as "Pignolo"), namely as stingy and arrogant. *Pignorati* were served at the beginning and end of the banquet, along with almonds, pistachios, raisins, and other sweets. It resembles the modern Italian pastry known today as *pignoli.*

SERVES: 45 pieces

TIME: 40 minutes

For the almond paste:

3 cups (360 g) whole blanched and peeled almonds

3 cups (360 g) icing sugar

2 (60 g) egg whites

1 tsp almond extract

1. Put the whole peeled almonds in the bowl of a food processor and pulse in three batches (approximately 30 seconds each). Once it resembles finely ground almonds, add the icing sugar, almond extract, and ¾ of the lightly beaten egg whites. Pulse again, this time in two batches for about 15 seconds each. Check the consistency. If it appears too dry, add the remaining ¼ of the egg whites. If it looks fine, stop here and do not add the rest of the egg whites. Take a rubber spatula and mix the ingredients until they form a large ball.

2. Shape the almond paste into a log and wrap it in plastic wrap to keep it moist. You can store it in the refrigerator for weeks.

(The recipe continues on the next page).

To make the *pignoli* paste:

8 ounces (220 g) almond paste

1 cup (200 g) sugar

¼ teaspoon salt

2 (60 g) egg whites

3 to 4 drops almond extract

1 cup (145 g) pine nuts

1. Preheat the oven to 375°F (190°C).

2. In the bowl of a food processor, break up the almond paste into small chunks. Add the sugar and salt. Pulse until combined, for about 30 seconds.

3. While pulsing, gradually add the egg whites, little by little (for approximately 30 seconds). Stop adding the egg whites once the mixture forms a sticky dough. You may need to use all the egg whites, depending on the moisture of your almond paste. The dough should be moist and sticky, but still rollable into balls between your hands.

4. Scoop out tablespoons of the dough and roll each one into a 1-inch ball, about 25 grams each. Work quickly as the warmth from your hands can soften the dough.

5. Place the pine nuts on a plate, and line a baking tray with parchment paper.

6. Remove a ⅜ oz (10 g) ball of the dough and roll it in the pine nuts in order to cover it. Try to avoid getting pine nuts on the side that will be in contact with the baking tray. Once the ball is almost fully covered with pine nuts, place it on the parchment paper-lined baking tray. Repeat until all the dough is used.

7. Bake until the pine nuts start to turn golden, approximately 15 minutes. Be careful not to overbake.

8. Allow the *pignorati* to cool on the baking tray for 4 minutes before transferring them to a cooling rack. Enjoy them with a cup of tea flavored with orange blossom water.

FORMIGO: WHITE GARLIC AND ALMOND SOUP
WITH PICOS CAMPEROS BREADSTICKS

The Spanish term "formigo" has an uncertain culinary origin. It resembles the Spanish term "hormigo," which also refers to various dishes made from flour. In the traditional Sephardic cuisine of Thessaloniki, the dish "formiho" is a kind of soup made with crushed almonds and milk that mothers would prepare for their daughters after giving birth.

In the Andalusian culinary heritage, there is a dish called "ajo blanco." It is a cold soup made from crushed almonds, garlic, oil, bread crumbs, vinegar, and salt. It pairs well with the short Andalusian breads known as "picos camperos."

Serves: 4 bowls and 45 breadsticks

Time: 20 minutes (soup) + 40 minutes (breadsticks)

For the soup:

2 cups (250 g) bread crumbs

Water

5.3 oz (150 g) blanched almonds

4 cloves of garlic

6.8 fl oz (20 cl) extra virgin olive oil

1 tbsp Vinegar

1 tsp Salt

Ice cubes

1. In a bowl, place the bread crumbs and add just enough water to cover the bread. Let it soak for thirty minutes, then transfer to a sieve to drain.

2. In a food processor, add the blanched almonds and peeled garlic cloves. Pulse at high speed for fifteen seconds.

3. Add the drained bread crumbs, olive oil, salt, vinegar, and two ice cubes to the food processor, and pulse at high speed for 30 seconds, until the texture becomes creamy.

4. Pour into small bowls and place an ice cube on top; serve cold.

(The recipe continues on the next page).

For the *picos camperos* breadsticks:

Starter (the day before):

⅔ cup (100 g) flour

¼ cup (50 ml) warm water

½ tbsp active dry yeast

1. In a bowl, mix all the ingredients. Then knead by hand and form a ball. Place it in a container, cover it with plastic wrap, and refrigerate overnight.

½ tsp (2 g) active dry yeast

1 cup (200 ml) water

3¼ cup (500 g) flour

Starter (from above)

¼ cup (50 ml) olive oil

1 tsp salt

1. In a small bowl, dissolve the active dry yeast in water. In a large bowl, combine the flour, salt, olive oil, starter, and the diluted yeast-water mixture. Mix everything together for 30 seconds with a spoon until you obtain a rough dough. Remove the dough from the bowl and place it on a floured surface. Knead it by hand until it becomes elastic.

2. Form a ball and lightly coat it with olive oil to prevent the dough from drying out. Place it back in the large bowl and cover it with a cloth. Let it rise at room temperature for 1 hour or until the dough has doubled in size.

3. Take the dough out of the bowl and knead it again. Form a ball and divide it into four equal portions. Divide each portion into pieces the size of a golf ball (1⅛ oz or 30 g) each (this will make it easier to shape the *picos*). Prepare a sheet of parchment paper and place it on a baking tray.

4. Take a small piece of dough and shape it into a ball. Gently flatten and then roll it to obtain a small breadstick about 1.6 inches (4 cm) long. Alternatively, you can roll the dough between your hands. Place the *pico* on the parchment paper, and repeat the process until all the dough is used. Cover with a cloth and let it rest for one hour.

5. Preheat the oven to 350°F (180°C). Place a container of water in the bottom of the oven to humidify the air. Bake for five minutes. Remove the water container and bake for an additional 15 minutes.

6. Turn off the oven, open the oven door, but leave the tray with the *picos* inside. After 10 minutes, remove the tray and let the *picos* cool outside of the oven.

SPAIN

HORMIGO
BREADCRUMB CHICKEN

The word *hormigo* appears several times in the trials of the Spanish Inquisition, but its meaning is unclear. The little information we have to describe this dish, also known as "hormiguillo," is that it is prepared with crumbled bread and resembles the couscous of the Moors. It is likely that it is a dish similar to *rfissa* from Morocco.

SERVES: 6 people

TIME: 2 hours

1 whole chicken, medium

2 tsp salt

5 large onions

½ tsp black pepper

½ tsp ground coriander

3 tbsp olive oil

⅛ cup (23 g) fenugreek seeds

2 tbsp sugar

For the bowl:

⅓ cup (66 g) olive oil

3 tbsp water

For the unleavened flat bread dough:

2 cup (300 g) flour

2 cup (300 g) extra fine semolina

1 tsp salt

2 cups (400 ml) lukewarm water

To decorate:

¼ tsp ground cinnamon

1 tbsp whole almonds

1 tsp cumin seeds

1. Cut the chicken into pieces, keeping the skin on.

2. Take a pot and add salt, sliced onions, black pepper, coriander, and oil. Stir and cook for 2 minutes over high heat. Then, add the cut chicken and add water until the halfway mark on the pot. Cover and cook over low heat for 30 minutes with the lid on.

3. Meanwhile, prepare the unleavened flat bread. In a large bowl, add the flour, salt and lukewarm water. Mix with a large spoon, then once the dough forms into a ball, knead with your hands for 15 minutes. The dough should be smooth. Cover it and put it in the fridge for 15 minutes.

4. Prepare the bowl of olive oil and water, and sprinkle some on the kitchen counter.

5. Take a chunk of dough the size of a golf ball (1⅛ oz or 30 g). Spread it with your fingers on the greased kitchen counter. Roll it out as thin as you can without letting it rip, keeping a disk shape. Be careful; it will be very fragile.

6. Then, fold it: the upper edge to the middle, then the lower edge to the upper edge, to form a strip of dough. Then take the right edge and fold it to the middle, followed by the folding the left edge to the right edge. The result should be a square with several folds. Do the same with the rest of the dough.

7. When all the squares are ready, heat a large greased pan to medium-high heat. Take the first square and use your fingers to spread it out, keeping the square shape and without breaking it, until it is three times the width of a hand. Put in the hot pan and cook for 2 minutes on each side. Once the puff pastry square is cooked, break it up into small pieces. Place these crumbs on a large serving dish.

8. Uncover the pot with the chicken. Take all the chicken pieces and roast them at medium heat in the oven for 10 minutes. Meanwhile, add 2 tbsp sugar to the broth and cook over high heat for 5 minutes, stirring frequently.

9. Then, take a large dish and spread out the flatbread crumbs. Put the chicken pieces on top, and drizzle the chicken and crumbs with all the onion sauce from the pot.

10. Decorate with whole almonds (preferably toasted), and sprinkle with cinnamon and cumin seeds.

YSABEL VELES'S STEWED CHARDS
WITH CHEESE AND BREADCRUMBS

SPAIN

Ysabel Veles was a new Christian from Almazán when her father died. A trial record from 1501 recounts that "a witness says that the day the aforementioned's [Ysabel, wife of Luis Veles] father died, he was a new Christian, they brought from the aforementioned's [Ysabel] house a stewed pot [*olla guisada*] of chard with cheese and breadcrumbs, and the aforementioned [Ysabel] and her husband and other relatives ate it at a low table, in a *portalejo* [a porch in front of the main entrance], where they did not usually eat, near the door, and they also brought from the house of the above the bowls [*escudillas*] in which they ate; and that they ate nothing else. And that before she died, the aforementioned ate at a high table that they had." What this text is describing is a funeral banquet, held at the death of a convert, where people eat at a low table.

For additional context, we read in the records of the Inquisition in Mexico, New Spain from 1646 about the consumption of "aveluz." These were hard-boiled eggs eaten without salt by the family members of the deceased to commemorate the pain of death.

SERVES: 2 people

TIME: 30 minutes

3 cups (about 250 g) Swiss chard (whichever color you prefer)

1 onion (yellow, white or red), sliced

1 clove garlic, slices

1 tbsp olive oil

½ cup (125 ml) vegetable broth

½ cup (100 ml) heavy cream

½ cup (50 g) Swiss cheese, grated

⅔ cup (90 g) breadcrumbs

1 tsp salt

1 tsp black pepper

2 tsp olive oil, for frying the bread crumbs

1. Wash the Swiss chard thoroughly and remove the end of the stems. Cut the leaves into bite-sized pieces. In a large pot (preferably a clay pot), heat the olive oil over medium heat. Add the slices onion and garlic, and sauté for about 3 minutes until they become translucent. Add the Swiss chard leaves to the pot and cook until they wilt, stirring occasionally, for about 1 minute.

2. Pour in the vegetable broth and bring to a simmer. Cover the pot and let it cook for about 2 minutes, or until the chard is tender.

3. Uncover the pot and stir in the heavy cream. Season with salt and pepper to taste. Cook for an additional 1 minute. Sprinkle with the grated Swiss cheese and cover.

4. In a separate pan, pour 2 tsp os olive oil and fry the breadcrumbs over medium heat until they're golden brown. Serve the Swiss chard stew hot, preferably in clay bowls, and sprinkled with fried breadcrumbs on top.

MAIMONIDES

Maimonides: "Bread should be eaten with almonds and seedless raisins."

Maimonides, in an text preserved in the Geniza, recommends that bread should be eaten with a syrup made of good, fresh dates mixed with water

Maimonides, as mentioned in a late Geniza source, reported that eight imprisoned people got cheese for both morning and evening meals, with bread.

MOROCCO

ḤARĪRA: FLOUR SOUP

This soup is reminiscent of the Moroccan soup that Jews prepare to break the fast of Yom Kippur today, and that Muslims eat to break the fast with each dinner during the month of Ramadan. Flour plays a key role in the recipe and it cannot be substituted; it serves to thicken the soup and give it a smooth texture. The *ḥarīra* recipe known today has tomatoes as a main ingredient. Consequently, it is not surprising that the first cookbook written in Spain, which dates back to the 13th century, the *Kitāb al ṭabīh*, does not mention a recipe for *ḥarīra* because tomatoes only arrived in Spain in the 16th century. One might think, on this basis, that this soup did not exist at that time, but that is not exactly the case. Maimonides, who settled in the Moroccan city of Fes in the 12th century, refers to the preparation of *ḥarīra* (חרירה) in his book *On Asthma*, which is a collection of health recommendations that were meant to treat the asthma of his anonymous patient. *On Asthma* is known from three Hebrew translations and two in Latin. Professor Gerrit Bos notes in his translation of the book that *ḥarīra* refers to a "A kind of soup of flour."

The first version I offer here does not contain tomatoes and may look like what *ḥarīra* was in the 12th century; it is only made with food available in the Old World at that time.

SERVES: 6 persons

TIME: 1 hour

---

1 large celery stalk, chopped very thinly

2 white onions, chopped very thinly

1 cup fresh cilantro, diced

½ cup olive oil

1 tbsp salt

1 tbsp turmeric

2 tsp ground ginger

6 cups (1.2 L) chicken or vegetable broth

10 strands of saffron or 1 tsp yellow food coloring

½ cup green lentils, washed and soaked in water for at least 3 hours

1 cup (200 g) chickpeas, cooked (or canned)

1 egg beaten

½ cup (70 g) flour

½ cup (100 g) Water

For topping the soup:

1 fresh lemon for juice

½ cup fresh cilantro leaves

---

1. In a large pot, add the olive oil and the chopped vegetables. Cook for about 10 minutes over medium heat until they are translucent. Add the salt, saffron, ground turmeric and ground ginger. Stir and cook for 2 more minutes. Then, add the broth, the soaked lentils and cooked chickpeas. Cover and simmer for about 35 minutes over medium heat, stirring frequently.

2. In a small bowl beat an egg. Then, add it to the pot and stir with a large spoon until you see that the white and yolk are cooked; it will make whisps of egg in the soup.

3. In a bowl, add the flour, and then add the water slowly, stirring constantly, until there are no lumps. Add this to the soup. It serves to thicken it and gave it a smooth texture. Stir for about 3 minutes over the heat until it thickens.

4. With a ladle, pour the *ḥarīra* into small bowls. Sprinkle each bowl with the fresh cilantro leaves and squeeze a few drops of fresh lemon over the top. Serve hot.

MOROCCO

MODERN *ḤARĪRA*

TOMATO AND FLOUR SOUP

Serves: 6 people

Time: 1 hour

1 large celery stalk, chopped very thinly (do not use the leaves)

1 white or yellow onion, chopped very thinly

5 big ripe tomatoes, peeled (or 1 can of tomato puree, with small tomato chunks)

5 tbsp tomato paste

1 cup fresh cilantro, diced

¼ cup olive oil

1 cup (200 g) fresh steak, cut into small pieces (optional)

1 tbsp salt

1 tbsp turmeric

2 tsp ground ginger

6 cups (1.2 L) chicken or vegetable broth

10 strands of saffron or 1 tsp yellow food coloring

½ cup green lentils, washed and soaked in water for at least 3 hours

1 cup of chickpeas, cooked (or canned)

¼ cup (25 g) short vermicelli noodles

1 egg beaten

¼ cup (30 g) flour

¼ cup (50 g) Water

For topping the soup:

1 fresh lemon for juice

½ cup fresh cilantro leaves

1. Blanch the tomatoes, peel them, and cut them into very small chunks (or use canned tomato puree).

2. In a large pot, add the olive oil, the chopped vegetables, and the tomatoes. Cook for about 10 minutes over medium heat until they are translucent. Add the steak (optional), salt, saffron, ground turmeric and ground ginger. Stir and cook for 2 more minutes. Then, add the broth, the soaked lentils and cooked chickpeas. Cover and simmer for about 35 minutes over medium heat, stirring frequently.

3. Uncover and add the short vermicelli noodles. Cook for about 3 minutes.

4. In a small bowl beat an egg. Then, add it to the pot and stir with a large spoon until you see that the white and yolk are cooked; it will make whisps of egg in the soup.

5. In a bowl, add the flour, and then add the water slowly, stirring constantly, until there are no lumps. Add this to the soup. It serves to thicken it and gave it a smooth texture. Stir for about 3 minutes over the heat until it thickens.

6. With a ladle, pour the *ḥarīra* into small bowls. Sprinkle each bowl with the fresh cilantro leaves and squeeze a few drops of fresh lemon over the top. Serve hot.

MAIMONIDES and bread practices in Egypt

Maimonides reveals information related to bread consumption in Egypt while he was living there. In his medical treatise *On Asthma*, he says that "Among the foods also eaten by the people of Egypt is bread seasoned with vinegar and skimmed honey or with vinegar and sugar and barley gruel. One should always have on one's table, especially in winter-time, squill vinegar, and one should dip some morsel [of bread] in it."

THE PORTRAIT OF LOZANA: THE LUSTY ANDALUSIAN WOMAN

RETRATO DE

la Loçana: andaluza: en lengua española: muy clarissima. Cõpuesto en Roma.

El qual Retrato demuestra lo que en Roma passaua y contiene munchas mas cosas que la Celestina.

Aldonza is *Lozana Andaluza*'s main character (*The Portrait of Lozana: The Lustry Andalusian woman*). This work of literature was composed in Rome in 1524 and is attributed to Francisco Delicado who was a Jewish *converso*. "The Portrait of Lozana" was printed in Venice four to six years later. It tells the story of a Jewish converted woman who arrived to Rome with her husband before the sack of the city in 1527. The *Lozana andaluza* narrates the tale of a young Andalusian prostitute from Córdoba who resided in Granada, Jerez de la Frontera, Carmona, and ultimately Seville.

Food is an omnipresent theme in "The Portrait of Lozana." As a crypto-Jew, Aldonza hides her customs, included her culinary practices. But her Spanish background allows the lector and also her female crypto-Jewish neighbors to understand who she is in a context where their religion must remain hidden. Aldonza can only be recognized as a Jew by how she behaves, including how she cooks. Silence and secrecy are essential for survival.

"The Portrait of Lozana" includes a number of Jewish dishes from al-Andalus, while testifying to the distrust that reigned among old and new Christians, as well as between Jewish converts themselves. Conversos were afraid of being condemned for betraying their continued Judaism through their practices, particularly those related to food.

The many dishes she lists are preparations that her grandmother taught her. It is an enlightening list, and includes dishes and ingredients cited in the narratives of the trials of the Spanish Inquisition nearly a century before, as well as (according to some) in Mexican texts. Her grandmother passed on to her the art of cooking and, thanks to her, Aldonza explains that she learned how to "make *fideos* [thin pasta/vermicelli], small stuffed pastries [*empanadillas*], couscous with chickpeas [alcuzcuzú con garbanzos] [. . .] and round meatballs made with green cilantro [*albondiguillas redondas y apretadas con culantro verde.*]." She praises the cooking talents of her grandmother, renowned in all of Andalusia, and adds that she also knows how to prepare "*hojuelas, pestiños, rosquillas de alfaxor, testones* of hempseed [*cañamones*] and sesame [*ajonjolí*], *nuégados* [small cakes], *xopaipas* [pastry disks pan-fried in oil], puff pastry [*hojaldres*], twisted *hormigos* with oil [*hormigos torcidos con aceite*], *talvinas, zahínas* and turnips without lard and with cumin [*nabos sin tocino y con comino*], Murcian cabbage with caraway [*col murciana con alcaravea*], and the resting pot [*olla reposada*], a more delicious one no man has ever tasted. And the *boronía* . . . and eggplant casserole *mojíes* [*cazuela de berenjenas mojíes*], [and] . . . stew of salted, dried fish [*cazuelas de pescado cecial*].

All of the dishes in the text are presented in this chapter.

FIDEOS: TUNA WITH VERMICELLI NOODLES

This recipe for thin and short pasta *fideos* is a classic of contemporary Spanish cuisine. Maimonides mentions them in his work *On Asthma* as well as in the *Regimen of Health*. Referred to as *itriya*, *tria* (*aletria* in Spanish), these dry and short pasta noodles have been prepared on a large scale since the 12th century, not far from Palermo in Sicily. The trade of these "vermicelli" is documented to have reached countries in the Mediterranean basin during that time and afterwards. As for their consumption, these noodles are included in dishes presented in the first Iberian cookbook that explicitly contains Jewish recipes, the *Kitāb al-ṭabīḫ*, under the name *fidāwīsh*. It was during this century that this type of pasta, native to al-Andalus, was created. Archives testify to a flourishing trade of these noodles in the Mediterranean basin since the 14th century, particularly in Sardinia, where Jewish merchants traded. Its capital, Cagliari, was then the main place of production and sale of *fideos* (also called *fideus* in northeastern Spain). Significant deliveries of these noodles from merchant ships to cities known for the presence of Jewish communities such as Barcelona and Valencia are documented. The inquisitorial archives of the Canary Islands also attest to the receipt of *fideos* among their goods between 1751 and 1796. The diasporic dimension of Sephardic history explains the preparation, consumption, and sale of *fideos* (*fidāwīsh*) among Jewish families in the city of Fes in Morocco in the 15th century. Today, *fideos* are consumed by both Sephardic Jews and non-Jews, but Moroccan Jews in particular prepare them for celebrating weddings, circumcisions, bar/bat mitzvahs, and for Shavuot.

The importance of the role of Jews in trade is well established. Whether it was textiles or consumables, the transport of goods was a lucrative activity where Jews, whether conversos, from Cyprus, the Mediterranean coasts (Genoa, Sicily, etc.) or the Atlantic coasts (Canary Islands, Recife, Veracruz, Bahia, Porto Alegre, Lisbon, etc.), played a significant role. The varied taste of Jewish cuisines is explained in part by the spice trade, which was an integral part of their activity. Spices were used in all types of dishes, including unleavened bread.

Here is a reconstruction of the dish, albeit including ingredients unknown to the area at the time such as green peppers and tomatoes.

SERVES: 4–5 people

TIME: 30 minutes

½ cup (100 g) olive oil

5 garlic cloves, chopped

3 tomatoes, chopped

1 onion, sliced

3 green peppers, sliced

3 tsp salt

3 cups (400 g) short vermicelli noodles

2 saffron strands (or ⅛ tsp food coloring)

½ cup (280 g) tuna (fresh or canned)

1 handful of mint, chopped

6 cups (1.5 l) water

---

1. In a pan, pour the olive oil, garlic, chopped tomatoes, onion, green peppers, and salt. Fry for 5 minutes. Add the vermicelli noodles and the saffron, mix well, and cook slowly for 2 minutes.

2. Boil the water separately and then pour it in the pan. Add the chopped mint and tuna. Mix carefully. You want a little broth in this dish. Cook over low heat for 15 minutes, and serve hot.

ALDONZA'S *EMPANADILLAS*

In Spanish, the suffixes "-ita" or "-illa" refer to something that is small. Using the term "empanadillas," Aldonza refers here to small *empanadas* (savory pastries with a crust). I am presenting a recipe for these small *empanadillas*, made with ingredients commonly consumed in Andalusia at the end of the fifteenth century, since the ancestral territory of Aldonza's grandmother is Cordova.

Serves: 25 pieces

Time: 45 minutes

For the dough:

3½ cups (490 g) flour

1 tsp (5 g) baking powder

½ tsp salt

7 tbsp (100 g) margarine

¾ cup (180 g) water

1. In a large bowl, combine the flour, baking powder, salt and margarine. Then, add the water little by little. Knead by hand for about five minutes, until you have a smooth and homogeneous dough. Form the dough into a ball, put it in a plastic bag, and cool it in the fridge for about 30 minutes (or overnight).

For the olive filling:

1 tbsp olive oil + ¼ cup olive oil

1 medium onion diced very finely

2 cloves garlic chopped

½ cup green olives (without pits)

½ cup black olives (without pits)

Instructions:

1. In a frying pan, pour 1 tbsp olive oil, the onion and garlic chopped very thinly. Cook for about one minute. Let it cool.

2. Over a chopping board, chop all the olives into chunks. And the salt and the dried thyme. Add the onion-garlic mixture from the pan, and mix with a spoon.

Making the *empanadillas*:

1. Line a parchment paper on a baking tray and flour it lightly, and place two other parchment papers on your counter.

½ cup purple olives (without pits; alternatively, use an additional ¼ cup black and ¼ green olives)

½ teaspoon salt

¼ cup dried thyme

Neutral oil for frying

2. Take the dough and cut it in half to make two balls. Put the first one on a parchment paper, cover it with the second parchment paper, and roll it between the two sheets until it is about ⅛ of an inch thick. Remove the paper from the top.

3. Use a cookie cutter to cut rounds of dough about 4-inches (10 cm) in diameter.

4. Place a round on the parchment paper in the baking tray. Take a small bowl of water and, using your finger, lightly water the outside edge of half of the circle. Fill the middle of the round with one tablespoon of filling, and fold the other half of the round over the top of the filling, pressing the edges of the dough to seal it. You can use a fork, pressing it over the edges, to seal it better.

5. Or, for a more aesthetic way to seal the *empanada*, use your fingers: With the arched edge of the empanada facing left, place the tip of your left index finger at the top corner of the sealed edge (with the palm of your hand facing up). Using the thumb of your right hand, push the dough from the right side of your left index finger over to the left until it covers the tip of your finger, and press a little once the dough touches the other side of your index finger. Repeat for all of the empanadas.

6. Cover the finished empanadas with a towel and cool them in the fridge for 30 minutes.

7. Take a frying pan and pour neutral oil up to about half of an inch deep, and heat it over medium heat.

8. Take the empanadillas and carefully fry them for about two minutes on each side. With a skimmer, take them out and put them on a towel paper to cool and drain.

9. Then can be dip into a pomegranate molasse and eaten with fresh goat cheese or labneh (cf. recipe p. 352) and a salad made with spinach leaves.

*See the photo on the next page.

COUSCOUS
WITH CHICKPEAS

In Italy, couscous was associated with Sephardic Jews from North Africa until the 16th century. This was particularly the case in Palermo (Sicily), a city that had a peak population of half a million Muslims, as well as small Jewish communities dating back to antiquity. Some of these Sephardic Jews had immigrated to this new Mediterranean territory where the three religions coexisted until the Norman invasion in the early 11th century. That's how couscous was adopted in Italy. While it is true that the first Italian recipe for couscous can be found in a culinary manuscript from the early 16th century copied in southern Italy, the "Manoscritto Lucano," it is entirely plausible that it had been consumed since at least the late 15th century. It is also worth noting that couscous is mentioned in a few trials of the Spanish Inquisition in the 16th and 17th centuries because eating couscous was considered evidence that a person was Muslim. In "The Portrait of Lozana," Aldonza's cooking practices reveal her religious identity: the act is more powerful than words. Beatriz, one of the crypto-Jewish women, says: "Let's tell [her] that we want to twist [*torcer*] *hormigos* or make couscous and, if she knows how to twist them, this way we will see that she is one of us, and [we will see] if she twists [*tuerce*] with water or oil." From this we understand that Sephardi women, from Spain, used to prepare and eat couscous. But here the most important point is the way they prepared it, and the food they used to make it. If Aldonza hadn't twisted the semolina with water and oil, she may not have been identified as Jewish.

SERVES: 4–6 people

TIME: 3 hours

For the meat:

6–8 pieces (2¾ lb/1.5 kg) of fatty lamb meat with bones (shoulder, neck, etc.)

6 tbsp olive oil

1 tbsp salt

½ cup (100 g) raisins

Water (to cover the meat)

For the couscous semolina:

4½ cups (1 kg) fine or medium wheat semolina couscous

2 tbsp + 1 tbsp fine salt (3 tbsp in total)

⅕ cup + 2 tbsp (130 g) 2 neutral oil (10 tbsp in total)

3 strands of saffron

6 cups water (2 cups + 2 cups + 2 cups)

For the vegetables:

2 white onions, sliced

15 carrots

6 turnips

2 pieces of squash

10 zucchinis

1½ cup (250 g) cooked canned chickpeas

½ cup (50 g) raisins (golden if possible)

For the spices:

1 tbsp turmeric

10 strands of saffron

1 tbsp ginger powder

1 tbsp coriander powder

1 tbsp caraway powder

1 tbsp cumin powder

1 tbsp nutmeg powder

¼ tbsp clove powder

1 tbsp pepper powder

Preparation of the spiced meat and vegetables:

1. In a couscous pot, pour in the olive oil (6 tbsp) and add the meat. Add all the spices and 1 cup of raisins. Cook over high heat for 5 minutes, turning the meat. Add salt (1 tbsp) and pepper (1 tbsp).

2. Add the sliced onions to the pot, along with the saffron. Mix well, and then add water. It should cover the meat by at least 2 cm (almost an inch). Cover and let it cook over medium heat while preparing the vegetables. The water should simmer. Alternatively, you can use a pressure cooker and cook it for about 45 minutes.

3. Wash and peel the carrots, squash, and turnips. Wash and peel the zucchinis, leaving some strips of skin. Cut all the vegetables in half lengthwise. Place them in a bowl, cover, and set aside.

Preparation of the wheat semolina:

1. Take a large wide-bottomed dish and pour the dry couscous semolina into it. Add the salt (2 tbsp), neutral oil (5 tbsp), and saffron. Mix with your fingers. Gradually add 2 cups (400 ml) of water. Mix with your hands until the wheat semolina has absorbed all the water. It should not form lumps. Cover with a cloth.

Couscous preparation:

1. Uncover the pot of meat. There should be steam escaping. If not, increase the heat; it should boil slightly.

2. Place the couscous basket on top of the pot. Gently take the wheat semolina and place it in the couscous basket. There should be no steam escaping between the pot and the top of the basket. You can use aluminum foil placed between the two parts to prevent steam leakage because the steam from the meat broth will make the couscous semolina swell. Once all the wheat semolina is in the basket, make sure it is evenly distributed and let it cook for about thirty minutes without covering.

3. After thirty minutes, steam will escape from the semolina. Take the basket and turn it over into the dish that was used to mix the semolina the first time. Be careful, it's very hot!

4. Add salt (1 tbsp) and oil (5 tbsp), and mix with a large spoon. Gradually add 2 cups (400 ml) of water, moistening the semolina everywhere. Mix and fluff it up with your hands. Make sure the semolina is sufficiently salted, mix it thoroughly, and take care that no lumps form.

5. Before putting the wheat semolina back into the basket, check that the broth level is high enough, and that the broth is sufficiently salty. It should cover three-quarters of the meat. If it doesn't, add hot water.

6. Delicately place in the broth and on top of the meat (in the following order): carrots, turnips, pieces of red squash, zucchinis, chickpeas, and raisins. Put the couscous basket back on top of the couscous pot and place the semolina back into the basket. Let it cook for about 15 minutes over medium heat.

7. After fifteen minutes, turn the basket over again into the dish used for preparing the semolina. Take a ladle of meat broth and pour it evenly over the semolina. Mix and fluff it up with your hands. Gradually pour the 2 remaining cups of water over the semolina while stirring it, and put the semolina back into the basket. Cook for another 10 minutes.

8. Finally, turn the semolina over one last time into the preparation dish. Be careful, it's very hot! Fluff it up with a fork.

Presentation:

1. Take a large serving dish, and spread the semolina on it, making it slightly higher around the edges. Using a large spoon, take the cooked vegetables from the couscous pot and place them on top of the semolina, starting with those on the outer edge of the dish. As soon as you uncover the meat, take the pieces of meat and place them in the center of the dish. Cover with the remaining vegetables, trying to alternate the different varieties. Once there are no more vegetables, use a slotted spoon to retrieve the chickpeas and raisins from the bottom of the broth. Arrange them in the dish. With a ladle, distribute the broth over the semolina, starting from the edges and finishing in the center.

2. The dish is best enjoyed very hot on the same day, but it remains excellent the next day when the semolina has fully absorbed the broth.

SMALL GREEN MEATBALLS
WITH CILANTRO

This dish is referred to as "albondiguillas redondas y apretadas con culantro verde" in the novel.

SERVES: 25 meatballs

TIME: 45 minutes

1 pound (450 g) chicken breast

¼ tsp black pepper

1 tsp salt

2 cups (100 g) chopped cilantro

10 chopped mint leaves

1 tbsp fresh or dried oregano or za'atar

1tsp ground cumin

2 spring onions strands, the green parts, chopped

¼ cup flour, to coat the meatballs

¾ cup (150 g) neutral oil, for frying

1. Wash the cilantro and finely dice it, including the stems, as that's where all the flavor is. Place them in a large bowl. Add the chopped mint leaves, salt, black pepper, fresh or dried oregano or za'atar, and cumin. Stir to mix the ingredients and set aside.

2. Take the chicken breasts and tenderize them by pounding them flat. Cut it roughly into smaller pieces, put the chicken in a blender, and blend for 20 seconds until it is ground.

3. Combine the chicken with the cilantro mixture thoroughly and place in the freezer for 15 minutes.

4. Heat oil in a frying pan over medium heat. Put the ¼ cup flour in a small bowl, and form small balls from the meat mixture; each one should weigh about 1⅛ oz (30 g), the size of a golf ball. Roll each meatball in the flour to coat it, and remove any excess of flour.

5. When you have enough meatballs to fit the pan (leaving space in between them), fry them for 3 minutes without moving them. Then, flip them over and cook for another 3 minutes until golden brown. Place the cooked meatballs on a paper towel to remove any excess oil.

6. Repeat the process to make all the remaining meatballs, and serve with a green salad and fried eggplants.

HOJUELAS: ROLLED AND FRIED PASTRY FOR ESTHER

This dish takes us on a long journey from Spain, to Italy, to Argentina. Aldonza learned how to make hojuelas from her Spanish Andalusian grandmother. Once she arrived in Italy, she shared this culinary practice with the Jewish communities there.

Today, all Sephardim are familiar with these rolled thin strips of pastry that are quickly fried and deliciously covered in sugar; they are impossibly tender and will melt in your mouth. They are known by many names (*fijuelas*, *fazuelos*, *hojuelas*), and are mainly prepared during the Jewish holiday of Purim.

For the *hojuelas* recipe, please see page 44.

PESTIÑOS
DEEP-FRIED PASTRY FROM ANDALUSIA

This Andalusian pastry, fried and soaked in honey, has the peculiar feature of being shaped like an ear. This recalls the "rekikim" (cakes) made from dough in the shape of ears, cooked in oil, and dipped in honey, thus called "ears."

The *Diccionario Crítico y Etimológico Castellano e Hispánico*, by Corominas and Pascual, mentions the year 1543 as the first appearance of the word "pestiño." It states that there is a direct connection between "prestiño" and the Occitan word "prestinh," which means "bakery" or "panadería" in Spanish, a place where bread and cakes are made. The etymology of the word likely derives from the Latin "pristinum," meaning the workplace of the baker. Therefore, this pastry is called "prestiño" in Castilian, which is supported by its presence in the *Lozana andaluza* novel. We have to wait until the *Diccionario de Autoridades* (1726–1739) to find the definition of "prestiño" as a "kind of dough fried in a pan, made with flour, eggs, cinnamon, in the shape of little tubes, which are fried in lard or oil, then glazed with warm creamed honey, and molded into little mounds in the shape of a pineapple or other things." The definition of "prestiño" provided by the *Diccionario de Autoridades* also brings to mind "gañote," a cylinder-shaped wafer that is one of the culinary specialties of Seville.

½ cup (100 g) neutral oil

2 tsp (10 g) anise seeds

3 oranges to make about ½ cup (100 g) fresh orange juice

½ cup (100 ml) white wine (optional)

1 tsp salt

3¼ cup (500 g) flour (if you don't use wine, put only 2¾ cup (400 g) flour)

¾ cup (200 g) honey

2 tbsp water (or orange blossom water)

1. In a sauce pan add the neutral oil and anis seeds. Cook for 2 minutes over medium heat, moving the frying pan constantly. Don't burn the seeds. Set aside to cool.

2. Make approximatively ½ cup (100 ml) fresh orange juice and add the white wine and the salt to it. Take a big bowl and mix the oil/anise seeds with the juice/wine. Add the flour, mix, and knead the dough for about 15 minutes. Cover and cool for about 30 minutes in the refrigerator.

3. Take the dough and roll it out with a rolling pin until it is about an inch (2 cm) thick. Use a pizza cutter to make squares as large as your hand (or smaller if you prefer).

4. In a sauce pan, put the honey and 2 tbsp water (or orange blossom water) over medium-low heat. Don't boil it!

5. Using your fingers, put a little water on two opposite corners of a dough square, then pull the two corners up and pinch them together; this should form a cylindrical space below where you connected the two corners.

6. Heat a frying pan over medium heat and fry each pestiños for about 4 minutes (2 minutes in each side). Once you remove the *pestiño* from the frying pan, put it in the saucepan with the honey and use a spoon to cover it completely with honey. Remove them a skimmer and put them on a plate.

7. You can add sprinkles to them if desired. These are delicious with a cup of tea.

HEMP NOUGATINE (BRITTLE)

Aldonza mentions the sweet treat called "testones de cañamones," which is a specialty of Villahermosa, a city located at the gates of Andalusia and about 200 km from Cordoba. It is a type of nougatine that can also be prepared between two sheets of wafer. It is mainly consumed during the Christian holiday of All Saints' Day, but it also seems to be connected to Jewish practices, based on a trial document drafted by the Spanish Inquisition. The document states that in 1484, Juan Sánchez Exarch, a converso from Teruel, was denounced for eating brown nougatine on the occasion of Sukkot (which usually falls in October): "They made huts with branches [for Sukkot] [. . .] where they did all the ceremonies that Jews used to do in those days, eating inside those and making collations with candy nougat and other thing."

SERVES: 4 people

TIME: 30 minutes

2 cups (250 g) hemp seeds (alternatively, you can use 1 cup [125 g] of almonds (with the peel) and 1 cup [125 g] of walnuts or hazelnuts)

¼ cup (50 ml) water

2½ cups (250 g) sugar

⅛ cup (30 g) honey

½ tsp fresh lemon juice

1 tbsp sesame seeds (golden or white)

2 wafer sheets (20 cm by 20 cm) (optional)

1. Preheat the oven to 350°F (180°C), and spread the nuts in a single layer on a baking tray.

2. Toast them for about 15 minutes. Be careful not to burn them; they should turn golden brown. Remove them from the oven and set them aside.

3. In a saucepan over medium heat, add the water, sugar, honey, and lemon juice. Stir constantly with a wooden spoon until you obtain golden caramel. Add the nuts to the caramel and continue stirring carefully with the spoon until the caramel browns slightly. All the nuts need to be covered with caramel. Add the sesame seeds.

4. Take a square baking pan about 8-inches by 8-inches (20 cm/20 cm). If you're using a wafer sheet, put it at the bottom of the baking pan. Pour all the brown nougatine in. It should be about half an inch (1 cm) thick. Be careful, it is very hot! Cover quickly with another wafer sheet and press. The surface needs to be flat. If you prefer making sticks, wait for 1 hour and flip the baking pan upside down. Take a long sharp knife and cut the brown nougatine into rectangles.

5. If you're not using wafer sheets, lightly grease the square baking pan with neutral oil and pour in the brown nougatine. Let it cool for at least two hours.

SESAME SEED NOUGATINE (BRITTLE)

As for the "testones de sésamo" mentioned above, this recipe makes a thin and sweet sesame nougat.

SERVES: 4 people

TIME: 30 minutes

¾ cup (150 g) fine white sugar

¼ cup (30 g) of white sesame seeds

Wafer sheets (optional)

1. Take a tray (or a silicone mat) and place a parchment paper sheet on top. If you are using wafer sheets, replace the parchment paper with the wafer sheets. Prepare another sheet of parchment paper (or wafer sheet) of the same size, and have a rolling pin nearby.

2. Take a saucepan and pour in the white sugar, spreading it evenly in a single layer. Do not move the saucepan once you've added the sugar. Heat over medium-high heat. As the sugar melts, caramel will start to form. Be careful, as the mixture can burn! When the caramel turns golden (if using a candy thermometer, it will be done at 320–338°F or 160–170°C), remove the saucepan from the heat and add the sesame seeds. Using a wooden spatula (not plastic as it could melt), stir for 30 seconds to coat all the seeds.

3. Immediately pour the mixture onto the parchment paper (or wafer sheet) and cover it quickly with the other sheet of parchment paper (or wafer sheet). If you are using a wafer sheet on top, still cover it with parchment paper to avoid piercing the sheet when flattening the nougatine with a rolling pin. Roll it out with a rolling pin to obtain a thin and uniform nougatine.

4. Wait for five minutes and gently remove the top parchment paper. At this stage, you can still shape the nougatine with your fingers into specific forms (using cookie cutters or a pastry wheel), but be cautious as the caramel is still very hot!

5. You can store it in a sealed container in the refrigerator for a long time. Use this sesame nougatine in a salad, on top of ice cream, or simply enjoy it as a treat on its own.

NUÉGADOS
ORANGE AND HONEY FRIED PASTRY

This dessert is part of the culinary heritage of Spain, particularly of the Northwest. What very few people know is that consuming this delicious dish led to the death of Spanish Jews and conversos, such as Diego Arias from Medina de Campo (1490), who was reported for gifting "nuégados" and other fried pastries. Often made with breadcrumbs instead of flour, the dish is also mentioned in the book *La Lozana Andaluza* by Spanish converso Francisco Delicado: in the story, the Andalusian conversa Aldonza arrives in Rome after fleeing the Spanish Inquisition and tells women how she learned to prepare nuégados from her grandmother. Today, there is a fried pastry from Italy called "pignolatta" and "pignoccata," and in the Campania region "struffoli." It looks exactly like the Spanish *nuegados*. In Monterrey, Mexico, renowned for its Sephardic Jewish community established in the late 16th century, a fried and honey pastry closely resembling nuegados is known as "muéganos."

For the recipe for *nuegados*, please see the instructions for *pignolata al miele* on page 245.

CORDOVAN *SOPAIPAS*
SMALL FRIED CAKES

Aldonza called these "xopaipas," but this dish remains the same to this day. Sopaipas are typical from Cordova, the town where Aldonza came from. These small round discs of unsweetened dough are fried and dipped in honey. As an evidence of the food's popularity in Jewish culture, sopaipas has spread beyond the Andalusian and Mediterranean borders. In Chile, *sopaipas* can be sweet but also eaten as a bread dipped in "pebre" (a sauce of chili pepper, onion, garlic and coriander).

SERVES: 15 pieces

TIME: 1 hour

½ cup (100 ml) water

1 tbsp of olive oil

1 tsp of salt

1 cup (150 g) flour

1 tsp of baking powder

Syrup:

5 tbsp (100 ml) of honey

1 small sprig of rosemary

⅛ cup (25 ml) water

Neutral oil for frying

1. In a small saucepan, combine the water, olive oil, and salt. Heat the mixture on low-medium heat without boiling it.

2. Take a large bowl, add the flour and baking powder, mix well, and add the water-oil-salt mixture. Stir with a spoon for two minutes, then knead by hand for 10 minutes. The dough should be smooth and free of lumps. Place the dough back into the bowl, cover, and let it rest in the refrigerator for thirty minutes.

3. Punch down the dough to release any air bubbles and divide it into small portions (around the size of a golf ball; 1⅛ oz or 30 g). On a floured surface, flatten each portion with your hands or a rolling pin to form round discs, about ¼ inch thick.

4. Heat a generous amount of olive oil in a large frying pan or deep pot over medium heat. Fry the sopaipas in the hot oil for about 1–2 minutes on each side, or until they turn golden brown and puffy. Remove the sopaipas from the oil and drain them on a paper towel-lined plate to remove excess oil.

Instructions for the syrup:

1. In a small saucepan, combine the honey, rosemary sprig, and water. Place the saucepan over low heat and stir the mixture until the honey is completely melted and well combined with the water.

2. Allow the syrup to simmer gently for about 5 minutes to infuse the rosemary flavor into the syrup. Remove the saucepan from the heat and let the syrup cool down. Once cooled, remove the rosemary sprig from the syrup.

3. Serve the sopaipas warm with the syrup poured over them.

4. Today, Andalusians eat sopaipas for breakfast or a snack, sometimes dipped in thick chocolate. Milk and tea pair well with sopaipas.

HOJALDRES
THE SIAM SQUASH PUFF PASTRY

"Cabello de ángel" is a sweet preparation made from the pulp of the Siam squash, sugar, cinnamon, and lemon. It resembles jam and is a typical delicacy from the city of Cordova. Today, it is mainly consumed sandwiched between two layers of puff pastry to make the famous "Pastel cordobés." It is not easy to find Siam squash, so the simplest option is to buy this jam commercially (although it is much better when made from scratch!).

For the puff pastry:

¾ cup (150 g) butter, at room temperature

1¼–1½ cup (250 g) flour

1 tsp (5 g) salt

½–⅝ cup (100–125 ml) cold water

2 tsp white vinegar

⅛ cup (30 g) butter

1 can (14 oz/400 g) of "cabello de ángel" jam

To sprinkle:

1 egg (for egg wash)

1 tbsp cinnamon powder

1 tbsp powdered sugar

½ cup sesame seeds

1. Take (near) room temperature butter and shape it into a square slab about 6 inches (15 cm) wide and half an inch (1 cm) thick. Wrap it in plastic wrap (ensuring no air is trapped) and refrigerate.

2. In a large bowl, mix the flour and salt. Add the cold water, white vinegar, and cold melted butter.

3. Mix all the ingredients, being careful not to overwork the dough. You can use a knife to cut and bring the dough together into a ball. Cover the bowl with plastic wrap and refrigerate for thirty minutes.

4. Lightly dust a work surface with flour, take out the dough ball, and make a cross-shaped cut on top with a knife (do not cut the dough in half, just make a shallow cut). Open up the four corners of the dough formed by the cut to create a square shape. Use a rolling pin to shape it into an even square.

5. Remove the butter square from the fridge. Remove the plastic wrap and place the flattened butter square onto the dough, turning it ¼ turn to the right (so it forms a diamond shape). Slightly stretch out the four corners of dough using the rolling pin. Fold the dough over the butter, creating an envelope.

6. Once the envelope is sealed, turn the dough ¼ turn to the right to that it resembles a square.

7. Use the rolling pin to flatten the dough upwards, forming a rectangle.

(The recipe continues on the next page).

8. Fold the dough like a letter: fold the bottom third of the dough over the middle third, then fold the top third over the middle third. You will now have a new rectangle. Wrap the dough in plastic wrap and refrigerate it for thirty minutes.

9. Take out the chilled dough and repeat this folding process two more times, and then chill again.

10. Preheat the oven to 350°F (180°C). Take the dough ball and divide it into two portions, with one slightly larger than the other.

11. Prepare two sheets of parchment paper. Place the first sheet on your working surface and place the smaller dough portion on top. Cover the dough with the other sheet of parchment paper. Using a rolling pin, flatten the dough into a round shape. It should be about 3 mm thick.

12. Take a 9-inch (24 cm) pie plate. Place the flattened dough into the pie plate, pressing it up against the sides, and carefully remove the top parchment paper. Use a fork to prick the dough all over; this will prevent it from rising too much.

13. Flatten the second portion of dough following the same process. Prick the dough with a fork, and place the parchment paper back on top of it to prevent the dough from drying out. Chill again.

14. In the pie pan lined with dough, spread the cabello de ángel jam evenly using the back of a spoon. It should be just under half an inch (1 cm) thick.

15. Take the second dough out of the fridge, remove the top parchment paper, and flip the dough to cover the jam. This second dough should be in contact with the jam and the edges of the first dough. Gently press to eliminate any air pockets between the dough and the cabello de ángel jam, and then press the edges of the two pieces of dough together and roll the edges for a better aesthetic.

16. Beat an egg, brush it onto the exposed dough on its top and edges, and prick the top dough again with a fork.

17. In a small bowl, mix the sugar and cinnamon. Sprinkle ¾ of this mixture over the dough, and then sprinkle with the sesame seeds

18. Bake for 16 minutes. Sprinkle on the remaining ¼ of the sugar-cinnamon mixture and bake for an additional 5 minutes. The top should be golden brown.

19. Remove from the oven. You can place a heavy tray over the puff pastry so it keeps flat while it cools. Cut and serve as you normally would slice a pie, and enjoy with a cup of mint tea.

HORMIGOS: HAND MADE SEMOLINA COUSCOUS

The ingredients in the dish called hormigos are not very clear, even though its preparation is fairly well understood. Various sources which mention the preparation of hormigos agree that it is a dish made of small rolled pieces of dough.

Both "The Portrait of Lozana" and the Spanish Inquisition trials mention the preparation of hormigos. What constitutes proof of the Jewish heritage of the person preparing this dish is that the dough is made of flour and oil, without yeast, and to make it, one must roll these two elements together into very small pieces of dough.

Evidence for this Jewish culinary practice is found in "The Portrait of Lozana" from the 16th century ("twisted hormigos with oil [*hormigos torcidos con aceite*]" ; "Let's tell [her] that we want to twist [*torcer*] hormigos or make couscous and, if she knows how to twist them, so we will notice that she is one of us, and [we will understand] if she twists [*tuerce*] with water or oil") as well as in the Spanish Inquisition trials (in 1486, 1491, 1501, and 1505).

3 cups (500 g) medium durum wheat semolina

5 cups (1 L) of salted water
(water + 1 tbsp salt)

1 tbsp olive oil

2⅔ cup (400 g) fine wheat semolina

1 tbsp salt

1. Take a medium-sized sieve and sift the semolina into a large bowl. In a second large bowl, pour the warm water with salt and mix until the salt is dissolved. Add the olive oil.

2. Using your hands, sprinkle the semolina with the equivalent of a glass of salted water and oil, and work it with the palms of both hands in circular motions. Small balls will start to form.

3. Sprinkle the medium semolina with a handful of fine semolina and continue rolling it for about fifteen minutes. The fine semolina will help the small balls dry and form better.

4. With one hand, gradually add salted water and then fine semolina, alternating between them. Continue rolling the couscous grains until they become round and form small pellets.

(The recipe continues on the next page).

5. Pass the semolina through a coarse sieve, and then through a fine sieve. Place the sieved semolina in a large dish. Repeat this process until all the medium semolina is used; once all the semolina is rolled, you can steam it.

6. Take a couscous steamer, and fill the bottom part halfway with water. Bring it to a boil. Then, in the top part of the couscous steamer, pour the rolled semolina grains. Do not stir the top basket of the couscous steamer and do not compact the grains. Cook for 15 minutes.

7. Take a very large flat-bottomed dish and invert the couscous steamer basket into it. The grains will fall, forming a large mound. Oil your hands with olive oil and gently separate the grains by rolling them between your palms. Add a little water with your hands to moisten the grains.

8. Crush a few grains together by placing them between your thumb and index finger to form large flattened crumbs. Then place all of the couscous back in the top part of the couscous steamer.

9. Cook again for 15 minutes. Repeat this process (rolling and crushing the grains with oiled hands and cooking). Once the hormigo crumbs have been cooked three times, you can transfer them to a dish and enjoy them.

10. The hormigo couscous can be served as a side dish or used in various recipes. They can be enjoyed with a drizzle of olive oil, sprinkled with grated cheese, or added to soups and stews for added texture and flavor.

TALVINAS: BARLEY PORRIDGE WITH SILAN

According to culinary sources found in Spain, this dish, also known as *talavina* or *atalavina*, dates back at least to 1495, as it is mentioned in Antonio de Nebrija's dictionary. The later *Diccionario de Autoridades* written by Covarrubias (1726) states that it is a puree made from almond milk. However, much older sources inform us that *talvina* was a porridge made from barley, milk, honey, and dates.

Talbina is also a preparation consumed in the Arab countries of the Middle East and is one of the dishes consumed to break the fast during Ramadan. In fact, the dish "Talbina" (التَّلْبِينَة) is mentioned in the Sunna Sunan Ibn Majah 3446 as one of the statements (prophetic sayings) for Muslims, describing it as a "beneficial dish."

SERVES: 2 small bowls

TIME: 20 minutes

2 tbsp (20 g) barley flour

1 tbsp water

1⅓ cup (260 ml) almond milk (or whole cow's milk)

1 tsp salt

1 tbsp (21 g) honey

5 Medjool dates, diced into small pieces

1 tbsp sumsumia (sesame paste with peanuts and honey)

Silan (aka date syrup) (see recipe on page 337)

1. In a small bowl, mix the barley flour with water. In a saucepan, add the milk and the barley-flour-water mixture. Mix and heat over medium heat, stirring constantly for 10 minutes. Add salt, honey, and continue stirring for another 5 minutes.

2. Pour the porridge into bowls. Drizzle with sumsumia and silan, and garnish with the diced dates.

ZAHÍNAS: SORGHUM AND ORANGE PORRIDGE

The term "zahína" is derived from the Hispanic-Arabic "saẖīna" and the classic Arabic "saẖīna." In Andalusia, it is used to refer to a puree made from flour that does not thicken. Similar to *talbina*, *zahína* can refer to both the type of flour used and the dish made with that flour. Zahína specifically refers to the porridge made with sorghum grain.

SERVES: 4 bowls

TIME: 20 minutes

4 tbsp (40 g) sorghum flour

¾ cup (150 ml) water

4 small strips of peel from one orange

4 tsp sugar

1 tsp ground cinnamon

1 tsp ground ginger

1 tbsp (21 g) honey

¼ cup (35 g) raisins (optional)

1. Add the water and sorghum flour to a saucepan, mix well, and then add the orange peels.

2. Stir and bring to a boil while constantly stirring to avoid lumps. Add 2 teaspoons of sugar.

3. Cook over low heat for about twenty minutes.

4. Pour the hot zahína into four small bowls, with one piece of orange peel in each bowl.

5. Sprinkle with the sugar, cinnamon, and ginger. Drizzle with honey, and garnish with a few raisins (to taste).

NABOS SIN TOCINO Y CON COMINO

TURNIPS WITH CUMIN SEEDS AND BREAD CRUST

In La Lozana Andaluza, the fact that Aldonza specifies that the turnip dish which her grandmother taught her to prepare ("Nabos sin tocino y con comino") does not contain lard highlights the fact that in 15th and 16th century Spain, turnips were commonly prepared with pork fat. However, the converted Aldonza and her Spanish grandmother used olive oil instead.

SERVES: 4 people

TIME: 1 hour 30 minutes

1¼ cup (175 g) wheat flour

Warm water

½ tsp active yeast

½ tsp salt

2 tsp olive oil

2 cloves of garlic

Rosemary leaves

Cumin seeds

12 medium organic turnips (preferably spring ones)

1 teaspoon salt

2 teaspoons cumin seeds

1 tablespoon olive oil

1 beaten egg (for egg wash)

Sauce:

1 tbsp olive oil

1 shallot, minced

1 tsp salt

¼ cup (50 ml) dry white wine

1¼ cup (250 ml) vegetable or veal broth

1. Wash the turnips. Place them into salted boiling water and cook them for about 15 minutes. You want them to soften. They should be cooked 80% soft. Then remove them from the water and place them on a paper towel to cool.

2. In the meantime, in a large bowl, prepare the bread dough by mixing together the flour, warm water, yeast, salt, and olive oil. Knead by hand for 15 minutes or using a mixer with a dough hook attachment for 7 minutes. Add the mashed garlic cloves, whole rosemary leaves, and cumin seeds. Knead for another five minutes. Cover the dough with a kitchen towel and let it rise for 1 hour.

3. Trim the base of each turnip to make it smooth, but do not peel them. Set aside.

4. Remove the dough from the bowl and press it to remove any air bubbles. Shape it back into a ball and refrigerate for thirty minutes.

5. Prepare a baking sheet, line it with parchment paper, and place the dough on a floured surface.

6. Divide the dough into balls of 2⅝ oz (73 g), the size of a baseball.

7. Take one ball and roll it out with a rolling pin to a thickness of about 3 mm. The diameter of the dough disc should be nearly twice the diameter of the turnip. Place a cooled turnip in the center of the dough disc. Sprinkle with some salt and a few cumin seeds. Drizzle a little olive oil over it, lightly moisten the edge of the dough of disc with water, an enclose the turnip with the dough, forming a ball. Press the top of the dough to seal it, then flip it over and place it on oiled iron skillet.

8. Brush the surface of the dough ball with the beaten egg and sprinkle with a few cumin seeds.

9. Repeat the process for all the other turnips. Let the dough rise for another 30 minutes.

10. Turn the skillet on to low-medium heat and cook the dough-coated turnips for about 20 minutes. Turn them carefully and cook them on all sides.

11. To prepare the sauce, heat the olive oil in a saucepan and add the minced shallot. Sauté for 3 minutes until golden brown. Add salt and pour in the white wine. Cook over low heat for two minutes, then add the broth. Let it simmer for five minutes to reduce.

12. Serve the turnips in their bread crust with cumin with the sauce. This dish pairs well with lamb meat.

OLLA REPOSADA: ADAFINA
THE ICONIC SEPHARDIC DISH

La olla reposada is one of the many names given to the emblematic dish of the Sephardic Jews in Spain. It is called "reposada," meaning "rested," because it would cook on the embers all night from Friday until Saturday noon. It was not to be "disturbed," meaning it should be left to rest without adding anything to it. Olla Reposada was also known by others names: *adefina*, *adafina*, *dafina*, *aní*, *hamín*, *caliente*, and *trasnochado*, but these all refer to one thing: the iconic Shabbat dish of the Sephardic Jews in the 15th century. The different terms which describe the dish, such as "buried" or "hidden" (*adefina*, *adafina*, *dafina*), "hot" (*aní*, *hamín*, *caliente*), and "cooked overnight" (*trasnochado*) could have been a way for Jews to conceal their identity from Inquisition officials, as the dish itself could have revealed their Jewish heritage.

To respect the historical context of this dish, the recipe below does not include the New World ingredients like potatoes and sweet potatoes which are commonly used by Sephardim today in *adefina* preparations.

Serves: 4–6 people

Time: 1 hour + overnight

½ lb (220 g) beef brisket, bone-in, or lamb neck

2 tbsp sugar

1 onion

⅓ cup (66 g) olive oil

2 bay leaves

1 tbsp salt

1 whole head of garlic

½ tsp ground cinnamon

½ tsp black pepper

½ tsp ground nutmeg

½ tsp turmeric

1 cup (200 g) softened chickpeas (soak for 24 hours in water beforehand)

6 eggs

10 dates

1 cup (175 g) boiled Swiss chard

10 mint leaves

Water

For the fried rice:

2 tbsp olive oil

½ cup (100 g) rice

1 clove garlic, chopped

½ tsp salt

½ tsp turmeric

6 saffron strands (or yellow coloring food)

A muslin cloth

1. Place the meat (bone-in) in a large ovenproof pot and add the sugar. Brown the meat over high heat for 5 minutes. Add enough water to cover the meat and boil for 10 minutes. Use a skimmer to remove and discard the layer of fat that forms on the water.

2. In the same pot, add the whole onion, olive oil, bay leaves, salt, whole head of garlic, ground cinnamon, black pepper, ground nutmeg, and turmeric (without overlapping if possible).

3. Add the soaked chickpeas, the raw whole eggs in their shells, dates, Swiss chard, and mint leaves.

4. Meanwhile, prepare the fried rice separately. In a frying pan, combine olive oil, rice, chopped garlic, salt, turmeric, and saffron. Brown the mixture over low-medium heat for 5 minutes. Allow it to cool, then place everything in a muslin cloth, tie it closed, and add the muslin cloth to the pot with the meat.

5. Add enough water to cover all the ingredients. Cover the pot and place it in the oven at 200°F (100°C) in the late afternoon. It will be ready the next day by the end of the morning.

6. You can serve the different components of the dish (rice, eggs, vegetables, broth, meat) in separate dishes.

COL MURCIANA CON ALCARAVEA

MURCIAN CABBAGE WITH CARAWAY

This dish, along with all of the other dishes presented in this chapter, is mentioned by Aldonza during her conversations with other crypto-Jewish women in Rome in the 16th century. It contains caraway, a seed also known as mountain cumin. Today, this cabbage dish, originating from the province of Murcia (a neighboring province of Andalusia), is one of the most popular dishes in this region.

SERVES: 4 people

TIME: 1 hour

1 medium white or red cabbage

2 tbsp olive oil + 1 tablespoon for frying the bread + 1 teaspoon of salt

4 small slices of bread (about half an inch/1 cm) thick

2½ cup (500 ml) water

2 cloves of garlic

1 tsp caraway seeds, crushed (or cumin seeds if caraway seeds are not available)

1 tsp black pepper

1 tsp salt

½ cup (75 g) fresh goat cheese

1 tsp cumin seeds

1. In a large pot bring the water to a boil. Cut the cabbage leaves into approximately 1½ inch (4 cm) pieces and add them to the pot. Cover the pot, reduce the heat to low-medium, and cook the cabbage slowly for about 30 minutes.

2. Crush the caraway seeds, garlic, olive oil and black pepper in a pestle. In a small frying pan, heat 1 tbsp of olive oil over medium heat. Once it is hot, add the whole slices of bread and sprinkle them with salt. Toast them for three minutes on each side or until golden. Set aside.

3. Using a skimmer or slotted spoon, place pieces of cabbage in a soup bowl. Pour broth and add the seasonings. Take the slices of bread and spread fresh goat cheese over them, and sprinkle with cumin seeds. This dish can be served hot or cold.

BORONÍA
EGGPLANT AND MEATBALL STEW

Boronía, also called *almoronía,* is a dish deeply ingrained in the culinary heritage of the Sephardic Jews from the Mediterranean basin, but especially from the Jews of Morocco. In the *Kitāb al-ṭabīẖ*, there are four recipes titled *būrāniyya, alburānya, burānya and boronía.* In the late sixteenth century in the Spanish city of Granada, the dish "boronia" was recognized and denounced as a Jewish dish, and boronía is also among the dishes mentioned by Aldonza.

What is interesting, however, is that the *Kitāb al-ṭabīẖ* recipe for *burānya* is preserved today by Moroccan Jews, who are the only ones still preparing it as it appears here: with meat and eggplant, and without peppers or tomatoes. Moroccan Jews consume the dish before starting (or after) the fast of Yom Kippur. Today, non-Sephardim make *alboronía* (as every Spaniard knows it) with tomatoes, peppers, onions, zucchini, and eggplant cooked in olive oil. Here is a recipe for *almoronía* in which the ingredients and method of preparation remain almost unchanged from the original.

SERVES: 4

TIME: 1 hour

- 4 large eggplants, cut into chunks
- 1 preserved lemon, cut into small chunks
- 10 green olives
- 10 purple olives
- ½ cup (100 g) olive oil
- 2 large spring onions with leaves, chopped
- 2 tsp vinegar
- 6 tsp salt
- 2 tsp black pepper
- 1 (60 g) fresh coriander, chopped
- 2 tsp ginger powder
- 2 tsp cumin
- 1 tsp cinnamon
- 6 saffron strands, crushed in 1 tbsp water

1. In a pot, add the eggplants, preserved lemon, olives, olive oil, salt, chopped onion, vinegar, salt, black pepper, coriander, ginger, cumin, cinnamon, and crushed saffron. Cook over medium-high heat for about 5 minutes. Then, lower the heat and keep covered and warm.

For the meatballs:

10.5 oz (300 g) ground lamb (or beef)

½ cup (30 g) fresh cilantro, chopped

1 tsp salt

1 tsp black pepper

½ cup (70 g) flour

½ cup olive oil (for frying)

To decorate:

⅔ cup (100 g) chopped almonds

For the meatballs:

1. Mix together the ground meat, chopped fresh cilantro, salt, and pepper. Form small meatballs the size of a heaped tablespoon. Put the flour in a plate, roll the meatballs quickly in the flour, and make sure to remove any excess flour. Place on another plate.

2. Take a frying pan and heat ½ cup of olive oil over medium heat. Fry the meatballs for 3 minutes, moving them every minute. You want them golden on all sides. When they're finished, set them aside.

3. Uncover the eggplant pot. Make holes in the eggplant mixture and place the meatballs in. Cover them with the eggplant sauce. Cook for about 5 minutes over low-medium heat.

4. Sprinkled with chopped almonds, and serve hot.

CAZUELA DE BERENJENAS MOJÍ
STUFFED EGGPLANT CASSEROLE

Eggplant casserole is a classic among Sephardic dishes because eggplant is an emblematic ingredient in Sephardic culinary culture, both from their own perspective as they consume it abundantly, and from the perspective of others, including non-Jews. The relationship between eggplant and Sephardic Jews was also shaped by the views of old Christians. The preparation of eggplant casserole, known as "caçuela de berenjenas," is mentioned in the records of the Spanish Inquisition, particularly the tribunal of Toledo. For instance, María (the wife who denounced her friend Catalina de Teva) testifies that one Saturday afternoon in 1509, she went to the house of Ximon de la Çarça and witnessed Catalina de Teva (Ximon's wife) and other women eating 'a casserole of stuffed eggplants, which was cold, and grapes and fruit [. . .] prepared the day before."

It is not surprising, therefore, that in "The Lozana Portrait," the converted Jew Aldonza from Cordova mentions that she learned the preparation of eggplant casserole, called "mojies," from her grandmother. The term "mojíes" comes from the Arabic term "muhsí," which means "stuffed." Cookbooks written under Christian influence, such as the "Regalo de la vida humana," contain recipes for "Eggplant casserole, stuffed" ("Berengenas en caçuela moxí") and "eggplant with *almodrote*" ("berengenas con almodrote)."

In one of Cervantes' plays entitled "Baños de Argel" (The Baths of Algiers, 1615), there is a story of a sacristan who steals a meal from a Jew. The meal is an eggplant casserole dish called "moji." The purpose of this theft is to ridicule the Jew's insistence on reclaiming his simple meal, which provides him "comfort" with its "aroma," and which he cannot cook again or buy back from the sacristan (who offers it to him) because it is Shabbat. The Jew's struggle to regain his modest dish aims to demean Jews not only in their culinary preferences and practices but also in their behavior.

SERVES: 4 people

TIME: 45 minutes

2 large eggplants

2 cloves garlic, crushed

2 tsp salt + 1 tsp black pepper

2 tbsp olive oil

2 cloves garlic, sliced

2 cups (300 g) cheese, like feta cheese

2 tsp ground cumin

1 tsp salt

¼ cup raisins,

2 hard-boiled eggs, mashed

1 egg, beaten

1 tbsp olive oil (to oil the pot)

1 cup breadcrumbs

¼ cup pine nuts

2 scallions, thinly sliced

1. Preheat the oven to 440°F (220°C), and line a baking tray with aluminum foil.

2. Crush the two cloves of garlic. Take a bowl, pour the 2 tbsp olive oil and mix in the crushed garlic. Cut each eggplant in half, and brush each half with the oil and garlic. Sprinkle with 2 tsp salt and 1 tsp black pepper.

3. With a knife, slash the flesh of the eggplant without cutting the peel. Arrange the eggplant halves in the baking tray, and cover with aluminum foil.

4. Bake for about 15 minutes, then remove the aluminum foil and bake for another 15 minutes until the top is golden. Check if the flesh is soft. If it isn't, bake for another 10 minutes. When you remove the eggplants, lower the oven temperature to 350°F (180°C).

5. Meanwhile, prepare the stuffing: pour 2 tbsp olive oil into a pan, heat over medium heat, and add the two sliced cloves of garlic. Cook the garlic for one minute, then add the cumin, salt, and raisins, and cook for another two minutes.

6. Once the eggplants are cool, take a spoon and remove the flesh carefully, without damaging the peel. Mash the flesh with a fork, and add the eggplant to the stuffing, along with the two hard-boiled eggs, the beaten egg and the cheese. Mix quickly all together.

7. Take a clay baking pan and grease it with 1 tbsp olive oil. Put the empty halves of eggplant in the pan, and with a large spoon, stuff the eggplants with the stuffing. Sprinkle with breadcrumbs and pine nuts, and cook in the oven for 10 minutes until the breadcrumbs golden. Broil for 3 minutes, and remove from the oven. Sprinkle with very thin slices of scallions.

FROM CORDOVA TO ROME

ROSQUILLAS DE ALFAXOR
HONEY STUFFED RINGS

These small wheel-shaped cakes that Aldonza claims to know how to prepare thanks to her grandmother are still made today in the town of Casar de Cáceres. It is also in this small town in Extremadura, northwest of Andalusia, where a Jewish community had settled and where they made a special cheese: a cheese without animal rennet. This cheese is still made today and is called "Torta de Casar."

These rosquillas de alfaxor are cakes made from wheat flour, oil, water, salt, and filled with a stuffing called "alfajor" made from bread crumbs, honey, and dried fruits. Small lines of holes decorate the rings, and grapes are often added on top.

SERVES: 8 pieces

TIME: 1 hour 30 minutes

For the dough:

2¼ cup (350 g) flour

½ + 2 tbsp (125 g) olive oil

½ tsp salt

For the *alfajor* stuffing:

¼ cup (80 g) honey

¼ cup + 2 tbsp (51 g) soft bread breadcrumbs

1 tsp Arabic gum (optional)

24 raisins

1. Pour the oil into a bowl and sift all of the flour into it. Add the water and salt, and stir with a spoon until the dough is homogeneous. Form eight balls of dough (about 2 oz/60 g each), place them in the bowl, cover them, and refrigerate for about 30 minutes.

The making of the *alfajor* stuffing:

1. Take a bowl and put the soft breadcrumbs in it. Add the honey and Arabic gum, and mash everything with a fork until you have a dough-like consistency. Cover it and place it in the freezer for 10 minutes.

2. Take a plate and cover it with parchment paper. Form eight balls (about ½ oz/15 g each) with the stuffing and roll each of them into sticks approximately a quarter of an inch (0.5 cm) thick. Place them on the parchment paper and let them cool in the fridge for 5 minutes.

3. Take a baking tray and cover it with parchment paper, and preheat the oven to 428°F (220°C).

4. To make the stuffed rings, flour your working surface, oil your hands, and take a ball of dough. Roll it into a stick shape approximately 6 inches (15 cm) long, and repeat for the other balls of dough. Make a groove in the stick of dough, and put an *alfajor* stuffing stick in the groove.

5. Cover the stuffing with the dough, ensuring that the stuffing is completely enclosed. Bend the stick of dough with the stuffing into a circle, and press the ends together to securely close the ring.

6. Lightly prick the top of the rings with a fork, and using a knife, make four small cuts on the top of the dough to allow the stuffing to come out slightly.

7. Press 3 raisins into the top of each rosquilla, and then remove them so they don't burn in the oven. Now you just want to indent their place in the dough; once the rosquillas are baked, you can replace the raisins in their places.

8. Repeat this process for each ball of dough, and place each ring on the parchment paper on the baking tray.

9. Cool for 15 minutes in the fridge, and then bake for 10–12 minutes. Rosquillas de alfajor are perfect when enjoyed with a glass of milk, hot chocolate, or a cup of tea.

ALFAJOR
HONEY AND NUT SANDWICH

The term "alfajor" is sometimes associated with the term "alajú" to refer to a preparation made with honey, nuts, almonds, and bread. Two thin sheets of dough are used to cover this filling. The term "alfajor" was more commonly used in the south of Spain, while the north of the country used the term "alajú." This sweet treat is now a specialty of the Spanish city of Cuenca, where an Inquisition tribunal was located. This preparation is similar to the one called "jūdhāb al-tamr" found in a recipe book from the 13th century: *Kitāb al-ṭabīẖ*, written by Al-Baġdādī. This sweet is made from dried dates (*tamr* in Arabic) that are cooked into two and a half times their volume. They should then be kneaded by hand and passed through a sieve. Sugar should be mixed with half its volume of honey, along with saffron, breadcrumbs (twice the volume of sugar), sesame oil (twice the volume of sugar), and blanched nuts (the same volume as the honey). Everything should be mixed until fully cooked, before being placed between two pieces of biscuit.

The following preparation of "alfajor" resembles the one made in the recipe "rosquillas de alfajor." However, this recipe uses two sheets of wafer paper or very thin biscuits. In his work *The Jews in New Spain: Faith, Flame, and the Inquisition*, Seymour Liebman notes that this sweet treat was prepared in the early 17th century and was traditionally served for Rosh Hashanah, the Jewish New Year.

SERVES: 4 people

TIME: 1 hour

¼ + ⅛ cup (125 g) honey

½ of an orange's peel

½ cup (60 g) breadcrumbs

½ cup (65 g) almonds, peeled and chopped

2 large round sheets of wafer paper

1. In a saucepan, pour the honey and add the orange peels. Heat gently over low heat, without boiling, for about 8 minutes. Remove the orange peels, add the breadcrumbs and chopped almonds, and stir. Continue cooking, stirring constantly, for about 7 minutes over medium heat, until the bottom of the sauce pan starts to turn golden.

2. Take one round sheet of wafer paper sheet and spread the honey-almond mixture all over the wafer. You want a very thin layer; about 3 mm (0.1 inches) thick. Flatten and smooth it gently with a spoon, making sure it reaches the edges of the wafer.

3. Cover the honey-almond mixture with the other round sheet of wafer paper. Press and flatten it carefully, and place a heavy plate on the alfajor so that the sheets stick to the filling and the almonds are evenly distributed. Wait for 10 minutes and then refrigerate it for 30 minutes.

4. Repeat the process with the remaining two sheets.

5. Using a sharp knife, cut into triangles.

LET'S COOK HISTORY

CREATIONS

SHORTBREAD WITH DATES

SERVES: 8

TIME: 1 hour 30 minutes

1½ cups (180 g) flour

½ + ⅛ cup (125 g) softened butter

⅛ cup (20 g) corn starch

2 egg yolks

1 cup (137 g) icing sugar

2 tablespoons (25 g) ground almonds

5 Medjool dates, chopped

1 egg yolk, beaten

1 teaspoon honey

1. In a bowl, combine the softened butter, flour, and starch until the mixture is homogeneous. Add the honey, icing sugar, and ground almonds. Mix everything together without overbeating, and then add the egg yolks.

2. Using a rubber spatula, quickly mix everything and transfer the dough into a plastic bag. Place it in the refrigerator for about 1 hour.

3. Preheat the oven to 392°F (200°C) and line a baking tray with parchment paper. Roll out the dough and shape it into a log about 2 inches (5 cm) thick. Using a knife, cut the dough log into slices that are about a quarter of an inch (0.5 cm) thick, and place them on the parchment paper.

4. Brush the date-filled shortbread cookies with a mixture of beaten egg yolk and 1 teaspoon of honey.

5. Bake for 15 minutes or until golden. Allow the cookies to cool on the baking tray for about 10 minutes without moving them. You can store the cookies in an airtight container at room temperature.

EID AL BANAT
FRIED AND HONEYED CROWNS FOR GIRLS' DAY

SERVES: 6 crowns

TIME: 2 hours 30 minutes

For the dough:

1 teaspoon (8 g) orange blossom water

1 cup + 1 tablespoon (214 g) water

⅛ cup (26 g) sugar

½ cup (90 g) margarine or butter

1 strand of saffron + 1 tablespoon hot water

3 cups + 2 tablespoons (470 g) flour

1. In a bowl, slowly mix together the orange blossom water, water, and sugar until dissolved. Add the margarine/butter.

2. In a small cup, combine the hot water and saffron strand. Stir, then add it to the previous mixture.

3. Gradually add the flour, mixing slowly (using a stand mixer over medium speed) or kneading by hand until the dough is homogeneous and not too sticky. Place the dough in a plastic bag and refrigerate for at least one hour.

For the honeyed syrup:

2½ cups (500 g) sugar

¼ cup (50 g) orange blossom water

1¼ cups + 2 tablespoons (285 g) water

1 cardamom seed

⅛ cup (20 g) bergamot or lemon fresh juice

4 tablespoons (85 g) honey

2 strands of saffron

1. In a saucepan, combine the sugar, orange blossom water, water, and cardamom seed. Heat over medium heat until the sugar is dissolved. Add the fresh juice, honey, and 2 strands of saffron. Stir gently. Keep the syrup over low-medium heat, making sure it doesn't boil, while preparing the crowns.

Frying:

1. Pour neutral oil into a frying pan and heat it to 350°F (180°C).

Making the crowns:

1. Take the dough and shape it into small balls the size of a golf ball (1⅛ oz (30 g)). Roll the balls into long and thin strands. You can shape them into a crown shape by making small pointed notches on the top of the dough with a pair of scissors, or leave them straight. Using a pastry wheel cutter, cut the strands into pieces that are as long as two hands and as wide as two fingers.

2. Take a round cookie cutter that is as wide as three fingers. Lightly oil the outer edges.

3. Take one strand of dough and wrap it around the cookie cutter, pressing the final part of the dough over the first part to close the circle.

Frying the crowns:

1. Take a fork and insert it into the dough circle which is still wrapped around the cookie cutter.

2. Carefully place it in the frying pan, rotating it very slowly to fry all of the dough in the oil. Each crown will take about 3–4 minutes. Transfer the fried crowns to a plate lined with a paper towel.

Honeying the crowns:

1. Heat the saucepan with the syrup over medium heat. Line a baking tray with a baking sheet.

2. Carefully dip one crown into the syrup for about 15 seconds. Use a skimmer to remove it. You can roll the crowns in sprinkles if desired. Place the honeyed crown on the baking sheet.

3. Do not move it for 5 minutes to avoid breaking.

4. Serve the crowns with mint tea. You can store them for up to 3 days by covering them with plastic wrap or, preferably, placing them under a glass plate.

---

*See the photo on the next page.

MANTECADOS
VELVETY CINNAMON SPANISH COOKIES

Even today, *mantecados*, also known as *mantecaos*, are part of the culinary heritage of the Sephardic Jews from Spain and Morocco. However, they can also be found on the tables of non-Jewish people, during celebrations or simply when hosting guests.

SERVES: 16

TIME: 1 hour

1½ cup (240 g) flour

½ cup + 2 tbsp (115 g) neutral oil

2 tsp vanilla essence

1 tsp bitter almond essence

1 tsp baking soda

¼ cup (80 g) sugar

4 tbsp (40 g) ground almonds

1 tbsp cinnamon + 1 tsp (for dusting)

½ tsp salt

1. In a bowl, combine all the ingredients until you achieve a smooth dough. Shape the dough into small balls (about 1⅛ oz or 30 g each), and place them on a parchment-lined baking tray. You can also roll out the dough to about ½ inch (1 cm) thick and use a round cookie cutter to shape them. Cover the tray and refrigerate for approximately 30 minutes.

2. Preheat the oven to 370°F (185°C), and bake for 10–12 minutes. Once the *mantecados* start to turn a slight golden color, remove them from the oven. They should maintain a creamy color. Using a sieve, sprinkle a light dusting of ground cinnamon over the top of the *mantecados*.

3. Allow the baking sheet to cool for at least 10 minutes before handling or removing the *mantecados*.

DATE AND POMEGRANATE CAKE
FOR ROSH HASHANAH

This cake smells so delicious; the combination of spices and dates will transport you.

SERVES: 1 large loaf (8 servings)

TIME: 40 minutes + 40 minutes baking

20 Medjool dates (10 diced and 10 for date puree)

½ cup (100 g) brown sugar

2 eggs

½ cup + ⅓ cup (100 g) flour

1 tsp (7 g) baking soda

¼ cup (60 g) neutral oil

1 tsp Salt

2 tsp Cinnamon

1 tsp ground nutmeg

½ Vanilla seeds

¼ cup (60 g) fresh pomegranate juice

To make date syrup:

1. Preheat the oven to 170°C (338°F).

2. Cut 10 of the dates in half and check for any defects. Add the 10 dates to a saucepan, along with the pits. Cover the dates with water (the water level should be twice as high as the height of the dates placed in the saucepan) and simmer for about 10 minutes. Once the pits and water start to darken, cook for an additional 5 minutes.

3. Remove the pits from the dates. Place the pitless dates in a muslin cloth, tie the top closed, and position it above the saucepan to drain the water from the dates into the saucepan. Once it has drained, open the muslin cloth and collect the puree obtained from the dates.

4. Boil the golden drained water (from cooking the dates) in the saucepan over medium-high heat. Stir and cook for about 25 minutes until the mixture thickens. This is silan, or date syrup.

5. Simmer and store the silan in a jar for future use.

To make the cake:

1. In a bowl, mix the brown sugar with the eggs, then add the flour and baking soda to the mixture. Pour in the oil and add the salt, cinnamon, nutmeg, vanilla, and pomegranate juice. Incorporate the date puree and the chopped dates into the batter.

2. Grease a rectangular baking pan (8 inches/19 cm long by 5 inches/12 cm wide) with neutral oil and dust it with flour to prevent sticking. Pour the prepared batter into the pan. If your oven is strong, cover the mold with aluminum foil to prevent quick cooking.

3. Bake in the oven for 40 minutes. Once baked, remove the cake from the oven and let it cool before taking it out of the baking pan.

4. This cake pairs well with mint green tea and vanilla ice cream for a delightful combination of flavors.

PASSOVER
CHOCOLATE
AND NUT BARS

Serves: 10 bars

Time: 40 minutes

1⅛ cup (120 g) unsalted butter, softened

¼ cup (50 g) brown sugar

¼ cup (50 g) white granulated sugar

1 egg

1 tbsp (20 g) tehina (sesame paste)

6 tbsp (56 g) almond flour

½ cup (70 g) corn starch

1 tsp baking powder

6 tbsp (50 g) hazelnut powder

⅔ cup (120 g) chocolate chips

4 tbsp (40 g) chopped hazelnuts

⅔ cup (100 g) chocolate (white, dark, or milk), chopped into small pieces, to coat

1 cup (100 g) slivered almonds (for coating the bars)

1. In a large bowl, mix together the softened butter, brown sugar, and white sugar until creamy. Add the egg and tahini, and mix until well combined. Gradually add in the almond flour, corn starch, baking powder, and hazelnut powder. Mix with a spoon until the mixture is homogeneous. Do not overbeat the dough.

2. Add the chocolate chips and chopped hazelnuts to the mixture, and quickly mix with a spoon. Lightly grease a rectangular baking pan (13 × 9 × 2 inches/33 cm × 23 cm × 5 cm) and line it with parchment paper, making sure to cover the sides. Pour the mixture into the pan, making sure to spread it evenly into the corners. Chill for 30 minutes.

3. Preheat the oven to 425°F (220°C), with fan mode on.

4. Toast the sliced almonds in a small frying pan or saucepan for 2 minutes until lightly browned. Once done, remove from the heat and transfer the almonds onto a flat plate in a single layer.

5. Bake the pan in the middle of the oven for 18 minutes. Once done, remove from the oven and let cool for 20 minutes in the pan at room temperature.

6. In the meantime, take a saucepan and melt the chopped chocolate over low heat, stirring constantly. Prepare a small flat plate that can fit into the refrigerator and cover it with parchment paper.

7. Once the baked dough has cooled down, remove it from the pan and place it onto a flat surface. Using a long knife, cut it into bars that are about 1 inch wide and 4 inches long (2 cm × 10 cm).

8. Pour the warm melted chocolate onto the parchment-lined plate. Take a bar and dip the bottom into the melted chocolate. Use a knife to remove the excess. Without waiting, place the bar with the chocolate-covered bottom into the plate with slivered almonds. The slivered almonds should stick to the chocolate. Turn it upside down so the chocolate can start drying.

9. Then place the bar on a small, parchment-lined tray. Repeat the process for all of the bars, and then put the tray with the bars into the fridge for approximately 30 minutes. The chocolate will harden and the almonds will firmly stick to the chocolate.

10. These chocolate and dried fruit bars are delicious when dipped in milk or eaten as-is.

SEPHARDIC MATZAH TOFFEE

SERVING: 6 people

TIME: 20 minutes + 1 h chilling

5 squares (3¾ oz or 125 g) matzot

5¼ oz (150 g) margarine or butter

¾ cup (150 g) brown sugar

2 tsp fresh orange juice

1 tsp orange zest

1¼ cup (200 g) dark chocolate chips

1 tsp salt flakes

¾ cup (90 g) almonds and hazelnuts, roasted and chopped

¾ cup (70 g) almonds, flaked

¼ cup (40 g) dry figs, chopped

¼ cup (30 g) cranberries

5 Medjool dates, chopped

¼ cup (35 g) sesame seeds, white and golden

Preheat the oven to 320°F (160°C).

1. Take a baking tray and cover it with parchment paper. Arrange the matzot in a single layer, without overlapping them.

2. In a saucepan, combine the butter/margarine, sugar, orange zest, and orange juice. Cook and stir the mixture constantly until it starts to brown (like caramel) and to form small bubbles on the top. Working quickly but carefully as the mixture will be very hot, spread it evenly over the matzot. Use a rubber spatula to ensure all the matzot are coated.

3. Bake in the oven for approximately four minutes.

4. Turn off the oven and remove the baking tray. Place it on a cool working surface and immediately sprinkle the chocolate chips over the hot matzot. Use the spatula to spread and cover the matzot with the melted chocolate. You can place it back to the oven if you want the chocolate to melt faster.

5. Quickly sprinkle the flaked almonds, chopped dry figs, and chopped almonds and Medjool dates onto the melted chocolate. Finally, sprinkle sesame seeds and salt flakes over the top.

6. Place a parchment paper over the topping and press to stick them to the chocolate.

7. Place the baking tray in the freezer for 30 minutes to 1 hour to allow the mixture to set.

8. Once frozen, break the matzah toffee into pieces and serve.

MOLLETE: FLOURED ROLLS FROM ANTEQUERA

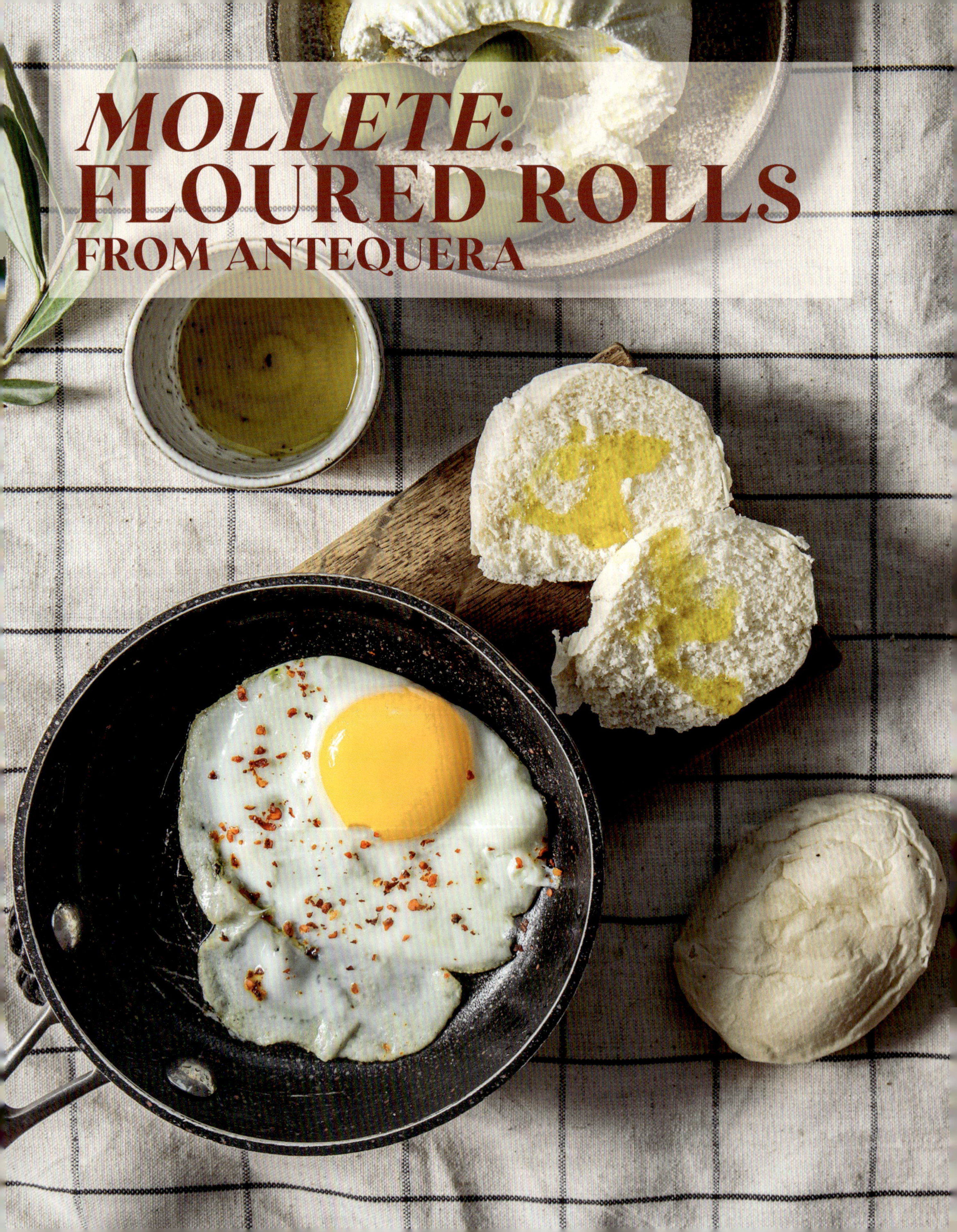

Mollete is a small, round, white, and soft bread that has a history dating back to at least the 16th century in Andalusia. It has become a traditional bread in the Andalusian city of Antequera. The basic ingredients of mollete are flour, salt, and a small amount of yeast. Interestingly, in the nearby Andalusian town of Archidona, there is a variation of mollete that can be made without yeast. This raises the question of whether this type of mollete could be used as matzah, a type of unleavened bread.

SERVES: 15 pieces

TIME: 50 minutes preparation; 2 h rising; 13 minutes baking; 5 minutes resting (3 hours 20 minutes total)

3¼ cups (500 g) fine-ground 00 flour (for pizza dough) + ½ cup (70 g) for covering the bread

1⅛ cups (225 g) warm water

½ tablespoon (12 g) fresh yeast or 1 packet of active dry yeast + 1 tablespoon warm water for dilution

½ tablespoon (10 g) salt

1. In the bowl of a stand mixer, using the dough hook attachment, combine the flour and warm water. Knead at medium speed for 10 minutes and let it rest for 30 minutes.

2. Dissolve the yeast in 1 tablespoon of warm water and add it to the dough. Knead the dough again for 10 minutes. Add the salt and knead for a final 10 minutes, and then cover the bowl and let it rise for 30 minutes.

3. Spread out a kitchen towel (not terry cloth) and lightly dust the surface with flour (this is where the molletes will be placed). Prepare another large towel to cover them.

4. Remove the dough from the bowl and divide it into 12 pieces.

5. Shape the pieces into balls and place them on the floured towel, spacing them about 1.5 inches (3 or 4 cm) apart. Dust them with flour and let them rise for 30 minutes.

6. Prepare a baking tray and line it with parchment paper. Dust it lightly with flour.

7. Using the palm of your hand, press the center of each mollete to flatten them. They should be about half an inch (1 cm) thick. Place them on the baking tray, spacing them about 1.5 inches (3 or 4 cm) apart. Sprinkle flour on top and cover them with the other towel. Let them rise for 1 hour.

8. Preheat the oven to 400°F (200°C). Remove the towel covering the molletes, but do not remove the flour. It should still cover the molletes.

9. Bake for 13 minutes. The flour may become colored, but it will protect the molletes. They will be cooked but remain white in color. Take them out of the oven and let them rest for 5 minutes. Transfer them to a wire rack to prevent the bottom from becoming moist.

10. Molletes are typically eaten for breakfast in Andalusia. They are sliced in half, toasted, and spread with olive oil. They can also be enjoyed with eggs, cheese, and other foods.

MIDDLE EASTERN COOKIES
WITH TEHINA, CHOCOLATE, SESAME, AND LABNEH

SERVES: 12 cookies

TIME: 30 minutes prep, 2 hours refrigeration, 10 minutes baking

½ cup + ⅛ cup (120 g) softened salted butter

½ cup (100 g) brown sugar

½ cup (100 g) dark brown sugar (brown vergeoise/panela/muscovado)

¼ cup (60 g) tehina (sesame paste)

¼ up to ⅓ cup (50 g) labneh (a type of fresh cheese, recipe on page 352)

1 egg

1 tsp baking powder

¾ cup (150 g) chopped dark chocolate

¾ cup (100 g) sesame seeds, toasted or not

¼ cup (50 g) halvah

1. Take a large bowl and add the soft butter, brown sugar, dark brown sugar, and tehina paste. Mix briefly. Add the labneh and mix, and then add the egg and mix all the ingredients together.

2. Pour the flour and baking soda into the mixture, and combine until everything is homogeneous. Do not overmix. Add the chopped dark chocolate and halvah chunks, and mix briefly with a spatula. Cover the bowl and refrigerate for 30 minutes.

3. Place a sheet of parchment paper on a tray or a large plate that can fit in the refrigerator. Pour the sesame seeds into a (separate) shallow dish.

4. Using an ice cream scoop, take balls of dough about 2 inches in diameter (approximately 70 g each). Place the ball in the dish of sesame seeds and roll it to coat it with seeds, then place it on the parchment paper. Arrange the dough balls in a staggered pattern, spacing them 4 cm apart. If there is not enough space on the baking sheet, do it in two batches. Repeat the process until all the dough is used up.

5. When all the balls are coated and placed on the parchment paper, cover them with plastic wrap, ensuring it touches the surface. Place the tray (or plate) in the refrigerator for 1.5 to 2 hours.

6. Preheat the oven to 200°C (392°F) with the fan on. Put the baking sheet in the oven, and reduce the temperature to 180°C (356°F). Bake for 10 minutes.

7. Remove the baking sheet from the oven but do not try to move the cookies.

8. Wait for 15 minutes before handling them to allow the outside to slightly firm up.

MEXICAN *SOPAIPILLAS* WITH SWEET CHIPOTLE SAUCE

In New Mexico today you can find *sopaipas* (also known as *sopaipillas*), which have a distinctive pillow-like appearance. While they are often served drizzled with honey, they can also be enjoyed alongside various foods or used for dipping in hot and sweet sauces.

Sopaipillas, which are related to the Sopaipas, are well known fried pastries in Chile. This is also the case in Northern Mexico as well. They are usually dusted with icing sugar and ground cinnamon, and served with honey or syrup. The Mexican Chef Daniel Ovadía and I presented sopaipillas as part of the menu for the event we hosted for Sukkot 2023 in Merkavá, one of his restaurants in Mexico City.

SERVES: 65 pieces

TIME: 1 hour 30 minutes

4 cups (600 g) flour

2 tsp salt

2 tsp baking powder

4 tsp vegetable oil or salted margarine

½ cup (100 ml) milk

1 cup (200 ml) lukewarm water

Neutral oil for frying

For the sweet chipotle sauce:

1 tbsp olive oil

1 clove garlic

½ red chile Costeño (optional)

2 red tomatoes

2 red onions

1 small red pepper, roasted

2 small chipotle pepper, in adobo sauce (use only 1 if you prefer a smoky flavor)

1 tbsp honey

1 tsp pomegranate syrup/molasse

1 tsp salt

1 tsp cumin

1 lime

2 tbsp heavy cream (optional)

1. In a bowl, combine the flour, salt, and baking powder. Stir well. In another bowl, pour the oil or melted margarine, milk, and water. Pour this mixture over the flour-salt-baking powder mixture, and stir with a spoon.

2. Flour a work surface and knead the dough for about 5 minutes. If you prefer, you can use a stand mixer with a dough hook and mix it for approximately 3 minutes, until the dough is no longer sticky. Place the dough in a greased bowl. Cover and let it rest in the refrigerator for about 2 hours, or overnight to obtain a wonderful pillow shape.

3. Divide the dough into six equally-sized balls. Take one ball and roll it out on a floured work surface until the dough reaches a thickness of ⅛ inch (0.3 cm).

4. Using a pastry wheel or a sharp knife, cut the rolled-out dough into squares about 1.5 inches (4 cm) wide, or into triangles.

5. In a deep pan, pour enough neutral oil so that the sopaipillas, when fried, do not touch the bottom of the pan. I recommend that the oil be around 4 inches deep for frying. Heat the oil over medium-high heat (400°F).

6. Carefully place three or four sopaipillas into the hot oil. Allow them to fry without touching them with a tool, as they will puff up and rise to the surface on their own. After a few seconds, use a spoon to pour hot oil over the tops of the sopaipillas. Finally, flip them over for an additional 10 seconds.

7. Using a slotted spoon or skimmer, remove the sopaipillas from the oil and place them on a paper towel to drain.

To make the dipping sauce:

1. In a saucepan, pour the olive oil and add the chopped garlic and sliced red onion. Cook for one minute. Add the salt and ground cumin. Set aside.

2. Chop the tomatoes and add them to the saucepan. Cook over medium heat for about 20 minutes.

3. Meanwhile, roast the red bell pepper on all sides using a flame or in the oven, positioning it four inches below the broiler, until it becomes charred (approximately 5 minutes). Place the roasted pepper in a plastic bag, seal it, and let it sit for about 20 minutes. Open the bag, remove the peel and seeds under running water. Slice the peeled bell pepper and add it to the mixture in the saucepan.

4. Add the chipotles, cover and cook slowly for about five minutes. Add water if it is too dry.

5. Pour in the honey and pomegranate syrup/molasses and stir. If the sauce is too thick, add water. If it is too runny, cook for an additional 15 minutes over medium-high heat, stirring constantly. If there are still chunks in the sauce, they should be small. Otherwise, you can blend the sauce in a blender for 15 seconds.

6. If the sauce is too spicy for your taste, you can add heavy cream and stir. Take small bowls and fill them with the sauce. Squeeze a little fresh lime juice over each serving.

---

*See the photo on the next page.

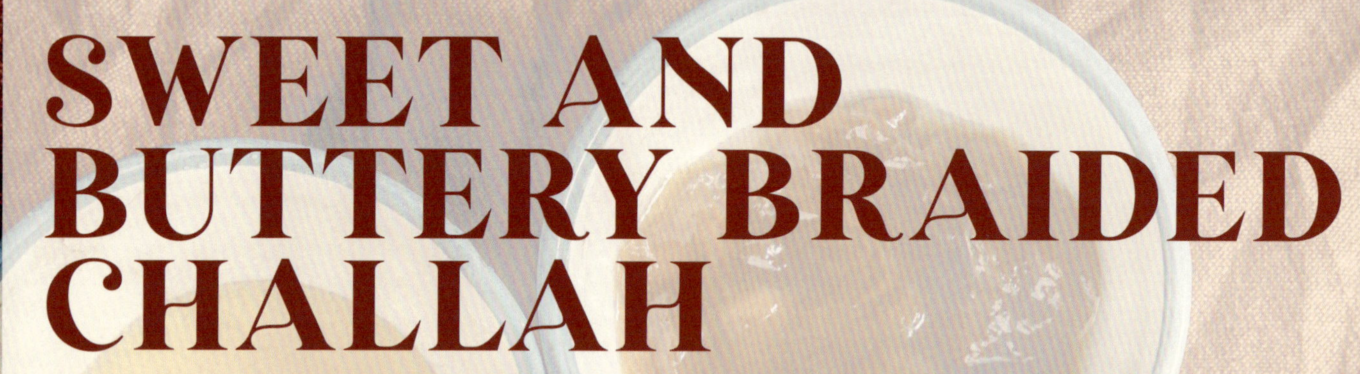

SWEET AND BUTTERY BRAIDED CHALLAH

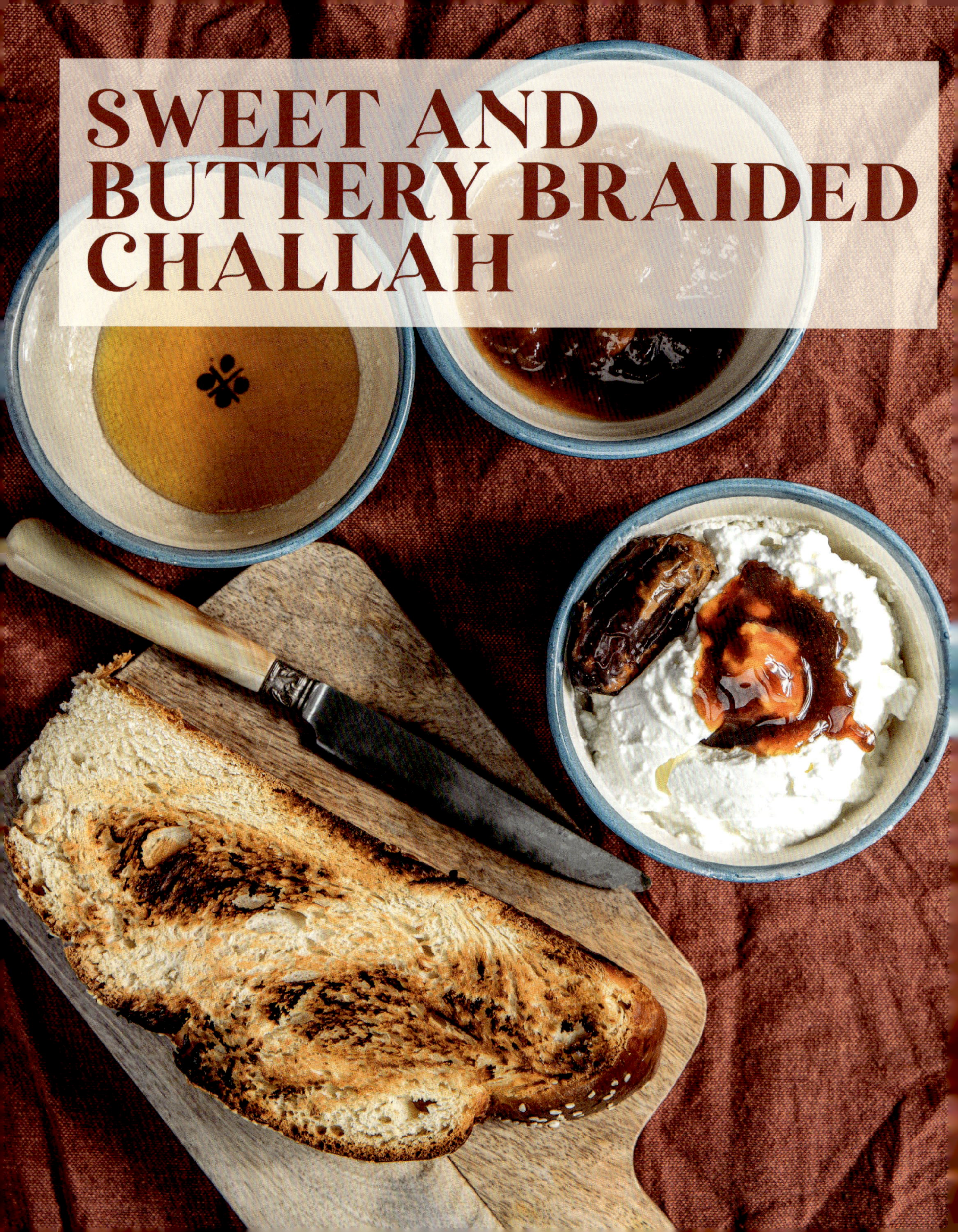

This braided challah is different from others because it follows the French brioche style. The strands are therefore more challenging to braid as they are softer, but the result is a buttery and long-lasting bread.

SERVES: 2 large braided loaves

TIME: Preparation time: 25 minutes prep, 3+ hours rising, 25 minutes baking

¼ cup (50 g) whole milk

2 tbsp (16 g) fresh yeast (or 1½ packets of active dry yeast)

2½ cup (650 g) flour

¼ cup (50 g) sugar

1 tsp salt

6 eggs (250 g)

½ cup (100 g) heavy cream

1 cup (200 g) softened unsalted butter

1 cup (140 g) sesame seeds (optional)

1 egg, beaten (for egg wash)

1. In a small bowl, warm the milk. Then add the yeast and mix.

2. In a large bowl or the bowl of a mixer, combine the flour, sugar, and salt. Mix for a few seconds, then add the milk-yeast mixture and mix for thirty seconds. Next, add the eggs one by one, followed by the cream and softened (not melted) butter.

3. Knead the dough by hand for 30 minutes or use a stand mixer on medium speed for 15 minutes. The dough should not be compact; it should be smooth and without lumps. Cover and let it rise for 1 hour 30 minutes.

4. After rising, press the dough with your hands to degas it. Shape it into a ball again and place it back in the bowl. Cover the bowl and refrigerate for at least one hour (you can also leave it overnight).

5. Remove the dough from the refrigerator and degas it again. Divide the dough into two equal parts to make two different braided loaves.

6. You can braid your challah in a variety of ways. The easiest is with three braids. Divide the first ball of dough into three equally-sized balls. Roll each ball into a smooth strand about 11 inches (30 cm) long. If you want to make a strand with sesame seeds, dip one strand quickly into a well-whisked egg wash, then roll it in sesame seeds previously placed on a plate.

7. Lay the strands side by side and pinch the tops together. Start braiding as if you were braiding hair: start with the right strand, placing it between the middle and left strands, and then take the left strand and put it between the middle and right strands, and so on. When you finish braiding, pinch the ends together and fold them under the loaf.

8. Place the loaf on a parchment-lined tray and let it rise in a warm place, covered with a kitchen towel, for 1–1.5 hours. Repeat the process with the second ball of dough. You can make a four to six braided loaf if desired.

9. Preheat the oven to 330°F (170°C). Lightly brush the challah dough with the egg wash (excluding the sesame seed strand). Bake for 25 minutes until golden brown.

10. Remove and let them cool on a tray for 20 minutes.

11. This bread is also excellent the next day when sliced thickly and toasted, enjoyed with jam or honey, or with labneh with tomato cherry and Persian cucumbers sliced.

ZA'ATAR AND NIGELLA CHICKPEA CRACKERS WITH LABNEH

I love labneh. My friend Emiliano Tatar (aka "Doc Cheese"), a local labneh specialist in Philadelphia and owner of Merion Park Cheese, gave me the tips below for making labneh.

According to documents from the great Cairo Geniza, the Jewish communities living in Egypt regularly ate fresh cheese. Some of this cheese was imported, but many documents from the Genizah mention the existence of local cheesemakers and the production of local cheeses. In a village near the city and capital of Tunisia Qayrawan, was a famous cheesemaker.

The establishment of a certificate of authenticity for kosher cheese dating back to the early 13th century, found in the Genizah, attests to the manufacture and sale of kosher Jewish cheese by the Jewish community of Sicily. In one document, a certain Fārājī Kohen, one of the Sicilian merchants who commuted to Alexandria, sold approximately 80 kilograms of kosher-stamped Sicilian cheese to a man named Bu'l-Faraj b. Barakāt.

SERVES: 6 people

TIME: 10 min prep, 10–25 hours resting time

4½ cups (1 kg) Turkish yogurt (10% fat)

1 tbsp kosher salt

5 black olives

Olive oil (optional)

Sumac (optional)

Za'atar (optional)

Aleppo pepper (optional)

Labneh:

1. In a large bowl, mix the Turkish yogurt and salt. Do not whisk the mixture. Let it rest for one hour; this allows the salt to distribute evenly in the yogurt.

2. Open a clean cheesecloth and place its center in the middle of another bowl, with the four corners hanging outside the bowl. Gently pour the salted yogurt into the center of the cheesecloth. Gather the four corners and close the cheesecloth to enclose the cheese. Hang the cheesecloth with the yogurt inside and place the bowl underneath to catch the whey (the liquid that drains out).

3. Let the yogurt drain at room temperature for 15 hours if it is not hot in the room. Then, using the same method, continue to let it drain in the refrigerator for 10 hours. Finally, carefully open the cheesecloth and with a spoon, transfer the labneh to a shallow plate.

4. I prefer my labneh slightly firm, so I let it rest for a longer time. If you prefer a softer labneh, you can reduce the resting time to 7 hours at room temperature and 3 hours in the refrigerator, or 10h in the refrigerator.

5. This labneh is delicious when topped with drizzled olive oil, sumac and za'atar.

SERVES: about 30 pieces

TIME: 1 hour (15 minutes prep, 20 minutes chilling, 20 minutes baking, 10 minutes cooling)

- 1 cup (150 g) chickpea flour
- 2 tsp olive oil
- 1 tbsp za'atar (hyssop) leaves, chopped
- 3 tbsp water
- 1 tsp nigella seeds
- ½ tsp baking powder
- 1 tsp salt
- 2 tsp honey + 1 tbsp melted honey, to brush
- 1 tsp coarse salt

Chickpea crackers:

1. Preheat the oven to 200°C/400°F. In a bowl, combine all the dry ingredients except for the 1 teaspoon of coarse salt. Gradually add the honey and water, kneading with your hands until you have a smooth and uniform dough ball.

2. Divide the dough into two balls. Take one ball, place it between two sheets of parchment paper, and roll it out with a rolling pin until the dough is about ⅛ of an inch thick, or as thin as possible. Chill the rolled-out dough in the refrigerator for 20 minutes.

3. Line a baking tray with parchment paper and carefully transfer the chilled dough onto it, removing the top layer of parchment paper. Lightly brush the entire surface of the dough with melted honey. Using a pizza cutter, cut the dough into 1.5-inch (4 cm) squares (or triangles), but do not separate them. Sprinkle the crackers with the coarse salt.

4. Bake in the preheated oven for 13 minutes. Allow the crackers to cool for 10 minutes before separating them.

Presentation:

1. Take a medium-sized plate with shallow edges, and place a full ladle of labneh in the center of the plate. Using a large spoon, spread the labneh from the center towards the edges of the plate in a circular motion. Arrange a dozen olives in the center of the plate, drizzle a bit of olive oil over the labneh, and sprinkle it with Sumac flakes or Aleppo pepper and za'atar. Place the crackers on one side of the plate.

2. Labneh can be stored in the refrigerator for several days and is delicious when paired with sun-dried tomatoes, olives, or slices of garlic-fried eggplant.

*See the photo on the next page.

POTATO MATZAH

These matzot are very light and easy to digest. They are a great alternative for those who do not consume wheat.

<u>Serves</u>: 6 pieces

<u>Time</u>: 20 minutes

1 cup (180 g) + ¼ (45 g) cup potato starch

½ cup (100 ml) boiling water

1 tsp salt

1. In a mixing bowl, add 1 cup of potato starch and the salt. Gradually add the ½ cup of boiling water while mixing with a fork. Continue to mix with the fork for one minute.

2. Once the starch has absorbed all the water, mix with your fingertips (not with the whole hand). Be careful, the dough will be sticky! Let it rest for 3–4 minutes. Add the other ¼ cup of starch, and mix again with your fingertips.

3. Form 6 equally-sized balls from the dough (about 1⅝ oz/47 g each). Sprinkle some starch on the work surface, and place one ball in the center. Using only the edge of your palm, flatten the ball. This helps to remove any lumps. Repeat this process 5 times and set the flattened ball aside. Repeat the same process for the remaining balls.

4. Take the first flattened ball and sprinkle some starch on the work surface. Using a rolling pin lightly dusted with starch, roll out the ball to obtain a disc with a maximum diameter of 4 inches (10 cm). The disc should be about 3–4 millimeters thick.

5. In a very hot, dry pan, place the disc. After one minute, you can move it a bit to prevent it from sticking to the pan. After 1 minute and 30 seconds, flip it over and let it cook for another 1 minute. Then flip it again for another 20 seconds. It will puff up.

6. Transfer it to a plate and cover it with a clean cloth or plastic wrap. This matzah will dry out quickly in the open air, so it's important to cover them. If you want to eat them later, moisten them slightly with water before gently reheating (preferably in the microwave).

PURPLE CORN TORTILLA AND FRIED EGGPLANT
WITH TEHINA, LIME AND CILANTRO SAUCE

SERVES: 10 tortillas

TIME: 2–2:30 hours

For the tortillas:

1½ cup (150 g) + 2 tbsp purple corn flour

1 tsp salt

1 cup (200 ml) boiling water

½ cup (60 g) tapioca flour

To make the tortillas:

1. Put the purple corn flour and salt into a bowl, and gradually add the boiling water while stirring with a fork. Continue to mix with the fork for a minute. Once the flour has absorbed all the water, mix lightly with your fingertips (not with your whole hand). Let it rest for 3–4 minutes, then add the tapioca flour and mix again with your fingers.

2. Form 10 balls from the dough (about 1⅜ oz/40 g each). Put some starch on the working surface, and place a ball in the middle. Using only the edge of your palm, flatten the ball. This helps remove any lumps. Do this for all the balls.

3. If you have a tortilla press, use it along with parchment paper (top and bottom) to press out the tortillas. You can also use a lightly starched rolling pin to roll out the balls to a maximum 10 cm diameter disk. The dough should be about an eighth of an inch (3–4 mm) thick.

4. Place the uncooked tortilla in a very hot (and dry) frying pan. After one minute, you can move it a bit to prevent sticking. After one minute and 30 seconds, flip it over and let it cook for another 1 minute and 30 seconds. After cooking, stack the tortillas on a plate and keep them covered with a clean cloth or plastic wrap.

For the eggplant:

3 eggplants (not very thick)

1 tbsp salt

½ cup (70 g) flour

1 tsp baking powder

¼ cup (30 g) corn starch

2 tsp smoked paprika

1 tsp salt

½ cup (100 ml) sparkling water (more or less)

½ cup (70 g) flour, for coating

1 cup (120 g) Breadcrumbs

Oil for frying

For the Tehina and Lime Sauce:

½ cup labneh (see p. 352) or heavy cream

¼ cup (120 g) tehina sesame paste

1 lime juice

2 tsp salt

½ cup (30 g) cilantro, fresh and chopped

1 tbsp Cumin seed

2 tsp Chili flakes

½ lime, cut

To prepare the eggplant:

1. Trim the stem of the eggplant and cut it in half lengthwise (do not slice it). Roughly peel the skin off of the eggplant, leaving some skin in place. Cut each half of the eggplant into sticks that are about ¾ of an inch (2 cm) wide. Sprinkle them with salt, place them on a wire rack, and let them drain for 20 minutes. Afterwards, pat them dry with paper towels.

2. In a bowl, mix together all the dry ingredients: flour, baking powder, starch, smoked paprika, and salt. Whisk to ensure there are no lumps. Gradually add sparkling water to the bowl, stirring until you have a liquid batter that is slightly thick, similar to pancake batter.

3. Place the coating flour on a plate, and prepare another plate with breadcrumbs. Keep the bowl with the batter close to you, and prepare a tray or large plate that can be placed in the refrigerator.

4. Take an eggplant stick and roll it in the flour to coat it, using a fork or kitchen tongs. Shake off any excess flour. Dip it into the batter, allowing any excess batter to drip off, and then place it in the breadcrumbs. Coat it evenly with breadcrumbs and place it on the plate. Repeat this process with all the eggplant sticks. Chill them in the refrigerator for 20 minutes.

5. Heat a deep fryer or deep-frying pan over medium heat, and prepare a plate lined with paper towels. Using kitchen tongs, carefully place the sticks in the deep fryer. Allow them to fry undisturbed for one minute before gently turning them to ensure even frying. Fry them for a total of approximately 3–4 minutes.

6. Using a slotted spoon or skimmer, remove the fried eggplant sticks from the fryer and place them on the paper towel-lined plate to drain excess oil.

To make the sauce:

1. In a bowl, combine labneh (or heavy cream), tehina sesame paste, the juice of 1 lime, and salt. Stir well to mix. Add cumin seeds to the sauce and stir again.

To serve the tortillas with the sauce:

1. Take a purple tortilla and spread a small spoonful of the sauce onto it. Place two eggplant sticks in the middle of the tortilla. Cover the eggplant sticks with another spoonful of sauce. Sprinkle with freshly chopped cilantro, chili flakes, and if desired, additional lime juice.

*See the photo on the next page.

CHEESE TAPIOCA MATZAH

I love the gelatinous texture of tapioca starch tortillas. This tuber is also known as mandioca, manioc, or yucca. When tapioca starch is mixed with boiling water, it forms a ball of soft and light dough that hardens if left to rest at room temperature for a while. This preparation is suitable for making dishes for Passover.

Serves: 6 pieces

Time: 20 minutes

- 1 cup (180 g) tapioca starch + ¼ cup (31 g)
- ½ cup (100 ml) boiling water + 2 tbsp
- 1 tsp salt
- 6 tbsp grated cheese (like Emmental)

1. Add the 1 cup of tapioca starch and salt to a bowl. Gradually add ½ cup of boiling water while stirring with a fork; continue to mix with the fork for a minute. Once the starch has absorbed all the water, mix lightly with your fingertips (not your whole hand). Be careful, the dough is sticky.

2. Let it rest for 3–4 minutes.

3. Add the other ¼ cup of tapioca starch, and mix again with your fingers. Form 6 equally-sized balls of dough (about 1⅝ oz/50 g each) and put some starch on a working surface.

4. Take a ball of dough, make a deep hole in the middle and stuff it with 1 tsp grated cheese. Seal the ball covering the grated cheese. Alternatively, you can combine cheese and dough.

5. Using only the edge of your palm, flatten the ball. This helps remove any lumps. Do this 5 times and set the ball aside. Repeat for the other balls.

6. Take the first ball again, and with a lightly starched rolling pin, roll out the ball to make a flat tortilla about four inches (10 cm) wide and 3–4 millimeters thick.

7. Place the dough in a very hot and dry frying pan. After one minute, you can move it a bit to prevent sticking. After one minute and 30 seconds, flip it over and let it cook for another 1 minute. Flip and cook for another 20 seconds. Place it on a plate and cover it with a clean cloth or plastic wrap.

8. This tapioca starch maztah recipe pairs well with avocado and fresh cilantro, as well as with meat.

MA'ASSAL: MOROCCAN LAMB STEW

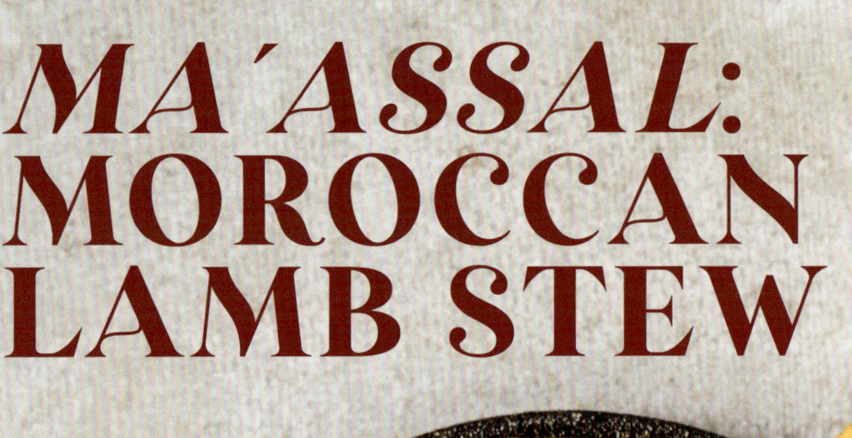

The word "ma'assal" refers to a meat confit for the Jews of Fes from the first half of the 20th century. In other cities of Morocco, ma'assal is also known as "muruzia," particularly in the Moroccan capital of Rabat. The first recipe for meat confit called "muruzia" can be found in the oldest cookbook of the Muslim West, in Andalusia, which dates back to the 13th century: the *Kitab al-tabih.* Interestingly, the Jews of Fes also refer to a jam made from dried grapes and walnut oil (or almonds) called "muruzia."

This lamb stew was presented for the dinner "Sephardic Feast with guest Chef and Author Hélène Jawhara Piñer and Chef Michael Solomonov" on March 17, 2022, at Chef Justin Severino's restaurant "Morcilla" in Pittsburgh, with the aim of promoting Sephardic cuisine. On the menu, it was called "Andalusian Lamb Stew" and was made with Elysian Lamb from a local farm. Chef Solomonov, Zahav Chef and co-owner, added his own twists to the recipe by incorporating pomegranate molasses, mint, and wine.

The Moroccan bread *Batbot* fits perfectly for this dish.

Serves: 4 people

Time: 2 hours (and overnight)

2.2 lbs (1 kg) Elysian Lamb shoulder

2 cups (½ liter) red wine

1 cup (250 g) golden raisins

½ cup (100 g) skinned almonds

1 chopped onion

2 tbsp honey

Water

2 tbsp oil

2 tsp salt

1 grated garlic clove

1 tsp of saffron

1 tsp ground ginger

1 cinnamon stick

1 tsp *ras el hanout*

Pomegranate molasses

Mint to decorate

1 tsp toasted sesame

1. Cut the meat into chunks. In a large bowl, place the meat pieces along with the salt, grated garlic, saffron, ginger, cinnamon stick, and spices. Pour in the wine to create a marinade. Mix well to ensure all the meat pieces are coated. Cover the bowl and let it marinate overnight.

2. Next, take a pot and add the marinated meat pieces, reserving the marinade. Sear the meat for about five minutes without adding the marinade. Once the meat is browned, pour in enough water to cover the meat and add the reserved spice marinade. Bring to a boil and then reduce the heat. Let it simmer for 1 hour. When the meat is nearly cooked, rinse the raisins and add them to the pot. Continue cooking uncovered for 10 minutes.

3. Finally, add the honey to the pot and continue cooking over low heat for 40 minutes until the mixture becomes syrupy. Stir in the pomegranate molasses.

4. In a separate large frying pan, heat neutral oil and fry the almonds until they turn golden.

5. To serve, place the meat on plates, spoon the sauce over the meat, and sprinkle with the fried almonds, mint leaves and sesame seeds.

6. Eat with small *Batbot* breads (below).

BATBOT: FLAT AND CHEWY MOROCCAN BREAD

SERVES: 6 large or 12 small flatbreads

TIME: 30 minutes prep, 30 minutes to rise, 30 minutes to bake

4 cups (600 g) flour

4 cups (600 g) extra fine semolina

1 tbsp salt

2 tbsp (35 g) fresh yeast (or 1½ tbsp active dry yeast, or 3 tbsp sourdough starter)

3⅓ cup (670 ml) lukewarm water

Nigella seeds, sesame seeds, and za'atar to sprinkle

1. In the bowl of a stand mixer, combine the flour, extra fine semolina, and salt. Attach the hook attachment and mix for 1 minute. Add the crumbled fresh yeast, and gradually pour in the lukewarm water in four batches.

2. The dough may appear slightly sticky, but that's normal. Continue mixing for at least 10 minutes. If you don't have a stand mixer, knead the dough by hand for at least 20 minutes. Prepare a tray or towel by lining it with parchment paper and lightly dusting it with flour.

3. Take portions of the dough, about the size of tennis balls, and knead them again until they become very smooth. On a lightly floured surface, use your fingers to flatten the dough portions into round disks. Place them on the prepared tray, ensuring they are lightly coated with flour, and cover them with a kitchen towel. Allow the dough to rise for 30 minutes.

4. Heat a skillet, preferably a cast iron one, over medium-high heat.

5. Carefully place a flatbread in the hot skillet. Moisten your hand slightly with water and gently dampen the top of the bread. Sprinkle sesame, za'atar, or nigella seeds over the top. After 2 minutes, gently flip the bread and cook the other side. It should turn golden.

PASSOVER *MURUZIA* JAM

SERVES: 1 small jar

TIME: 1 hour 15 minutes

1 cup (160 g) golden raisins

¼ cup (50 g) sugar

¼ cup (50 g) water

1 seedless lemon

¾ cup (100 g) walnuts, crushed

1. Rinse the raisins, and put them in a saucepan with the sugar and lemon juice. Cook covered for about 15 minutes over medium heat, stirring regularly, until the water has evaporated.

2. Remove the raisins from the pan and mash in a mortar.

3. Spread the walnuts on a baking sheet and toast them under the broiler for a few minutes until they are fragrant.

4. Put both the walnuts and the raisin puree back into the pan and stir gently over low heat for a few minutes.

5. The jam can be eaten hot or cold, and can be stored in a jar.

APPLE *BUNUELOS* WITH TEA AND HONEY

Like many people, I make donuts for Hanukkah and Rosh Hashanah. The following recipe is for *buñuelos de manzana* (apple donuts). I usually use honey instead of sugar in my dishes. And when Rosh Hashanah is around the corner, honey takes an even more symbolic meaning. Apple and honey are the perfect combination, and the touch of tea gives these donuts a very unique and enjoyable flavor.

SERVES: 15 donuts

TIME: 45 minutes

2 cups water

3 apples (Braedburn, Reinettes) cut into thin (¼ inch/0.5 cm) slices

1 tbsp black tea (if possible, Arya Tara)

1 cup (150 g) flour

½ tsp kosher salt

2 eggs (separate yolks and whites)

¾ cup (145 ml) milk

⅛ cup (30 g) sugar

⅓ cup hot honey

1. Boil 2 cups water and add the tea in a strainer ball. In the meantime, peel the apples and cut them into slices. Once the tea is ready, remove and reserve one tablespoon of it (to be used with the honey later in the recipe).

2. Place the apple pieces in a small bowl and pour the very hot tea over them. Cover the bowl with plastic wrap and cook in the microwave for about 2 minutes. Drain the cooked apple slices and set them aside to cool.

3. Slowly combine the flour, sugar, and salt together, then add the two egg yolks. Gradually pour in the milk while mixing to prevent lumps. The dough should have a thick paste-like consistency. In a separate large bowl, beat the two egg whites for about three minutes until stiff peaks form. They should be firm but not hard. Carefully fold the beaten egg whites into the dough mixture.

4. Heat oil in a frying pan until it reaches 375°F (190°C), and prepare a plate lined with paper towels to absorb excess oil.

5. Take an apple slice, dip it into the dough (ensuring there is no excess dough clinging to it, and then fry it for approximately two minutes per side until golden brown.

6. Transfer the cooked buñuelos to the plate lined with paper towels. Repeat the process with the remaining apple slices.

7. Pour the honey onto a separate plate and add the one tablespoon of tea water that was set aside earlier in the recipe. Mix well to combine.

8. Take a buñuelo and dip it into the honey-tea mixture for about five seconds per side.

9. Place the coated buñuelos on a clean plate.

10. You can also glaze or coat the buñuelos with chocolate, sugar-cinnamon, or any other desired toppings.

"Ocho Kandelikas" (Eight Little Candles) is a Ladino (judeo-Spanish language of the Sephardim) song celebrating the holiday of Hanukkah, written by the Jewish-Bosnian-American composer Flory Jagoda (1923–2021) in 1983. She received a National Heritage Fellowship from the National Endowment for the Arts for her efforts in passing on the tradition of Sephardic songs sung in Ladino:

Hanukah linda sta aki,
ocho kandelas para mi,
Hanukah linda sta aki,
ocho kandelas para mi, O . . .

Una kandelika, dos kandelikas, tres kandelikas,
kuatro kandelikas, sintyu kandelikas,
sej kandelikas, siete kandelikas,
Ocho kandelas para mi.

"Muchas fiestas vo fazer, kon alegrias I plazer,
Muchas fiestas vo fazer, kon alegrias i plazer,
Los pastelikos vo kumer, kon almendrikas i la myel,
Los pastelikos vo kumer, kon almendrikas i la myel. O . . ."

Una kandelika, dos kandelikas, tres kandelikas,
kuatro kandelikas, sintyu kandelikas,
sej kandelikas, siete kandelikas,
Ocho kandelas para mi.

Una kandelika, dos kandelikas, tres kandelikas,
kuatro kandelikas, sintyu kandelikas,
sej kandelikas, siete kandelikas,
Ocho kandelas para mi

OCHO CANDELIKAS
HANUKKIAH CHALLAH CANDLES

In tribute to Flori Jagoda and her song "Ocho candelikas" I present this recipe for a challah shaped like a Hanukkiah with eight branches and a central candle.

SERVES: 1 large Hanukkiah challah

TIME: 3h

1 tbsp lukewarm milk

1 tbsp fresh yeast

3¾ cup (575 g) flour

½ cup (55 g) sugar

½ tsp salt

¾ cup (140 ml) lukewarm water

1 tbsp orange blossom water

2 eggs

2 egg yolks

¼ cup (40 g) oil

1 egg, beaten, to brush

Coloring gel (orange and yellow)

1. In a small bowl, warm the milk and stir in the yeast. In a large bowl or the bowl of a mixer, combine the flour, sugar, and salt. Mix for a few seconds, then add the warm water and the milk-yeast mixture.

2. Knead for 15 seconds, then add the orange blossom water, whole eggs, egg yolks, and oil. Knead by hand for 20 minutes or use a stand mixer on medium speed for 10 minutes. The dough should be smooth. Cover and let it rise for 1 hour and 30 minutes.

3. After the dough rises, gently press the dough with your hands to release the air. Divide the dough into 12 equally-sized balls (about 2⅞ oz/84 g each), except for one which should be slightly larger. Cool in the refrigerator for 20 minutes.

4. Oil your hands lightly, take 8 of the regular-sized balls of dough, and divide each into three equal pieces of dough the size of a golf ball (1⅛ oz or 30 g) each. Roll the pieces in between your hands to make 3 strands, around 6 inches/15 cm long each, and braid them together. Pinch the ends of the strands together to secure the braid. Repeat this process with the remaining seven balls.

5. Take another dough ball and roll it into a thin rope about 8 inches (20 cm) long. This is the *shamesh*. To make a twist, hold one end and roll the rest of the strand under the palm of your hand.

*See the photo on the pages 372–373.

6. Take the largest ball, and shape it into a long rope (16 inches (40 cm) that will serve as the base for the candles.

7. Divide the eleventh ball of dough into three parts and braid them as before; this will serve as the trunk of the hanukkiah.

8. Shape the last ball into a rope that will serve as the base of the hanukkiah.

9. Prepare a baking tray and line it with parchment paper.

10. Make the hanukkiah directly on the parchment paper: place the base of the hanukkiah horizontally across the long side of the baking sheet. In the middle and perpendicular to it, place the braided trunk, and press the ends together to connect them. Place the other rope parallel to the base, with its center at the end of the braided trunk. Pinch the dough together to connect them. Place the twisted *shamesh* in the middle of the hanukkiah, in line with the braided trunk, and press to connect it. Finally, add the eight remaining candles (the first eight balls) on either side of the central candle, and press the lower ends onto the base rope to connect them.

11. Pinch the top of each candle to form a small flame, and paint the flame with food coloring gel.

12. Leave the Hanukkiah to rise in a warm place, covered with a kitchen towel, for 1–1.5 hours.

13. Preheat the oven to 330°F (170°C), and lightly brush the hanukkiah with the beaten egg.

14. Bake for 25 minutes, and allow it to cool for 20 minutes before removing it from the baking tray.

BURNT BASQUE CHEESECAKE

Cheesecake is not exclusive to the United States. In the north of Spain, there exists a fresh cheese cake, baked for a long time in the oven, with a top that is so cooked and caramelized that it almost becomes black. As a big fan of cheese and cheese-based cakes, I propose here a recipe that can be prepared for every day, and even for Passover, Shavuot or Hanukkah.

SERVES: 8 people

TIME: 40 minutes prep, 1 hour resting (and overnight)

18 oz (510 g) full-fat cream cheese

1 cup (230 g) labneh (or mascarpone)

1⅓ cup (320 g) heavy cream

1 cup (200 g) sugar

½ tsp salt

4 eggs

3.5 tbsp (30 g) corn starch, potato starch or almond flour

1. Preheat your oven to 400°F (210°C) for traditional baking (not convection), and lightly grease an 8-inch (20 cm diameter) springform pan. Take a single large sheet of parchment paper and moisten it with water. After crumpling it up, press it to drain any excess water, being careful not to tear it. Line both the bottom and sides of the springform pan with the parchment paper, ensuring that the paper extends above the baking pan's sides.

2. In a large bowl, mix the cream cheese, labneh, heavy cream, and salt. Do not whip the mixture. Add the sifted corn starch/potato starch/almond flour to the mixture, and mix carefully until homogeneous.

3. In a bowl, beat the eggs with sugar for about 3 minutes until the batter becomes smooth and creamy. Then, add it to the cheese-flour mixture and stir well. Pour the mixture into the lined springform pan, and tap it on the table to remove any air bubbles.

4. Bake for 25 minutes. When finished, it should be jiggly in the middle (more than a traditional American cheesecake), and the top should be dark. If the top is not dark enough broil the cheesecake for 4 minutes.

5. Then turn off the oven and open the door, but leave the cheesecake inside for 10 minutes. After 10 minutes, the center should still jiggle when you shake it, but less than before.

6. Remove from the oven and let it cool at room temperature for 1 hour. Then put it in the fridge for at least 3 hours (but overnight is better). Carefully remove the cheesecake from the mold and parchment paper, and put it on a plate.

7. You can enjoy this cheesecake plain or with quince jelly or orange marmalade.

ANDALUSIAN ANGEL HAIR CHALLAH

This challah is the one I make most often. It reminds me of my Andalusian roots on my father's side, because of its strongly spiced flavor and aroma and because it is made with "angel hair" made from strands of Siam squash.

SERVES: 2 medium loaves

TIME: 30 minutes of prep, 7+ hours for rising, 25 minutes for baking

1½ cup (300 ml) warm water

5 tsp active yeast

¾ cup (150 g) sugar

2 cups (300 g) flour +2 tsp ground cinnamon

2 tsp salt

1 tsp ground ginger

2 ground cardamom seeds

2 eggs

½ cup (125 g) angel hair jam ("Cabello de ángel")

⅓ cup (66 g) neutral oil

5 cups (750 g) flour

½ cup white sesame seeds

1 egg, beaten + 1 tbsp heavy cream

1 tbsp bergamot syrup, to brush (optional)

1. In a small bowl, mix the warm water with the yeast until dissolved, and let it rest for 5 minutes.

2. In a large bowl or in the bowl of a mixer, combine ¾ cup of flour, cinnamon powder, salt, ginger powder, and cardamom. Mix for 30 seconds, and then add the yeast-water mixture and mix for 30 more seconds.

3. Add the eggs, angel hair jam, and oil, and mix again for 30 seconds. Add the remaining flour. Knead in a stand mixer for 15 minutes at medium speed (or 25 minutes by hand).

4. Remove the dough from the bowl and shape it into a ball. Lightly oil the bowl with 1 tablespoon of oil and place the dough back in. Cover with a cloth and let it rise at room temperature for 1.5 hours. The dough will double in size.

5. Remove the dough from the bowl and deflate it by pressing it with your hands. Shape it back into a ball, and place it back into the same bowl and cover it. Place the bowl in the refrigerator for at least 6 hours, or overnight.

6. Remove the dough from the bowl and deflate it by pressing it with your hands. Shape it back into a ball, and divide it into 10 equally-sized balls to make 2 braided loaves with 5 strands each. If you braid each loaf with 3 strands, divide the dough into 6 equally-sized balls.

7. Place a sheet of parchment paper on a baking sheet. Sprinkle sesame seeds in two lines where the loaves will be placed, with space between them.

8. Lightly flour a work surface, and braid your loaves (without pulling the strands too tightly, or the dough may tear). When finished, place them on the prepared sesame seeds. Cover the loaves with a light cloth and let them rise for 1 to 1½ hours in a warm place, protected from drafts.

9. Preheat the oven to 340°F (170°C). Before baking, beat an egg together with the heavy cream. Gently brush the loaves with this mixture. Bake for 25 minutes, until golden brown color.

10. When out of the oven, lightly brush the surface of the loaves with bergamot syrup (optional).

11. Let them cool. This hallah is delicious plain or as a complement to various dishes.

---

*See the photo on the next page.

SALMOREJO AND MATZAH: COLD TOMATO SOUP
FROM ANDALUSIA

This chilled soup is traditionally made with regular bread, but using matzah bread adds a delicate and velvety twist to the dish.

SERVES: 4 people

TIME: 15 minutes of prep, 3 hours to chill

7 red ripe tomatoes, diced

2 teaspoons of salt

1 or 2 cloves of garlic, crushed

3 large pieces of plain matzot, broken into small chunks

¼ cup of vinegar (preferably Jerez vinegar)

½ cup of olive oil

½ cup of ice

To garnish:

2 hard-boiled eggs

1 tablespoon of olive oil

Dried beef (optional)

1. Boil the eggs until hard-boiled. Once cooked, cool them under cold water and then mash them with a fork. Set aside.

2. In a large bowl, combine the tomatoes, salt, crushed garlic, and matzot pieces. Pour the vinegar and olive oil over the mixture. Stir well to ensure everything is evenly soaked. Cover the bowl with plastic wrap and refrigerate for about 3 hours to chill and allow the flavors to meld.

3. Transfer the chilled mixture to a blender and blend until smooth. Add the ice to the blender and continue blending until you achieve a velvety texture.

4. Pour the salmorejo into 4 small bowls. Sprinkle the crushed eggs in the center of each dish, add small chunks of dried beef if desired, and drizzle 1 tablespoon of olive oil lightly over each serving. Serve cold and enjoy.

BIBLIOGRAPHY

Abbott, Lyman, and Thomas Jefferson Conant. *A Dictionary of Religious Knowledge, for Popular and Professional Use: Comprising Full Information on Biblical, Theological, and Ecclesiastical Subjects. With Several Hundred Maps and Illustrations*. Harper & Brothers, 1885.

Abrahams, I. *Jewish life in the Middle Ages*. Philadelphia: Jewish Publication Society, 1930.

Alberro, Solange. Chapitre II. Résistances et assimilation In: Inquisition et société au Mexique: 1571–1700. Mexico: Centro de estudios mexicanos y centroamericanos, 1988 (generated 09 février 2023). https://doi.org/10.4000/books.cemca.2613.

Azevedo Mea, Elvira. *Sentenças da Inquisição de Coimbra (II) em metropolitanos de D. Frei Bartolomeu dos Mártires (1567–1582)*. Porto: Arquivo Histórico Dominicano Português, 1982.

Baer, Yitzhak. *Historia de los judios en la España cristiana*. Barcelona: Riopiedras, 1998.

Baroja Caro, Julio. *Los judíos en la España moderna y contemporánea*. Madrid: Ariel, 1961.

Beinart, Haim. *Records of Trials of the Spanish Inquisition in Ciudad Real, vol. 1: 1483–1485*. Jerusalem: Israel National Academy of Sciences and Humanities, 1974.

Beinart, Haim. *Records of Trials of the Spanish Inquisition in Ciudad Real, vol. 2: 1494–1512*. Jerusalem: Israel National Academy of Sciences and Humanities, 1977.

Beinart, Haim. *Records of Trials of the Spanish Inquisition in Ciudad Real, vol. 3: 1512–1527*. Jerusalem: Israel National Academy of Sciences and Humanities, 1981.

Blázquez, Juan Miguel. *Inquisición y criptojudaismo*. Madrid: Kaydeda, 1988.

Blásquez, Juan Miguel. *Toledot, Historia del Toledo judío*. Toledo: Arcano, 1989.

Boeglin, Michel. *L'Inquisition espagnole au lendemain du concile de Trente: Le tribunal du Saint-Office de Séville (1560–1700)*. Presses universitaires de la Méditerranée, 2004.

Boleslao, Lewin. *Singular proceso de Salomon Machorro (Juan de Leon): Israelita liornes condenado por la inquisicion (Mexico, 1650)*. Buenos Aires, 1977.

Carbonell, Pedro Miguel. *Opusculos inéditos del cronista catalan Pedro Miguel Carbonell*. Volume 2, 1865.

Carrete Parondo, Carlos. *Fontes Iudaeorum Regni Castellae, vol. II: El Tribunal de la Inquisición en el Obispado de Soria (1486–1502)*. Salamanca: Universidad Pontificada de Salamanca, Universidad de Granada, 1985.

Carrete Parondo, Carlos. *Fontes Iudaeorum Regni Castellae, vol. III: Proceso inquisitorial contra los Arias Dávila segovianos: un enfrentamiento social entre judíos y conversos*. Salamanca: Universidad Pontificada de Salamanca, Universidad de Granada, 1986.

Carrete Parondo, Carlos & Fraile Conde, Carolina. *Fontes Iudaeorum Regni Castellae, vol. IV. Los judeoconversos de Almazán (1501–1505). Origen familiar de los Lainez*. Salamanca: Universidad Pontificada de Salamanca, Universidad de Granada, 1987.

Chabrán, Rafael. "Dr. Francisco Hernández Ate Tacos: The Foods and Drinks of the Mexican Treasury." *Diálogo* 18 no. 1 (2015): Article 4.

Code of Jewish Law: Kitzur Shulchan Arukh. Translated by Chaim N. Denberg. Montreal: Jurisprudence Press, 1954.

Cole, Pete. *The Dream of the Poem. Hebrew Poetry from Muslim and Christian Spain 950–1492*. Princeton: Princeton University Press, 1997.

Cooper, John. *Eat and be Satisfied: A Social History of Jewish Food.* New Jersey: Jason Aronson, 1993.

Corominas, Joan, and José A. Pascual. *Diccionario Crítico Etimológico Castellano e Hispánico*. Gredos Editions: 1954.

Covarrubias Sebastiian de. *Diccionario de Autoridades*. Madrid: Real Academia Española, 1726.

Delgado Martínez, José and Amir Ashur. *La vida cotidiana de los judíos de Alandalús (Siglos X–XII). Antología de manuscritos de la Guenizá de El Cairo. University of Cambridge.* Córdoba: UCO Press, 2021.

Escobar Quevedo, Ricardo. *Inquisición y Judaizantes en América Española (Siglos XVI–XVII)*. Bogotá: Universidad del Rosario, 2010.

Freidenreich, D. *Foreigners and Their Food. Constructing Otherness in Jewish, Christian, and Islamic Law*. Berkeley: University of California Press, 2011.

García, Genaro, and Carlos Pereyra. *Documentos inéditos ó muy raros para la historia de México, Vol. 28–30*. Toronto: Toronto University Press, 1905.

Gerber, Jane. *The Jews of Spain: A History of the Sephardic Experience*. New York: The Free Press, 1994.

Gitlitz, David. *Secrecy and Deceit: The Religion of Crypto-Jews*. Philadelphia: The Jewish Publication Society, 1996.

Gitlitz, David, and Linda Kay Davidson. *A Drizzle of Honey: The Lives and Recipes of Spanish Secret Jews*. New York: Saint Martin's Press, 1999.

Gitlitz, David. *Living in Silverado: Secret Jews in the Silver Mining Towns of the Colonial Mexico*. Albuquerque: University of New Mexico Press, 2019.

Goiten, S.D. *A Mediterranean Society, Volume IV: The Jewish Communities of the Arab World as Portrayed in the Documents of the Cairo Geniza. Volume 4: Daily Life*. Berkeley: University of California Press, 2000.

Gottreich, Emily Benichou. *Jewish Morocco: A History from Pre-Islamic to Postcolonial Times*. Bloomsbury Publishing, 2020.

Gampel, Benjamin R. *Anti-Jewish Riots in the Crown of Aragon and the Royal Response, 1391–1392*. New York: Cambridge University Press, 2016.

Gandz, Solomon. *The Code of Maimonides. Book Three. The Book of the Seasons*. Translated by Hyman Klein. New Haven: Yale University Press, 1961.

Guillaumond, Catherine. *Cuisine et diététique dans l'Occident arabe médiéval. D'après un traité anonyme du XIIIe siècle. Étude et traduction française*. Paris: L'Harmattan, 2017.

Hajjar, Rachel. "The Air of History Part III: The Golden Age in Arab Islamic Medicine. An Introduction." Dans *Heart Views: The Official Journal of the Gulf Heart Association*. Vol. 14. N ° 1, janvier-mars 2013: p. 43–46.

Huici Miranda, Ambrosio. *La cocina hispano-magrebí en la época almohade Según un manuscrito anónimo del siglo XIII*. Gijón: Trea, 2005.

Ibn Razīn al-Tuǧībī. *Relieves de las mesas acerca de las delicias de la comida y los diferentes platos (Fuḍālat al-Ḫiwān fī ṭayyibāt al-ṭa'ām wa-l-alwān)*. Edited and translated by Manuela Marín. Gijón: Trea, 2007.

João Capistrano Honório de Abreu. "Confissões da Bahia, 1591–1592: Primeira Visitação do Santo Ofício às Partes do Brasil." Kindle edition.

João Capistrano Honório de Abreu, *Primeira Visitacao Do Santo Officio as Partes Do Brasil Pelo Licenciado Heiter Furtads de Mendoca: Confissoes Da Bahia, 1591–92*, Sociedade Capistrano De Abreu: Hardpress Publishing, 2013.

Kraemer C, David. *Jewish Eating and Identity Through the Ages*. London: Routledge, 2008.

Liebman, Seymour B. *The Jews in New Spain. Faith, Flame, and the Inquisition*. Coral Gables: University of Miami Press, 1970.

Loewe, Herbert. *Mediaeval Hebrew Minstrelsy, Songs for the Bride Queen's Feast*. London: James Clark and Co., 1926. https://zemirotdatabase.org/view_song.php?id=36

MacDonald, Nathan. *Not Bread Alone: The Uses of Food in the Old Testament*. New York: Oxford University Press, 2008.

MacDonald, Nathan. *What Did the Ancient Israelites Eat? Diet in Biblical Times*. Grand Rapids, MI: William B. Eerdmans, 2008.

Maimonides. *Hanhagat ha-Beri'ut (Regimen Sanitatis)*. Edited by Solomon Munter. Vol. 1, no. 6. Jerusalem: Mosad ha-Rav Kook, 1957.

Maimónides. *Obras médicas I. El régimen de salud. Tratado sobre la curación de las hemorroides*. Edited and translated by Lola Ferre. Barcelona: Herder, 2016.

Maimónides. *Obras médicas I. El régimen de salud. Tratado sobre la curación de las hemorroides*. Edited and translated by Lola Ferre. Barcelona: Herder, 2016.

Maimónides. *Obras médicas II. El libro del asma*. Edited and translated by Lola Ferre. Barcelona: Herder, 2016.

Maimonides. *On Asthma: A parallel Arabic-English edition*. Edited, translated, and annotated by Gerrit Bos. Leiden: Brill, 2002.

Maimonides. *On the Regimen of Health: A New Parallel*. Edited, translated, and annotated by Gerrit Bos. Leiden: Brill, 2019.

Mohlo, Michael. *Usos y costumbres de los sefardíes de Salónica*. Madrid: Consejo Superior de Investigaciones Científicas, 1950.

Monaco, Farell. "Breads of the Gods: An Ancient Greek recipe for the Pharmakos Barley Cakes with Cheese and Figs." In *Tavola Mediterranea*, July 24, 2020. https://tavolamediterranea.com/2020/07/24/bread-for-the-gods-pharmakos-barley-cakes-with-cheese-and-figs/

Nebrija Antonio de. *Gramática sobre la lengua española. Vocabulario español-latino*. Madrid: Real Academia Española, 1494.

Nirenberg, David. *Neighboring Faiths: Christianity, Islam, and Judaism in the Middle Ages and Today*. Chicago: University of Chicago Press, 2014.

Pérez Alonso, María Isabel. "La olla judía del Šabbat: estudio lexicológico y lexicográfico de adafina, Ḥamín, caliente(s) y otras denominaciones." *Espacio, tiempo y forma. Historia Medieval* 28 (2015): 441–458.

Pilar Bravo Lledó. "Las costumbres judeoconversas en Alcalá de Henares." Museo Casa Natal de Cervantes, Archivo Histórico Nacional, 2012.

Piñer, Hélène Jawhara. "El patrimonio culinario judío de la Península Ibérica a través de un manuscrito del siglo XIII. Ejemplos de la pervivencia de recetas en la cocina de los sefardíes de España y de Marruecos." *Ladinar* 12 (2020): 45–62.

Piñer, Hélène Jawhara. "Maqruḍ المقروض or Maqrūṭ المقروط: A Moroccan Sephardi Recipe for Ramadan." *Sephardi Weekly*, May 2018.

Piñer, Hélène Jawhara. "Almoronía: A Moroccan-Jewish Recipe from the 13th Century Andalusia." *Sephardi Report*, March 2019.

Piñer, Hélène Jawhara. "Making Mufleta, History's Oldest Jewish Pastry, for the Holidays." *Tablet Magazine*. September 7, 2018.

Piñer, Hélène Jawhara. *Jews, Food and Spain: The Oldest Medieval Spanish Cookbook and the Sephardic Culinary Heritage*. Boston: Cherry Orchard, 2022.

Qusṭā ibn Lūqā's medical regime for the pilgrims to Mecca : Risālā fī tadbīr safar al-ḥajj, Edited and translated by Gerrit Bos. New York: Brill, 1992.

RELMIN projet. "Le statut légal des minorités religieuses dans l'espace euro-méditerranéen (V[e]-XV[e]siècle)." Digital edition, Institut de Recherche et d'Histoire des Textes - Orléans http://www.cn-telma.fr/relmin/extrait252359/.

Roden, Claudia. *Le livre de la cuisine de la cuisine juive*. Portugal: Flammarion, 2012.

Romanow, Katherine. "Mufleta, Zaban, and Sushi: The Development of the Mimouna and its Foodways from Morocco to Montreal." Unpublished Thesis in The Department of Religious Studies Presented in Partial Fulfillment of the Requirements for the Degree of Master of Arts (Judaic Studies). Concordia University, Montreal, 2013.

Romero Castelló, Elena. "El olor del sábado: la adafina, del Arcipreste de Hita a las versiones 'light.'" In *La mesa puesta: leyes, costumbres y recetas judías: XVI curso de cultura hispanojudía y sefardí de la Universidad de Castilla-La Mancha: en memoria de Iacob M. Hassán*, edited by Uriel Macías and Ricardo Izquierdo Benito. Cuenca: Universidad de Castilla la Mancha, 2010.

Romero, Elena. "Canciones y coplas sefardíes de contenido gastronómico." In *La mesa puesta: leyes, costumbres y recetas judías: XVI curso de cultura hispanojudía y sefardí de la Universidad de Castilla-La Mancha: en memoria de Iacob M. Hassán*, edited by Uriel Macías and Ricardo Izquierdo Benito, 171–214. Cuenca: Universidad de Castilla la Mancha, 2010.

Safra, Edmond (ed.). *Chumash*. Translated by Aharon Marciano. New York: ArtScroll Series, 2017.

Samrakandi, Mohammed-Habib and Georges Carantino (eds.). *Manger au Maghreb: Part 2. Approche pluridisciplinaire des pratiques de table en Méditerranée du Moyen Âge à nos jours*. Toulouse: PU du Mirail, 2009.

Sánchez Moya, Manuel, and Jasone Monasterio Aspiri. "Los judaizantes turolenses en el Siglo XV." *Sefarad* 32 (1972): 105–140.

Sefaria. "Exodus 16." Accessed April, 18, 2017. https://www.sefaria.org/Exodus.16?ven=The_Koren_Jerusalem_Bible&lang=bi&aliyot=0.

Sefaria. "Shabbat 119a." Accessed April, 18, 2017. https://www.sefaria.org/Shabbat.119a.8?lang=bi&p2=Jastrow%2C_חֶ%D6%BCבָל.1&lang2=bi&w2=Shabbat&lang3=en.

Selke de Sanchez, Angela. *Los Chuetas y la Inquisición. Vida y muerte en el ghetto de Mallorca.* Madrid: Taurus Ediciones, 1972.

Shafer-Elliott, Cynthia. *Food in Ancient Judah. Domestic Cooking in the Time of the Hebrew Bible.* Bristol: Equinox Publishing, 2013.

Shapiro, Benjamin. "The Hidden Jews of New Mexico." *Avotaynu: The International Review of Jewish Genealogy* 5.4 (1989): S4.

Shatzmiller, Maya. "Professions and Ethnic Origin of Urban Labourers in Muslim Spain: Evidence from a Moroccan Source." *Awraq* 5 (1983): 152–153.

Sierro Malmierca, Feliciano. *Judíos, moriscos e Inquisición en Ciudad Rodrigo*. Salamanca: Diputación de Salamanaca, 1990.

Siqueira, Sonia. *A Inquisição portuguesa e a sociedade colonial: a açao do Santo Oficio na Bahia e em Pernambuco na época das visitações.* São Paulo: Atica, 1978.

Toaff, Ariel. "Le couscous et l'histoire des juifs en Italie." In *Couscous, boulgour et polenta. Transformer et consommer les céréales dans le monde*, edited by Hélène Franconie, Monique Chastanet, and François Sigaut, 143–44. Paris: Karthala, 2010.

Toro, Alfonso (ed.). *Los judíos en la Nueva España: documentos del siglo XVI correspondientes al ramo de Inquisición.* México: Archivo General de la Nación: Fondo de cultura económica, 1982.

Uchmany, Eva Alexandra. *La vida entre el judaísmo y el cristianismo en la Nueva España (1580–1606).* Mexico City: Archivo General de la Nación, 1992.

Weingarten, Susan. *Haroset, A Taste of Jewish History*. London and New Milford: The Toby Press, 2019.

Williams, Jillian. *Food and Religious Identities in Spain, 1400–1600.* London: Routledge, 2019.

Yerushalmi, Yosef Hayim. *Sefardica.* Paris: Chandeigne, 1998.

ACKNOWLEDGMENTS

I have a deep appreciation for bread, including matzah—savoring its taste, texture, versatility, and aroma. Its uses are as diverse as the friends and individuals who have crossed my path since the publication of *Sephardi*, inspiring, encouraging, and supporting me in writing 'Matzah and Flour.'

Special gratitude goes to the Academic Studies Press team—Alessandra, Diana, Matthew, Becca, Kira, Daniel, and Maria—for their enduring patience, support, and enthusiasm throughout this project.

As a Broome and Allen fellow, I express my thanks to the American Sephardi Federation and its executive director, Jason Guberman-Pfeffer, for their support.

I extend a special thank you to Paul Freedman, Chester D. Tripp Professor of History at Yale University, for hosting my lecture at this esteemed institution. His impressive knowledge in Food Studies serves for me as an exemplary career to follow.

Similar sentiments are extended to Heather J. Sharkey, Professor and Chair of the Department of Near Eastern Languages & Civilizations at the University of Pennsylvania. Professor Sharkey's vast knowledge is matched only by her kindness, and our collaboration since my lecture at Penn has been invaluable in spreading awareness about Food Studies.

A heartfelt tribute is dedicated to my late friend and mentor David Gitlitz, a distinguished historian and specialist in crypto-Jews. His influence since our meeting at the Society for Crypto-Judaic Studies in 2017 continues to light my path.

Recognition is due to the documentary consultation service of the General Archives of the Nation (AGN) of Mexico for their invaluable assistance in accessing various manuscripts. Similar acknowledgment goes to the Kislak Library of the University of Pennsylvania for facilitating my access to unknown manuscripts of the Inquisition. I am thankful to have been awarded a Visiting Research Fellowship at the Schoenberg Institute for Manuscript Studies at the University of Pennsylvania Libraries to conduct research in 2024.

I thank Professor Emeritus Gerrit Bos of the University of Cologne for facilitating my access to the analyses he conducted on Maimonides and for sharing his knowledge on the topic.

I would like to thank Daniel Wagman, a junior at the Dalton School in New York, for his enthusiasm about my work and for inviting me to the Dalton School for a talk and cooking session. He also created fascinating maps on Sephardic foods around the world for me. Your involvement and passion for the topic are very encouraging.

I express my deep gratitude to Chef Michael Solomonov for his support and advocacy of Jewish food culture and Sephardi cuisine, engaging in conversations and events, and for having faith in my work.

Thank you to Chef Daniel Ovadía for our wonderful collaboration in organizing the Sukkot dinner at Merkavá, one of his Mexican restaurants.

I appreciated collaborating with Chef Julien Ruffin from Valantin Bakery in Bordeaux while we worked in recreating the "Monte Sinai" pastry. Similar thanks also go to caterers Loïc and Clotilde from "La Manufacture du Bayon" in Bordeaux for their help in recreating a pigeon crust.

I appreciate the ongoing opportunities provided by the New York-based organizations Moise Safra Center and DOROT to talk about and cook Sephardi cuisine.

Warm appreciation goes to Barbara Kupetzky Tannenbaum and Josh Tannenbaum, my dear friends from New York, for their support in spreading the word about my work. Similar sentiments are extended to my "guardian angel" Candice Kiss for her steadfast support and guidance.

Thanks to Estrella Abudarham—and Billy—with whom I regularly exchange ideas, and to all those who, even though I've not yet met in person, virtually share a slice of Sephardic culinary life.

I extend warm appreciation to cookbook author Adeena Sussman for inviting me to her home and for our meaningful discussions on food practices. Special thanks go to Chef Susan Barrocas from *Savor*, Danielle Kranjec from Hillel International, and Dr. Yonatan Elazar for their support and shared insights.

A special recognition is due to my sister Marianne for creating and sewing the *sambenito* tunic. Your talent knows no bounds!

Heartfelt thanks go to my husband and children—especially my daughter Laly for agreeing so many times to help in the kitchen and take photos—for their unwavering support and patience, for enduring numerous tastings, and for their emotional support. I love you all dearly.

INDEX

D

M